IN THE NAME
OF THE LAW

OTHER BOOKS BY DAN COLLINS

I, KOCH (with Arthur Browne and Michael Goodwin)
THE MILLENNIUM BOOK (with Gail Collins)

IN THE NAME
OF THE LAW

Confessions of a Trial Lawyer

THOMAS P. PUCCIO

WITH

DAN COLLINS

W · W · NORTON & COMPANY

NEW YORK LONDON

Copyright © 1995 by Thomas Puccio and Dan Collins
Printed in the United States of America
First Edition

The text of this book is composed in 11/12.5 Garamond Simoncini
with the display set in Adobe Garamond Semi-Bold
Composition and manufacturing by the Haddon Craftsmen, Inc.
Book design by Margaret M. Wagner

Library of Congress Cataloging-in-Publication Data
Collins, Dan (Dan J.)
    In the name of the law / Thomas Puccio with Dan Collins.
        p.   cm.
    Includes index.
    1. Puccio, Thomas P.   2. Lawyers—United States—Biography.
3. Defense (Criminal procedure)—United States.   4. Criminal justice,
Administration of—United States.   I. Puccio, Thomas P.
II. Title.
KF373.P83A3   1995
345.73'01—dc20
[347.3051]   94-41705

ISBN 0-393-03728-2

W. W. Norton & Company, Inc., 500 Fifth Avenue, New York, N.Y. 10110
W. W. Norton & Company Ltd., 10 Coptic Street, London WC1A 1PU

1 2 3 4 5 6 7 8 9 0

This book is dedicated to my wife, Kathy, and my son, Matthew—and to the memory of the relationship that existed among the three of us. I loved Matthew in the way only a father can. Kathy, his stepmother, loved him as much as I did, and he returned that love to both of us in his own unique and wonderful way.

CONTENTS

Acknowledgments

I HAVE HAD more than my fair share of successes as a lawyer, both for my clients and for myself. The pages of this book reveal many of them. What no narrative can adequately reveal, however, is the debt of gratitude I owe to others. I began my career in the profession with an organization that gave me an unparalleled opportunity to learn, to grow, and to excel—the United States Department of Justice. During my thirteen-year tenure at the department, I had the privilege of working with highly skilled career professionals, such as Dave Margolis and Gerry McDowell, as well as public-spirited individuals, such as Phil Heymann and Irv Nathan, who left prestigious positions outside government to join the department for a period of time, thereby adding their valuable insights and expertise to our efforts. My respect for these lawyers, and countless others I worked with at Justice, and for the institution itself, has deepened over the thirteen years since I left.

Two others deserve very special mention—my good friends and mentors, Ed Korman and Dave Trager, now both sitting federal judges in the Eastern District of New York. Without their sound advice, encouragement, and support, both on an intellectual level and as confidants and colleagues, many of the accomplishments mentioned herein would never have been attained. Today, the legal community and the public continue to be the beneficiaries of the wisdom, integrity, and professionalism that have been their hallmark with me over the years.

One cannot easily undertake a project such as this without the patience, support, and understanding—not to mention inspiration—provided by a caring family. Our son, Matthew, who was tragically taken from us this year and whom we miss beyond what words can express, our daughter, Mary, and new son-in-law, Chris, all contributed in one way or another to what is good in the pages that follow. So did my parents. They were devoted to me and had high hopes for me which I hope in some measure were realized.

But most of all I am indebted to my beloved wife, Kathy, who has brought me more happiness than I have ever known, as well as comfort during times of adversity—my partner for life whose exquisite beauty is equaled only by her keen insight, lively wit, and sparkling intelligence. Kathy read and inspired every page of the manuscript of this book with her ideas and suggestions. Without her I can truly say it would never have been written.

INTRODUCTION

MOST AMERICANS hate the legal profession. If you went outside my Manhattan office and asked the first ten people you saw: "Do you like lawyers?" nine of them would undoubtedly say no. The tenth would be a lawyer himself.

I've been a lawyer for twenty-five years, and I've had a lot more adventures than I ever dreamed about when I was a kid in Brooklyn, planning vaguely on a career as an English teacher. I can't say I've done it all—I haven't represented any terrorists or Mafia bosses, nor have I wanted to. But I've prosecuted crooked cops and crooked congressmen, defended everybody from a tennis star accused of buying cocaine to a socialite charged with injecting his comatose wife with potentially lethal insulin.

Fascination with the law has never been higher. Neither has hatred of lawyers. I'm pretty well inured to both sentiments. I've made use of the media a time or two myself in my career, parading a client around the block for the benefit of Dan Rather's cameramen, or "spinning" a swarm of courthouse reporters in the hope of convincing them that my client's case was one of mistaken identity.

I must admit I do feel a little uncomfortable when I open *People* magazine and see the lawyer of the week sitting by his pool with his poodle, right next to a spread on Michael Jackson's plastic surgeon. Sometimes the profession seems to be turning into one long movie of the week or CNN special. But I've never found it surprising that people are interested in the work we do. Three of the cases I've worked on have been the subject of movies—*The French Connection, The Prince of the City,* and *Reversal of Fortune,* Alan Dershowitz's version of the Claus von Bulow story. And I've always thought the Abscam investigation, in which we dressed up federal agents as Arab sheiks to get evidence against crooked politicians, would have made the best movie of all.

Truthfully, some of what happens behind the scenes in the legal profession *does* seem like a scriptwriter's fantasy. I've never had a witness break down and confess on the stand, as they always did on the old "Perry Mason" shows. But I did have one who was so conscience-stricken he sought me out to admit that he had lied before a grand jury and offer gold-plated testimony to convict his cousin, a corrupt FBI agent. I've met CIA agents with secrecy fetishes so surreal they make the old "Get Smart" comedies look like docudramas. And there were scenes that would have fit comfortably into an early Woody Allen script: a ferocious turf war in which rival federal prosecutors stormed the control tower at Kennedy Airport, where they demanded that startled tower personnel send a radio message to the plane carrying an important mafia witness to New York. After some browbeating, the message was dispatched and the witness was handcuffed in midair, rushed off the plane by federal drug agents after it landed, and bundled into a car for an unscheduled trip to Manhattan. (Watching the abduction was a team of red-faced FBI agents I had sent to the airport to pick him up.)

The last time I looked, our law schools were graduating about thirty-eight thousand new attorneys every year. I'm sure a lot of them are like I was—attracted less to the idea of The Law than to steady employment. Like me, they probably had relatives who followed them around the house demanding to know how they were going to pay the rent with a degree in English literature.

I always thought my career goal would be to work my way up on Wall Street—to become a partner someday in one of those fancy white-shoe law firms. I became a prosecutor only because the fancy firms were totally disinterested in a Fordham Law School grad from Brooklyn named Puccio. Still, the dream of a white-shoe partnership stayed with me, throughout my government career, and even during my first years in private practice. The only way I got rid of it, frankly, was by having it come true.

After moving through three law firms (including one that I founded myself) I was invited to join Milbank, Tweed, Hadley & McCloy, a venerable old Wall Street law firm that fairly shouted You've Made It! You're Now Part of the Establishment!

It was only after I'd been there a few years that I realized my dream job was not what it was cracked up to be. I can remember going to a partners' meeting and discussing the case of another lawyer who was thinking of leaving the firm. "Anybody who's been here twenty-odd years and hasn't thought of leaving is either brain-dead or has no options," I said. It didn't get a big laugh. Looking around, I realized a lot of the people I was talking to had been with Milbank Tweed since I was in high school, and probably never once thought about jumping ship.

A prominent lawyer who served as attorney general of the United States once said: "It took me twenty-five years to become part of the establishment, I'll be damned if I'm gonna leave it." It didn't take me quite that long to become part of it, and it didn't take me very long to decide to leave it. I guess I wasn't really part of it to begin with.

I have come a long way from my early days as an eager young prosecutor in Brooklyn who walked a few short blocks to work every morning. Today, I am just as likely to start my work day at the Dolder Grand in Zürich or the Plaza Athenee in Paris as I am to be in my office on Park Avenue. My clients, no longer federal agencies such as the FBI or the IRS, are investment bankers, wealthy investors, Fortune 500 companies, politicians, society figures, and often other lawyers. Instead of masquerading as wealthy Arab sheiks as we did in Abscam, I am now representing them. Instead of prosecuting major corporations, I am now defending them. Instead of ferreting out crime on Wall Street, I am now committed to showing how little crime there really is. Securities law has, for the most part, replaced the penal law as my stock-in-trade. However my plate is normally filled with a variety of criminal and civil cases. And sooner or later, I know, I'll wind up in another high-profile criminal trial.

Being a lawyer often involves endless meetings and pushing paper. But as I think this book will make clear, the inside of a courtroom is where I'm most comfortable. There's nothing quite like a big trial. A trial should be much like a theatrical production. A well-prepared lawyer (director) knows the script by heart and the answers his witnesses will provide to his questions. Nevertheless, the most exciting moments in the law are those times when something unanticipated pops up during a major trial. You're forced to improvise, to scramble for a solution on the spot. Law schools don't teach you how to react when your client's glamorous ex-lover emerges from hiding in an effort to put him behind bars for the rest of his life. But that's exactly what happened when soap opera actress Alexandra Isles showed up in Providence, Rhode Island, to testify against Claus von Bulow.

Like most really intense careers, the legal life inflicts a lot of scars. As a federal prosecutor, I put away some very sympathetic people. As a defense lawyer, I've kept some people on the street who you might prefer to see serving life at the state penitentiary. I don't apologize for either. Who wants a society where prosecutors only go after people they don't like, or where only lovable defendants get their day in court?

Still, people ask me all the time how I could go from prosecuting the "bad guys" to defending them. It's the second most frequently asked question in my life. (The first is: "Did Claus von Bulow really do it?") All I can tell them is that in my opinion, our system is best served when the lawyers perform well on both sides of the courtroom. You don't want the lawyers making decisions about who deserves to go to jail, any more than you want doctors deciding who deserves to live or die.

The real emotional pains I've suffered in my career have been personal rather than philosophical. Once, when I was prosecuting the Abscam corruption cases, the Justice Department itself asked me to take a polygraph test, to prove I wasn't leaking information to the press. That hurt. A friend and colleague—who is now Mayor Rudy Giuliani—once approved the FBI's bugging of a conversation I was having in an apparent attempt to catch me in some kind of wrongdoing. The fact that I was totally innocent in both cases didn't mitigate the sense of betrayal and isolation I felt.

There is no perfect job in the law. Even legal aid lawyers, who really do God's work representing indigent defendants, are often harassed by clients who feel—rightly—that the over-worked attorneys aren't giving their cases enough time. On the other end of the spectrum, Ed Williams, probably the twentieth-century's greatest criminal trial lawyer, candidly remarked to me that the best client is one who is very scared and very rich. All this is probably why lawyers' groups tend to give out so many awards. They figure if they don't honor one another, nobody else will. But I prefer to keep my distance from other lawyers, too. I don't think clients are best served by a counsel who feels that he or she is part of a great club.

As I said, it's not a warm, fuzzy occupation. In court, the lawyers are engaged in a sort of ritualized dance that limits one's ability to act spontaneously, or even humanely. We witness moments of terrible pain but are not usually able to respond very sympathetically to the wrenching things we see and hear.

Going back over my career for this book, for instance, I remembered a woman, who was divorced from a crooked cop, sitting in court and listening to his attorney suggest that her ex-husband was not the father of their youngest child. It was a moment of terrible anguish.

That claim was made during a sidebar, a moment in a trial when the lawyers get together with the judge near the bench to discuss things out of the jury's earshot. Some of the most interesting exchanges in court go on during sidebar. They eventually become part of the written record, but only the major players can really pick up the dialogue.

One idea I had in writing this book was to bring everybody up to the bench, to hear the things that happen when all the voices drop low. Everyone comes from somewhere, and this book is about where I came from as a lawyer. It has been over twenty years since I prosecuted a bank robbery, a narcotics conspiracy, or a police corruption case. Yet the skills I developed in those days are invaluable to me today when I walk into the offices of the SEC or the antitrust division defending a client. I hope the following pages will tell why.

IN THE NAME
OF THE LAW

1

COPS AND ROBBERS

YOU MIGHT SAY that if it hadn't been for organized crime, I never would have been born. My mother's father left Sicily and came to America because of the Mafia. He was a fish merchant, and the mob's incessant extortion demands outraged him so much that he decided he'd rather emigrate than continue paying.

That's the story as it was handed down in my family, anyway. I can't say it made much of an impression on me as a boy. My grandfather, who opened up a fish store in Yonkers, New York, didn't seem to thirst for vengeance. My own ideas about the mob were largely shaped by "The Untouchables" on television.

Both my parents' families arrived here around the turn of the century from the same small seacoast village, Sciacca. My father's family lived the classic immigrant life on the Lower East Side—cold-water flat on top of a six-story walk-up, hard work for little pay in the garment industry. My dad, Matthew Puccio, had to drop out of school in the eighth grade to help support his four brothers and sisters. Otherwise, I'm sure, he would have made a great lawyer. He had a tremendous love for the law. As a young man, he'd cap a long day of work by slipping into night court to watch the judges and attorneys in action for hours at a time. But he never had the opportunity to pursue that kind of life himself.

Still, he managed to put the tenements behind him long before I was born in 1944. He eventually became a purchasing agent for the General Services Administration, the federal agency that provides everything from pins to pianos for U.S.

government offices. Anybody working at GSA in a purchasing capacity entered into multimillion-dollar contracts with a variety of suppliers. Unsurprisingly, unsolicited gifts arrived at our apartment from time to time. But my father would always send them back. He had a reputation for honesty that I more or less took for granted as a boy. It was years later before I discovered that my father's behavior wasn't the norm for all government employees.

My parents provided me, an only child, with a comfortable, middle-class upbringing. My mother, Jeanette Delacato Puccio, quit her job as a secretary to raise me. She'd spent most of her free time in the library as a young girl and never missed a chance to lecture me about the importance of reading. She typed all my school reports and helped me to write some of them. When I told her I was going to write a book, my eighty-year-old mother proclaimed herself ready to type it.

We lived in a four-room apartment in the Kensington section of Brooklyn. The rent was fifty dollars a month. It was a neighborhood of brick row houses that contained a mixture of Jews, Italians, and Irish. We attended a church with the tremendously Catholic name of Immaculate Heart of Mary. I went to a public grammar school a block from our home and hung out in the schoolyard. As an only child, I got just about anything I wanted. For a time during the 1950s, 3-D comic books became a rage among kids, but there were none available in the local stores. My mother went into action and managed to find a woman who worked at a plant where they were printed. I was soon sporting 3-D glasses.

When I was about eight, my father discovered something better than night court to feed his fascination with the world of law. He came home with a table model RCA television set, and it became our window to the world. Dad would root for Rudolph Halley, the chief counsel for the Kefauver Committee, admiring his relentless questioning of the mob boss Frank Costello during the televised hearings in New York. And he thought Joe Welch, the lawyer for the army in the army-McCarthy hearings, was magnificent.

As you might imagine, my dad had an opinion of what his

only child should be when he grew up. But even though I was generally eager to please my parents, I couldn't work up any enthusiasm about becoming an attorney. Like my mother, I loved literature, and I fancied myself a scholar.

One of my grammar school teachers, a wonderful woman named Maureen McDonald, thought I was a good enough student to apply for admission to Brooklyn Prep, a Catholic boy's high school run by the Jesuit fathers. She even came to my house once a week to tutor me for the admissions test. All her work paid off, and I was chosen to enter Brooklyn Prep in the fall of 1958.

The Jesuits were the most intellectual of the priestly orders, but Brooklyn Prep, like other Catholic high schools of the era, had a touch of San Quentin about it. The prefect of discipline, Frederick Engel, was a priest who'd been a boxing champion in the U.S. Navy. We called him Fred. If Fred's eagle eye spotted a student cutting up in a hallway or at an assembly, he would rush to the scene of the crime much like an NFL fullback. Any student standing between Fred and the perpetrator had an excellent chance of being knocked to the ground. Once on the scene, Fred administered instant justice with a few well-placed blows. (It was very easy to get into trouble in this way, since students were forbidden to talk or make noise above the first floor of the building.)

Detention was then a common form of punishment for misbehaving high school students, but Brooklyn Prep did things with a flair. Boys sent to detention (or the "jug," as it was called) for violating one of the school's numerous rules and regulations were made to assemble in the schoolyard. They then marched around the yard in single file for an hour (or two), like a little chain gang. Fred would watch the parade from a window in his office. Wayward boys might also be required to do push-ups, sit-ups, or to hold bricks or stones with their arms outstretched.

Boys unfortunate enough to be suspended from school for a serious infraction of the rules (twice getting caught smoking, for example) did not sit out their punishment at home. They reported to school each day just like everybody else and stood in the hallway outside Fred's office from 9 A.M. to 4 or 5 P.M.

I was so intimidated I probably would have studied hard on my own—even if the Jesuits had not required my parents to sign a form every week that certified I was doing at least three hours of homework each night. But despite the jailhouse trappings, I thrived at Brooklyn Prep. I finished fourth in my class and won full scholarships to Georgetown, Holy Cross, and Notre Dame. The Jesuits exerted tremendous pressure on us to attend colleges run by the order. Other Catholic colleges were acceptable, though the good fathers made it absolutely clear they had no enthusiasm for such institutions. Non-Catholic colleges were utterly taboo in their eyes. They would literally write "not recommended" on your school records if you applied to a non-Catholic college. I had more or less settled on Georgetown, but my father died of pneumonia six months prior to my graduation from high school in 1962.

I decided it was important to stay with my mother. So I enrolled at Fordham University, the Jesuit college in the Bronx. I spent four years shuttling back and forth between our home in Brooklyn and the Bronx. The commute, by subway, took a total of four hours, and I didn't do much in the way of extracurricular activities at school.

I did manage to maintain my enthusiasm for literature. I was interested in Thomas Hardy and Henry James, Updike and Bellow, Dante and Shakespeare. I wanted to get a doctorate and teach English at the college level. But my mother, as it turned out, secretly shared my father's ambition for me—she was just too clever to pressure me herself. I had a cousin Michael who was an accountant, the only person in our family with a job as a professional. My mother began inviting him to dinner at our apartment with the express intent of talking me out of a life of letters.

"How are you going to pay the bills? Write a poem?" he would ask.

To please my mother I made last-minute applications to several law schools and was accepted at Boston College Law School. To pay my board and tuition at BC, I was given a job as a dormitory counselor. I showed up at the Chestnut Hill campus in August 1966 and discovered that I would be the "counselor" for members of the BC football team. It was not my idea of a dream job. I fled BC in the dead of night and, with the help of a former professor, managed to get myself enrolled at Fordham Law School.

It wasn't long before I discovered my parents had understood me better than I understood myself—I flourished in law school. Despite my intellectual pretensions, I never did fully grasp Kant and Heidegger, or Teilhard de Chardin's theory of the universe. But judges were a different story. I understood their meaning perfectly. The law, I came to realize, was very often an exercise in nuts-and-bolts pragmatism. By the time I finished Fordham Law in 1969, I really was looking forward to being an attorney.

I graduated with a very conventional ambition: I wanted to become a Wall Street lawyer. I did a little research and found a sprinkling of Fordham graduates who were partners at some of New York's leading white-shoe law firms. Writing to them was enough to get me in the door for interviews, but I quickly discovered that law firms that recruited the best students from the nation's best law schools had no interest in an Italian graduate of Fordham who hadn't been on the *Law Review*.

One of the partners who interviewed me was Edward Neaher of Chadburne, Park, Whiteside, & Wolff. The interview went well enough, and at one point, Neaher leaned over to me and said, "Look, I'm going to be appointed as the United States attorney for the Eastern District of New York. Would you be interested in working for me as an assistant United States attorney?" I had lived in Brooklyn all my life, but I never knew the Eastern District even existed, and I had never even considered the idea of becoming a prosecutor. I told Neaher I'd like a little time to think it over.

On the same day, I went to Davis Polk and Wardwell for an interview with an attorney named Robert Fiske. Fiske was kind enough to gently point me in the right direction. "The young man I interviewed before you went to Harvard Law School and clerked for Earl Warren," he said. "It might be very hard for you to get an offer at a place like this."

I considered all this overnight and called Neaher the next day to sign on as a $9,500-a-year assistant U.S. attorney for something called the Eastern District. I only learned later that I was joining the losing team as far as federal law enforcement was concerned. The Eastern District, which represented the interests of the United States government in Brooklyn, Queens, and Long Island, had been created during the Civil War. For precisely that long, it had been overshadowed by the Southern District in Manhattan, the crown jewel of the federal law enforcement system.

An appointment to the Southern District was an honor, and a ticket to a future career at New York's most prestigious law firms. Getting a job in the Eastern District, on the other hand, was generally a political favor. The place had always been dominated by clubhouse politicians who approved all the appointments. They did not go out searching for the best and the brightest. As a result, the FBI and other federal agencies steered clear of the Eastern District, directing all the high-profile investigations across the harbor to Manhattan.

When Richard Nixon was elected in 1968, the Eastern District offices virtually emptied out. Most of the lawyers appointed by the local Democratic machine loyally resigned and moved into the gritty world of the Brooklyn bar. The stampede into the private sector was a mixed blessing. The Eastern District certainly couldn't afford to lose the few capable prosecutors it had to begin with. On the other hand, it was a chance for Neaher to clean house and bring in young lawyers of merit, and after 1969 things slowly began to change. But even Neaher had to pay a certain amount of attention to political reality.

"Oh, by the way," Neaher told me after I'd accepted his offer. "There's a man by the name of John Crews with an office on Court Street. Why don't you drop in and say hello to him?"

I found out later than Crews was one of the most powerful Republicans in the state. He was head of the Brooklyn Republican organization and a very important figure in New York politics. I took Neaher's invitation to mean "If you have a chance," rather than, "Get your ass down there and see John Crews and get clearance."

Two days before I was scheduled to start work, I attended the swearing-in ceremony for Neaher as U.S. attorney at the federal courthouse in Brooklyn. I got on the receiving line to shake his hand after the ceremony. He looked at me gravely and said, "By the way, get down and see John Crews." It finally dawned on me that meeting John Crews was not an optional assignment. I duly made the appointment through Tony Durso, the Brooklyn county clerk. Durso told me to report to his office in Borough Hall in downtown Brooklyn. Then he took me across the street to meet the Don, so to speak. I was ushered into a big, empty office with not much more than a chair and a desk. Behind the desk was an old, bald man who was wearing sunglasses.

I sat down in a chair in front of Crews and handed him my résumé. I still didn't have the foggiest notion about who John Crews was or that I was being cleared for my job by the Republican organization.

"Have you done any work for the party?" he asked.

"No," I replied.

"I see here you live in the Heights. My dentist lives in your building," Crews said. "Maybe you can get involved."

That was it. Durso, who spent all his time fawning over Crews during the brief meeting, ushered me out of the office.

"OK, kid, we'll call you," Durso said.

Happily, they never did. The symbolic nature of this ring-kissing ceremony was pretty much lost on me at the time. Ignorance is bliss.

I was sworn in as a member of the bar on December 18, 1969, by the legendary New York gangbuster, Tom Dewey. Personally, I had no interest in fighting the mob myself, despite the legendary wrong inflicted on my ancestor's fish business. I still had my eye on Wall Street, and I requested a job in the Civil Division.

I was made a Justice Department bill collector in the office of fines and claims. The guy who ran the office was an old Democratic clubhouse lawyer with a handlebar mustache. He had remained on after Neaher and the Republicans took power, and he treated me like a real kid. But nothing could dampen my enthusiasm. I was told to collect big unpaid fines, so I dusted off the old records and discovered that a man named Joe Valachi owed the government $50,000, a lot of money in 1969. I began making calls. I was going to get that money. Very quickly, the Justice Department in Washington demanded to know the identity of the crazy kid in Brooklyn who was trying to collect $50,000 from the government's greatest witness ever against the Mafia. They were ready to send the men in white coats for me. Fortunately, my stint as a hyperactive bill collector lasted only a couple of weeks.

Neaher called me into his office and said, "We have a real crisis in criminal cases. Nearly all of our prosecutors have resigned. They were hired for political reasons, and they're leaving for the same reasons. We want you to work in the Criminal Division for a short period of time."

I broke into a cold sweat. I was absolutely terrified at the prospect of going to the Criminal Division.

"I came here to work on civil cases, gain experience, and get a job on Wall Street," I protested.

"Well, do this for a few months," Neaher replied.

It was not a request.

I reluctantly became a criminal prosecutor in January 1970, dawn of the decade of leisure suits, Watergate, fondue sets, the Partridge Family, and the kidnapping of Patty Hearst. I was twenty-five years old.

There were only a handful of lawyers in the entire Criminal Division and an enormous backlog of cases. Things were very, very disorganized. Neaher had begged some of the Democratic clubhouse lawyers to remain on, but only a few had chosen to do so. I was one of only three new lawyers in the division.

Neaher had brought in Tony Lombardino, a veteran state prosecutor from Queens, to be the new chief of the Criminal Division. Lombardino was a short, heavyset man with a pockmarked face and wavy black hair. He was backed by the Queens Republican organization.

Tony was not an intellectual lawyer, but he was a ferocious investigator with great courtroom instincts. He also loved gambling and nightlife. Tony was a cop at heart. He hung out with cops and went out on raids with them whenever possible. He also carried a gun. He would come into the office in the morn-

ing, take off his jacket, and slip the gun into a closet.
He was, to my young eyes, larger than life.
Tony was my mentor in matters of the law. He took a seat-of-the-pants approach to lawyering but had great courtroom instincts. During my first trial, he functioned much like a paramedic called to the scene of a bad accident. He would flit in and out of the courtroom periodically, dispensing on-the-spot advice and instructions.

Criminal prosecutors wield enormous power. A wrongful indictment can ruin a man's reputation, destroy his career, and bankrupt him. Conviction can lead to the harshest penalties society levies on its members—imprisonment or even death. A poorly prosecuted case can have equally devastating results if a murderer or rapist is allowed to go free. That's why society has established exacting standards for certain critical occupations. Given the importance of my job, you'd figure a prosecutor would go through a rigorous preparation, sort of like an airline pilot. You wouldn't want to step onto an airplane and see the pilot studying a book on how to fly. And you'd have reason to be shocked if you entered the courthouse on the night before an important trial and saw the prosecutor fumbling through a ponderous, three-volume set of *Goldstein's Trial Technique,* which was exactly what I was doing on the eve of my first trial.

My first case was a bank robbery in which two hardened stickup men had badly beaten a guard during the holdup of the Republic Bank in the Williamsburg section of Brooklyn. I had never even attended a criminal trial, much less prosecuted one. My sole experience with the administration of justice had come one day when I wandered into the federal courthouse in Manhattan and watched a mean-looking old judge sentence a guy in a wheelchair to twenty years in jail. Basically, I was going on "Perry Mason." Law school does not prepare you for criminal trial work, or for any other practical aspect of the law.

The night before the trial began, I sat glumly in my small, windowless office (a former storage room) in the Brooklyn federal courthouse. I had spread out the evidence in the case on the desk in front of me, but I wasn't sure I knew how to get it introduced as evidence at the trial, the *Goldstein* tomes notwithstanding. My only immediate source of comfort was a sandwich I'd picked up at a nearby deli.

I was munching away, contemplating the stacks of stolen bank bills, when a terrible thought occurred to me. I began frantically trying to figure out if I had bought my sandwich with money stolen in the holdup.

"Your Honor, the government inadvertently used some of the evidence in this case to purchase a pastrami on rye," I imagined myself saying to an unsympathetic judge and sniggering defense lawyers. I remained in a real panic until I checked my wallet, counted the bank bills, and determined I had used my own money to buy my sandwich.

After an uneasy night, it was time to put up or shut up. My goal was to survive the trial without completely embarrassing myself. My adversaries were Ed Kelly, the head of the Legal Aid Society, and Willie Thompson, a New York City councilman. They were defending Edmund Leroy Pierson and Fletcher Faison, a pair of professional bank robbers who looked just as tough as they were.

I was scared out of my mind as I gave a ten-minute opening statement. Fortunately, seated next to me at the prosecution table was Tom Sheer, the FBI agent who had investigated the case and captured Pierson and Faison. Sheer was a granite-jawed ex-marine and a terrific agent with great informants. He radiated self-confidence, and that helped to make me confident. Unfortunately, Tom was also a guy who never bothered to comb his hair. He walked around with his hands thrust into the pockets of an old trench coat. By the three-piece-suit-and-watch-fob standards of the FBI, Sheer was a veritable Beatnik. Despite Tom's tremendous talent, I believed (wrongly as it turned out) that he would never get ahead in the Bureau.

One of the defense witnesses was a jeweler who said that he remembered selling Faison a ring at the exact moment the bank was being robbed. At Sheer's suggestion, I had reviewed hundreds of the jeweler's sales receipts prior to the trial and discovered that he had once sold a cuckoo clock.

After the jeweler told his story on the stand, I was ready to cross-examine him.

"How many rings have you sold over the years?" I asked.

"Oh, thousands," he casually replied.

"Well," I said, "did you ever sell a cuckoo clock?"

He paused, and answered, "I do recall selling one cuckoo clock."

"Well, who did you sell that clock to and when?"

Of course, he couldn't remember who'd purchased that cuckoo clock or any other detail. His credibility was totally impeached.

Things were going well, I thought, but Willie Thompson gave such an inspired, dramatic, and forceful closing argument that when the judge called a recess, I walked out of the courtroom scared shitless. I felt like a punch-drunk fighter trying to find his way back to his corner.

Someone who saw the sad shape I was in must have dialed 911. Tony Lombardino raced to the rescue. He could see that I was dazed and immediately administered verbal smelling salts.

"Look at me," Tony commanded. "I want you to march back into the courtroom and tell that jury exactly what happened at the Republic Bank."

That was the Eastern District's version of a pep talk. But it turned out to be all I needed. I pulled myself together, returned to the courtroom, and did just what Tony said—delivered a routine recitation of the facts. My address has yet to be reprinted in any law journal, but the jurors didn't start scratching their heads or howling with laughter.

I then staggered back to my office to await the verdict. Instead of growing more apprehensive as the jury deliberated, I became completely relaxed. I was overcome by a sense of total serenity. (Unfortunately, it was a feeling I have never been able to recapture. With each succeeding case, jury deliberations became a little more nerve-racking. Now, as a defense lawyer, jury deliberations are the worst moments in my professional life.)

After four hours, I returned to the courtroom to hear the jury foreman return guilty verdicts on Pierson and Faison. I suppose this is a golden moment in the life of any young lawyer, but my elation lasted only an instant.

Faison, who had the cold eyes of a killer, pointed at me and screamed: "You're going to die for this!"

I was dumbfounded.

My mind flashed back to a recent dinner I'd had with friends from law school. They kidded me about becoming a prosecutor and talked about an old 1930s gangster movie with Edward G. Robinson in which the judge says to Robinson: "Do you have anything to say before you are sentenced?" And Robinson turns to the prosecutor and says: "If it's the last thing I do, I'm going to get you."

It almost seemed as if my law school chums had hired Fletcher Faison to play a little joke on me. Fletcher, unfortunately, didn't smile or playfully wink an eye at me.

I was a marked man, but more importantly, I was a *winner.* The guilty verdicts in my first trial inflated my ego to Olympian proportions. I moved into the Clarence Darrow stage of my fledgling career. Regrettably, it only lasted about two weeks.

I was assigned to prosecute a routine income tax evasion case before a judge named Jack Weinstein. Today, the IRS pursues criminal prosecution in cases involving major tax cheats, but in 1970, the IRS prosecuted beauticians, waiters, cab drivers, blind paper boys, and other little people. The defendant in my case was a small businessman.

Now Judge Weinstein, a brilliant jurist, was reputed to be very liberal politically—to my mind definitely not the kind of guy who looked favorably on the criminal prosecution of grocery store owners and newspaper vendors. The defense lawyer in the case wanted to waive his client's right to a jury trial and place the decision in the hands of the judge. I cannily refused to go along with this arrangement, reasoning that Weinstein would surely acquit the defendant.

I then proceeded to lose the case in record time, with the jury quickly acquitting the businessman on all counts.

"You put on a really great case," Weinstein later told me. "I would have found the guy guilty on every count."

I've always considered that this was the moment I actually became a lawyer. I now understood that I was not going to win every case, and that even if I did everything right, I couldn't always count on a jury to deliver a rational verdict. I also learned not to take things at face value, such as Weinstein's status as a Great Liberal. The judge had great intellectual honesty and reverence for the law. He might have fined that small businessman $2.50, but he would have found him guilty. Unfortunately, I had to find out the hard way.

During my first year as a prosecutor, I also learned, once again, that I was the worst possible judge of what work I'd be best suited to do with my life. I loved criminal trials. Once I got over my initial stage fright, I realized I was good at thinking on my feet, organizing a prosecution in a way that made sense to a jury, and wrapping all the evidence up in the package of a final argument.

If left to my own devices I'd probably have still been in graduate school, trying to think of something new to say about Thomas Hardy. But the fates were kind, and instead I was becoming a specialist in prosecuting bank robberies.

In 1970, bank robberies were still a very big deal to the FBI. The Bureau in the Hoover era was very comfortable with this kind of crime. It was cops and robbers, literally. It was also a great way for a young guy with no experience to learn how to handle himself in a courtroom. Bank robbery cases are usually simple and clear-cut. In many forms of white-collar crime, defense lawyers can forcefully argue that no crime was committed, as they did in the complex insider trading cases of the 1980s. No such confusion or legal nuance attended bank robbery trials.

With the help of FBI agents like Tom Sheer, I put away some of the toughest bank robbers of the 1970s. Nevertheless, I wasn't as smart as I thought. Gary Brooks proved that.

Gary was an only child and the product of a broken home. His mother did her best to raise Gary the right way, but she was unable to control him. He dropped out of school and, at age fifteen, became a member of one of the most dangerous bank robbery gangs of the era. The gang, which had about fifteen members, was led by a professional bank robber named George Collins. George, who was in his early forties, was hardly a devotee of Frantz Fanon and Che Guevara. But he had no difficulty adopting the quasi-political style affected by the angry ghetto youths in his gang. That meant black berets, dark sunglasses, black three-quarter-length coats and clenched-fist Black Power salutes. The Collins gang was a lethal knockoff on the Black Panthers.

The gang carried out a dozen bank robberies in Queens over an eighteen-month period. Four or five suitably attired members of the gang armed with enormous Magnum revolvers would enter a bank and order everybody onto the floor. They would then scoop up all the available cash (usually $30,000 to $50,000) and flee in one or two getaway cars driven by other members of the gang.

During this era, the FBI still regarded bank robberies as one of their main reasons for being. And the specter of wild-eyed-revolutionary-militant-Communist-black bank robbers must have been close to the supreme nightmare for the Bureau's Hoover-era bureaucrats. The Collins gang quickly made the Bureau's list of most-wanted bank robbers. Wanted posters promising a reward of $10,000 went up all over the city. Barry Goas, a bright young FBI agent with the striking good looks of a male model, was placed in charge of the case. Barry used bank surveillance photos of the robbers and information gleaned from informers to piece together an accurate picture of the gang and its activities.

Following an FBI raid of the Brooks's home that turned up no trace of Gary, George Collins and three other members of the gang fled the city and wound up taking refuge in a women's dormitory at the University of Massachusetts. The FBI learned of his whereabouts but was fearful an effort to take Collins might produce a bloodbath. George and his companions played the role of black revolutionaries being hunted by the pigs during their stay at UMass. But George, who at age forty-two must have looked positively ancient to the students, proved to be a bad militant. The black students hiding George suspected that he was really a police narcotics agent. Thereafter, Collins and his friends "dropped out" of college in great haste. George was later arrested at a YMCA in Philadelphia thanks to an informer whom Barry Goas paid $10,000 in cash for the tip.

About a week after the raid, Gary Brooks phoned the FBI and said he wanted to surrender and cooperate with the government. But Gary insisted that the FBI would have to make it look as if he had been captured.

"I'll get killed if they find out I came in on my own," he told Goas. Gary then outlined a plan in which the FBI would apprehend him on a street corner under an elevated subway line in Queens. Goas and another agent duly went forth and "captured" Gary at the appointed time and place.

Gary Brooks was really a boy—a tall, slender, good-looking black kid with a cherubic face and a wonderful, winning smile. He was very intelligent and well spoken for somebody with very little education. He was also eager to please, and there was an aura of vulnerability about him that made you want to step in and help him.

Gary was treated differently from other prisoners from the very beginning. As a sixteen-year-old, he was immediately separated from older prisoners at the Metropolitan Correction Center. Barry Goas went out of his way to do little favors for Gary. Not too many federal prisoners were eating home-cooked meals lovingly prepared by Mom. Thanks to Barry Goas, Gary did.

Barry brought Gary to my office a day or two after the "capture." I quickly worked out an agreement with Gary's lawyer to make him a cooperating witness. I was tremendously impressed with him.

Gary told me he had been drawn into the gang by two older boys, William Trusty and Robert Earl. It was through Trusty and Earl that Gary was introduced to George Collins and his son, Ray, who was also a bank robber. Gary said he had been fooled by the gang's revolutionary pretensions. He thought that they wanted to help the black community. Gary very soon learned that wasn't true, but having fallen in with dangerous men like George Collins, he was afraid to stop.

I was delighted to discover that Gary had a photographic memory and a tremendous eye for detail. His testimony would be devastating. As we prepared for the trial of George Collins and two other gang members, Gary slowly became part of the family. I was determined to get him a walk (a suspended jail sentence). We celebrated Gary's birthday in the office with a cake. He was more like a surrogate son to me and Barry than a cooperating witness.

The trial got under way and went smoothly enough until it was Gary's turn to testify. Gary was being held in a cell in the basement of the courthouse. Goas, who went downstairs to retrieve him, found Gary marching in a circle around his cell in the rigid, jerky, quasi-military way that Black Panthers marched. He refused to speak to Barry. This was not a good omen.

Gary took the stand and calmly identified the defendants. He admitted his own role in the bank robberies and then named as his accomplices several people I had never heard of. He went on to assure the jury that the men on trial were completely innocent.

I hastily called for a recess. One of those things that only happen in the movies had just happened to me. I spent the next day and a half standing in the courtroom with transcripts of Gary's grand jury testimony. In order to impeach Gary's bogus story and get in real testimony about the crime, I repeatedly confronted him with what he had said before the grand jury.

"Were you asked this question and did you give this answer?" I asked him over and over again.

"Yes, but it was a lie," said my star witness.

Perhaps the most bitter pill I had to swallow was watching George Collins and his codefendants. These cutthroats wore grins from ear to ear.

Gary, however, was full of surprises. After a day and a half as a witness for the Collins gang, he decided to rejoin the government. I think an impassioned plea from his mother turned the tide.

"Is it too late to go back on your side?" he asked.

I was delighted to have Gary back on the team. He told me that he became terrified when he saw Collins and the others in the flesh. He decided he couldn't go through with his testimony. I knew it was true that smiling George and his men would have happily run Gary's body through a wood chip machine, had there been one handy in the courtroom. I also knew that Gary was a young kid, a boy really, who had been testifying in the friendly environment of a grand jury. Going face-to-face against these birds in a courtroom must have been frightening indeed. Gary got back on the stand and started to tell the truth. George Collins, et al., stopped smiling and started listening. They were all convicted.

Gary went on to become a wonderful witness in five other trials over a two-year period. Several members of the Collins gang went to prison. Over the months these trials unfolded, a grimmer picture of Gary Brooks began to emerge. I learned, for example, that Gary was the de facto "brains" of the Collins gang. At sixteen, Gary was much too young to be accepted as a leader, but he was by far the smartest member of the gang. George Collins tended to be a spontaneous soul who, when he wanted to rob a bank, went out and robbed one. Gary proposed watching the bank before it was robbed and giving each member of the holdup team a specific task to perform. Many of his ideas were accepted by the gang.

These were not the actions of a badly scared kid who had gotten in over his head with the wrong crowd. But I pushed such uncomfortable facts into the back of my mind.

Judge John Bartels, who had presided over several of the trials, had the reputation of being a notoriously tough jurist, but he actually was soft hearted. Judge Bartels was more impressed with Gary than I was. He wanted to use his influence to get Gary admitted to a prep school like Andover. Needless to say, I encountered no difficulty in persuading the judge to give Gary a suspended sentence. Barry Goas and I pursued what we regarded as a more realistic educational goal for Gary by helping him get into Harlem Prep, a private high school that was just right for a talented but troubled kid. From then on, Gary was never a stranger.

He would drop by periodically to talk about his hopes and dreams. He would first talk a mile a minute to my secretary, Lilly Grant, and then sheepishly make his way into my office. Gary would tell me how well he was getting along and how he hoped to attend MIT when he graduated. He always addressed me as "Mr. Puccio."

I received one of the great jolts of my own young life when I opened the New York newspapers on the morning of June 6, 1975. Gary was charged with murdering a sixty-three-year-old security guard during the robbery of the bookstore at St. John's University in Queens. He had stolen $177. The police described Gary as a heroin addict who had robbed the bookstore at Queensborough Community College three times earlier in the year.

I couldn't believe it. I just couldn't believe it. It didn't seem possible that there could be a murderer behind that sweet face. But the surprises just kept coming. Following Gary's arrest, I spoke with the lawyer representing him. I discovered that on days when Gary committed a crime, including the day he shot and killed that elderly security guard, he made it a point to visit me at the U.S. attorney's office. Gary had not only fooled me, he had obviously used me in an effort to set up an alibi for himself.

I never spoke with Gary again. I guess I showed youthful arrogance, presuming it was that easy to pull someone out of a life of crime and turn his life around. Maybe the die was already cast with Gary by the time he first walked into my office. All I know is that over time most lawyers build an emotional wall between themselves and the needy people they deal with every day. My wall began with Gary Brooks.

BANK ROBBERY CASES make it very easy for young prosecutors to separate the good guys (us) from the bad guys (them), the white hats from the black. But less than two years after I'd become one of the good guys, I began a discovery process that made these comfortable moral categories much more murky. I would spend much of the next ten years prosecuting "good guys" who had betrayed the public trust in places that ranged from the precinct house to the halls of Congress.

I got my first taste in 1971, with a case known in the office as the Kosher Caper. It involved a group of Hasidic Jews from the Williamsburg section of Brooklyn who were heavily involved in selling stolen goods. A large shipment of stereo systems had been stolen from a New York pier and then sold at a retail electronics store run by the defendants.

The stolen stereos had been seized in a series of raids carried out by a squad of New York City police officers attached to the Brooklyn district attorney's office. The case was relatively straightforward, or so I thought. But as I prepared the case for trial, I discovered that the number of stereo sets seized was much, much larger than the number of sets that were actually in police custody.

I was baffled by the discrepancy. I made inquiries and soon learned that the police never dreamed that the case would be prosecuted by the federal government. So they had simply walked off with the evidence, like so many office paper clips. Of the hundreds of stereo systems seized in the raid, only a handful were left. (One of the few remaining sets had been set up in a police squad room.)

This was somewhat of a predicament. Here I was readying a trial of people charged with theft, and now it appeared the real thieves were New York's Finest. As the trial approached, more and more of the stereos were turned in by the cops, but many units were still missing by the time the trial got under way.

This was my first encounter with official corruption and the beginning of a decade-long education. Since the stolen stereos involved the local cops, it was easy enough to shrug off what had happened. Sure, cops were members of the criminal justice system, but not my part of it. I was working for an organization with an unimpeachable record of honesty and integrity, or so I thought.

Early in 1972, I was approached by Ed Korman, a top aide to the new United States attorney, Robert Morse. (Ed Neaher had resigned to take a federal judgeship.) Korman gave me a very carefully drawn perjury indictment against a low-level hoodlum who had been charged with hijacking a truck. He wanted me to prosecute the case. The suspect was one of three men who had been arrested by the FBI for hijacking a truck from Kennedy airport.

Only two of the hoodlums, however, had been indicted. (They were subsequently tried and acquitted.) The third man simply went free. The suspect I prosecuted was charged with perjury for testimony given in his own defense at the hijacking trial. This was a highly unusual procedure, and one that was much frowned upon by the Justice Department. The prevailing view was that if the government couldn't get you for committing the crime, it shouldn't be trying to get you for having denied doing the crime. You needed approval from Washington to pursue this kind of a prosecution.

I still couldn't understand Korman's insistence on pursuing the matter. The hijacking was one of hundreds of routine cases handled by our office that never received any publicity. Why in the world did Korman indict this guy, and why had the Justice Department given him permission to do so?

The answer was contained in a hundred-page FBI report given to me by Korman. About a year previously, a high-level FBI informer in the Mafia had reported that a case had been fixed in the U.S. attorney's office. The FBI informer said a prosecutor in our office was paid $25,000 by a well-known Brooklyn lawyer to make sure that one of the three men arrested in the hijacking case was passed over by the grand jury.

The FBI investigation also uncovered another problem. It was discovered that $30,000 in cash was stolen from the Eastern District's evidence safe. I knew this money well. It was evidence in the case of Ronald Raymond Ravitch, a notorious bank robber I'd put into jail. The $30,000 was lifted from a suitcase containing several hundred thousand dollars stolen by the energetic Ravitch. Looking for suspects, the FBI quickly zeroed in on four New York City police detectives attached to the department's Special Investigating Unit. The SIU was an elite group of narcotics detectives who specialized in cases against major drug dealers. Regrettably, some SIU detectives were also major-league criminals. Comparisons to Ali Baba and his forty thieves are not misplaced when discussing the history of this police unit. But the darker side of SIU had not become known.

The Bureau, which generously referred to this outrageous crime as a "mysterious disappearance," was never able to come up with any proof against the SIU foursome.

It would be difficult to exaggerate the impact this entire messy affair had on me. In later years, I would be accused by some of my colleagues of being excessively secretive, even mysterious. I plead guilty. But I was genuinely shocked by the allegation that one of my fellow federal prosecutors was corrupt. It was also hard for me to believe that the U.S. attorney's office could be the location for a grand larceny in which the suspected thieves were well-regarded police detectives. I became very cautious and circumspect in my dealings with others.

My work as a prosecutor had pleased my superiors. In 1972, I was named chief of the Eastern District's one-man (me) Narcotics Bureau. That was fine with me. I was ready to take on the world's biggest dope dealers. I didn't, however, anticipate that I'd be doing battle with the world's most corrupt police officers.

2

COPS AS ROBBERS

A FRIEND who recommended me for the Narcotics Bureau job
told the Eastern District brass that I was a bright young lawyer
who was "killing himself" by spending unbelievably long hours
in the office. I think it was the hope that I might indeed be sui-
cidally work-obsessed that got me the appointment.

Despite the fact that the war on drugs was supposed to be a
priority under the Nixon administration, the word had not yet
trickled down to the Eastern District. There were plenty of drug
arrests, thanks to the fact that Kennedy Airport falls within the
district's borders. But if it had not been for all the small-timers
caught trying to smuggle narcotics in via commercial jet, our record would have looked really embarrassing.

I learned later on that everybody involved in the war on drugs
didn't work in a one-man bureau. In 1973, after I had managed
to "smash" (as the tabloids like to say) several international narcotics rings, I was invited to Mexico for a high-level meeting on
drug trafficking. Jerry Strickler, a Drug Enforcement Administration official, and I were ushered into the huge office of the
American ambassador in Mexico City. As we walked in, I noticed a marine guard stationed next to a mysterious curtain.
Without ceremony, the marine threw back the curtain he was
guarding to reveal a glass bubble big enough to take up most of
the space in the medium-size room that the curtain had concealed. Wires were hanging from the ceiling of the bubble, and
inside were a conference table and chairs.

It reminded me a little of the "cone of silence" in the old "Get
Smart" television series. For comic effect, Max and the chief

would hold their supersecret meetings by sticking their heads under a cheap plastic cone that descended from the ceiling. But no one in Mexico City was laughing. I watched as the marine guard opened the hatch on the bubble by turning a wheel, much as you might spin the wheel on a bank vault. Strickler and I were invited to step inside the bubble with a delegation of officials from the embassy. The purpose of all this, of course, was to prevent our precious words from being intercepted by our then-numerous Communist enemies and any other international outlaws who might be listening in.

No one took note of the fact that we were in a bubble, much less protested the arrangement. To show my own cloak-and-dagger savvy, I quickly decided to act as if I had been meeting in a bubble all my life.

Once we were seated inside, the meeting began, though not before the hatch had been shut. The embassy officials who dealt with narcotics trafficking went around the table introducing themselves to me and Strickler. The last official introduced himself as the "agricultural attaché."

"Excuse me?" I asked.

"CIA! CIA!" the man responded in a tone of mock irritation. Laughter filled the bubble.

That was the way they did business in the big leagues, I guess. And while I did pretty well at building up the Eastern District's drug enforcement operation, nobody ever offered to give me my own security bubble. Or even an agricultural attaché.

The best thing that my superiors did give me in the early days was the services of Tom Dugan. Tom was a federal narcotics agent acting as a liaison between the old federal Bureau of Narcotics and Dangerous Drugs and the Organized Crime Strike Force. Since the strike force wasn't doing narcotics-related investigations, I was permitted to take him on as my investigator.

Tom was known as the "silver fox" because of a distinguished mane of gray hair. He had a keen mind and an encyclopedic knowledge of the international drug trade. It was rare to find an agent with a detailed grasp of the entire international narcotics business. Dugan was also a renegade and a loner. I didn't know it then, but those were the exact qualities you'd want to look for in a recruit from an agency I later learned had been thoroughly corrupt.

Dugan taught me how to make conspiracy cases against major drug dealers. Conspiracy cases were ideal for a young prosecutor with virtually no resources, money, or manpower. There would be no need for wiretaps, bugs, or undercover agents. Instead, I would use drug traffickers already in jail to implicate their bosses in a conspiracy to import heroin or cocaine into the United States. The key to this low-cost strategy was persuading some very tough customers to become witnesses for the U.S. government. In this regard, I had a couple of advantages. Prison sentences for drug-trafficking were Draconian, making it easier to get cooperation. And most of the people I was interested in were foreigners, Frenchmen and South Americans who were alone and isolated in American prisons. They wanted desperately to get out of jail and go back to where they came from.

Thinking big was another asset I brought to the job. I had no interest in wasting time and energy on small-time drug dealers. I wanted to nail the men at the top—the men responsible for importing heroin into the United States.

At the time, heroin was the drug of choice, and it followed a trail from the poppy fields of Turkey to processing plants in Marseilles and then to the United States via South America. At the apex of the international narcotics trade was a cartel run by French and Corsican criminals. There were five drugs rings within the cartel that cooperated with one another. It was just like OPEC.

Many of the top French and Corsican narcotics dealers had fled France to avoid prosecution. They were routinely convicted in absentia by French courts and sentenced to death. The dealers took refuge in South America, where they were protected by corrupt government officials in countries like Argentina, Uruguay, and Brazil. From the safety of their South American sanctuaries, the dealers shipped tons of heroin into the United States in expensive Jaguar automobiles, fish cans, hollowed-out ski poles, and anything else they thought might escape detection at the border.

Once inside the United States, the heroin was turned over to distributors—most of them Hispanic, Italian, or black. These distributors were the men Americans most often thought of as big-time drug dealers. A multimillion-dollar heroin transaction in New York might take place in a Manhattan restaurant by the simple act of turning over the claim check for a Jaguar parked in a nearby garage. The heroin was then sold on the street at enormous markups. Virtually all of it flowed into America's black ghettos. Blacks were thus whipsawed. Tons of drugs were flooding their neighborhoods while hundreds of millions of dollars in scarce cash were flowing out to pay for the heroin.

My approach to battling the heroin problem was more scholarly than two-fisted. It centered on becoming the convicted dealers' biographer. I'd find an important drug trafficker who was languishing in jail and invite him to my office to tell me the story of his life. I would never begin by demanding information that I would find useful in building a case. I always made it a point to find out what the convicts' problems were, rather than what I needed from them. This was no ploy. I had an enormous curiosity about the details of their lives, both in prison and in the countries they came from.

So, I would invite the trafficker to tell me all about his concerns before gently leading him through the story of his life from childhood through incarceration. I would take the narrative, which typically ran to forty or fifty pages, and begin a process of "footnoting" by documenting the story I was told. An informer might say he or one of the people he delivered narcotics to was arrested. I'd go to the law enforcement agency responsible for the arrest, get the case folder, and obtain confirmation. If my storyteller stayed at a hotel in Marseilles, or made transatlantic telephone calls, those facts too were subject to corroboration. Sometimes, important players were known only by nicknames. Dugan obtained hundreds of photographs from Interpol that were shown to our cooperators. More often than not, the people known only by nicknames were fully identified. Since the narcotics conspiracy was worldwide, jurisdiction was really no problem. It did not matter how strange or exotic the places the traffickers described to me were as long as part of the story took place in New York.

The end result of this effort was enough material to provide the basis for the indictment of perhaps thirty people. Given the nature of the international narcotics trade, twenty-nine of them might be outside the country and seemingly beyond our reach. My policy was to go after these men—wherever they were— through extradition or expulsion. A coup d'état could have unpleasant consequences for major drug dealers who had been protected by officials in the government that was overthrown.

I found out very quickly that most of my cooperators didn't speak English. I would need interpreters. Being a court translator is a job that is usually thought of as a nuts-and-bolts support service, like being a stenographer or transcriber. I felt otherwise. While watching television one night, I'd seen evangelist Jimmy Swaggart preaching to a large crowd at an outdoor stadium in Chile. Swaggart was a smashing success, but as I watched it became clear that the crowd was actually being excited by the oratorical skill of the translator rather than Swaggart, who was speaking in English. It taught me a lesson: An accurate interpreter with a great voice and great presentation was extraordinarily valuable in a courtroom setting. The witness could be a total disaster, but the jury would be hanging on the words of an articulate translator.

Prosecutors with witnesses who spoke no English traditionally hired translators on a free-lance basis from a pool of men and women who did this kind of work in the courtroom. You took your chances on whether your selection would be good or bad. I decided that this was not the way I was going to proceed. I wanted somebody who could do for me what that guy in Chile did for the evangelist. So I conducted a search for the top translators who worked in the court system and came up with two marvelous women—Lydia Clancy and Marguerita Mensa. I put both of them on my payroll full-time. It was a decision I never regretted. The man sitting in the witness chair might be a sleazy inarticulate drug dealer, but the person the jurors kept their eyes on was my honest, forthright translator.

I also set out to make my drab, government-issue office a friendlier place for these frightened foreigners. A visitor in late 1972 or 1973 would have found an espresso machine and a buffet of Chilean, Italian, and Mexican dishes. And of course there would be Lydia and Marguerita in the middle of it all, engaged in animated conversations with my informers and their families. While all of this was going on, I might be letting one of my cooperators slowly tell his story, or I might be trying to help one of them out.

Being useful to people who helped me was something I worked on very hard. If a drug dealer was willing to become one of my informers, I'd break my neck to persuade the judge in his case to be lenient. I got one dealer facing a hundred-year sentence off on probation. Through word of mouth prisoners soon learned that I was a prosecutor who could get you a really good deal. So many drug dealers wanted to cooperate with me that some people began to think I was a defense lawyer.

One of the first people I helped was an Argentinian heroin trafficker named Jack Grosby. Grosby had been extradited to the United States from Switzerland. The extradition generated some excitement and attracted some headlines, but Grosby quickly became a nonperson after arriving on our shores. He was languishing in the Bergen County, New Jersey, jail when I became interested in him. Grosby supposedly had detailed knowledge of international narcotics trafficking, but no one in law enforcement had made a serious effort to get him to open up.

So I had Grosby brought to my office for a chat. He was cautious, and clearly knew a great deal more than he was telling me. I decided to invite him back for a second visit—lunch the following Saturday. Grosby was more forthcoming then, describing some of his drug dealings to me in a general way.

At the end of a long day of conversation, I said, "Jack, look, this is very helpful to me. There's got to be a way to make cases here. Are you sure there isn't more that you could fill in here?"

And Grosby said, "There's a guy in the Atlanta penitentiary doing forty years named Eduardo Poeta."

"I know Poeta," I replied.

Poeta had been the codefendant in the case of Luis Stepenberg, a major narcotics trafficker who was convicted in Brooklyn. Between the time of his conviction and his sentencing, Stepenberg committed suicide in prison. That left the judge in the case, Jacob Mishler, with just one person to sentence. The judge gave Poeta forty years, even though he was a secondary figure in the case.

It turned out that Poeta and Grosby were friends. And Grosby wanted to help his pal.

"Speak to Poeta," Grosby told me, "and then I'll speak to you."

I had Poeta brought to Brooklyn from Atlanta, where Dugan went to work on him. Spanish-speaking defendants who Dugan had helped in other cases were used to convince Poeta to cooperate. Dugan is OK and Puccio is OK, Poeta was told again and again. Within a couple of days, Poeta started to come around.

"Look, Eduardo, you're doing forty years, your appeals have been turned down," I said. "Help us and we'll help you. We know that Stepenberg arranged to have major shipments of narcotics sent to the United States. We know that you were important, because you were here in the United States getting the deliveries."

And Poeta said: "Thousands of kilos have passed through my hands. I picked it up from the French and gave it to the customers in New York."

This guy was the link between the major French Connection dealers and their customers in the United States. We debriefed Poeta for months. He named some of the biggest narcotics dealers in the world. Then Grosby came in and told us how he and Stepenberg had made the deals overseas. So we had Grosby overseas, cutting the deals, and Poeta here when the stuff arrived picking it up and making the deliveries.

By the time I was ready to hand up my first indictment on international narcotics dealing, the anteroom and the hallway into my office had twenty or thirty of the most important people in narcotics enforcement in New York waiting, looking on as my secretary, Lilly, was typing the proposed charges.

In November 1972, all this effort bore fruit with the indictment of twenty major narcotics traffickers, including Christian David and Michel Nicoli, Frenchmen who ran huge heroin smuggling rings from the safety of Brazil—or so they thought.

Only four of the suspects were Americans, but my investigation luckily coincided with a CIA effort to expel narcotics traffickers from South America. As I've said, Nixon put the CIA into the war on drugs, and the agency was very, very powerful in Latin American countries.

David and Nicoli were not extradited by the agency's friends in Brazil's military junta. The two drug lords were simply picked up, brutally tortured, and then summarily kicked out of Brazil without the niceties of an extradition hearing or other legal proceeding. I had to have David hospitalized when he arrived in New York. I liked to think of myself as a tough prosecutor, but I must have looked like Father Christmas to David after his encounter with the Brazilian authorities.

David, by the way, was a cutthroat who had already been sentenced to death in France for murdering a police commissioner. I soon had a chance to make a deal with the French fugitive. I offered him a choice of returning to France and the guillotine or cooperating with me and spending the rest of his life in a U.S. prison. He chose jail in the good old United States. His cooperation was much less than I had hoped for, however. David offered to give us the identities of corrupt American narcotics agents, but he refused to give up anyone in his drug operation. (Today, David is offering the contents of a sealed envelope that supposedly contains the truth about the Kennedy assassination to anyone who frees him from prison. There have been no takers.)

The rings headed by David and Nicoli were responsible for about 10 percent of the world heroin market. We determined that they shipped about 1,100 pounds of heroin worth $250 million into the United States from 1968 to 1971. At the time, these were astonishing figures.

When people ask me how to fight the war on drugs today, I always point out that the only significant reduction in the amount of heroin being imported into the United States came during the 1970s, when the prosecution of high-level international drug traffickers coincided with the ban on poppy growing in Turkey. The shortage of heroin produced a "panic" on the streets of New York. My little Eastern District operation became an integral part of this effort. French prosecutors would come to

New York and take detailed statements from many of the traffickers I had persuaded to cooperate. They then returned to France, where the sworn statements obtained here were used as evidence in criminal cases that were brought against high-level French narcotics dealers. About thirty top narcotics people in Marseilles alone were jailed largely on the basis of statements from my cooperating witnesses.

But prosecution has its limits. Absent diplomatic measures to halt the flow of drugs from the country of origin, you are not going to stem the flow of narcotics into the United States. Prosecutions, investigations, and large seizures are helpful, but no more than that. There is just too much "product" and too many ways to bring it into the country.

Still, in the 1970s hopes were high that the "war" really was being won for a time. I managed to get Grosby and Poeta out of jail in exchange for their cooperation. This did my reputation no damage among other heroin traffickers in U.S. jails.

All of a sudden, we were in the big time, and for more than a decade thereafter, the Eastern District overshadowed the Southern District in terms of the quality and importance of major criminal prosecutions. Naturally, this didn't happen without a battle. The Southern District had an established narcotics unit that for many years had handled all of the major drug cases in the New York area. Now I was aggressively challenging their hegemony. Wally Phillips, the chief of the Southern District's Narcotics Unit, had no intention of surrendering. The result was war.

To give you an idea of how intense that war got, let me tell you about an encounter that I lost:

One of the drug traffickers rounded up by the Brazilian police was an Italian named Bennie Buschetta. Brazil planned to ship Buschetta back to Italy, where he was wanted for a variety of serious crimes. But I wanted him in Brooklyn, where I believed his cooperation could be very useful to my effort to shut off the flow of heroin from South America to the United States. Unfortunately, I didn't have enough evidence to obtain an indictment against Buschetta. So I came up with what I thought to be an ingenious solution. I arranged with Brazilian authorities to have

Buschetta sent back to Italy by way of New York. Once Buschetta was in New York, I would go into my "Let's Make a Deal" mode, giving him a choice of remaining in the United States and cooperating with me or returning home to spend the rest of his life in an Italian prison.

Little did I know that other creative minds were at work. Across the East River, perhaps a mile from my office as the crow flies, Wally Phillips was laying plans to get Buschetta for the Southern District. Someone in federal law enforcement had tipped Phillips off about my interest in Buschetta and my plan to secure his cooperation.

The two law enforcement districts are supposed to cooperate in the never-ending war against the underworld, but in fact these two arms of the United States government are often quarrelsome, suspicious, and competitive. Powerful Mafia bosses and petty street hoodlums alike are oblivious to the federal bureaucratic boundaries that separated places like Manhattan and Brooklyn, the Bronx and Queens. Since criminals do business in both districts, jurisdictional quarrels are guaranteed. The conflict between the two districts, like the troubles in Northern Ireland, is endless. The rivalry is greatly intensified by social factors. Prosecutors in the majestic Southern District tend to look upon their Brooklyn-based counterparts as the Dead End Kids of law enforcement. Eastern District prosecutors from law schools like Fordham and St. John's naturally resent this second-class citizenship.

There was no doubt in my mind about the source of the Buschetta leak. For a number of years, federal narcotics enforcement had been hampered by an ongoing blood feud between the Bureau of Narcotics and Dangerous Drugs and the Customs Service. Both agencies regarded halting the flow of drugs into the United States as their sacred mission. The two agencies would battle over cases, compete for turf, and when things grew especially heated, arrest each other's drug-dealing informants. In Buschetta's case, I asked a Customs agent to go to Brazil to determine if he had valuable information and if he would be receptive to making a deal with me. Customs was very enthusiastic about my plan. The BNDD, however, expressed no enthusiasm for a scheme that gave a key role to its hated rival.

BNDD carried word of my desire to bring Buschetta into the fold to Phillips and entered into an alliance with the chief of the Southern District's narcotics unit. In January 1973, a few days before Buschetta was scheduled to arrive in New York, Phillips filed a sealed indictment against Buschetta charging him with using a phony ID in some of his previous travels between the United States and Brazil. This was a minor charge, to say the least, but it meant that Phillips could have Buschetta arrested when he arrived in New York and carted off to the Southern District.

I was quickly tipped off to Phillips's plan by my own reliable sources. I decided to retaliate by developing my own case against Buschetta. I had the Italian drug smuggler indicted on draft law violations in the Eastern District and asked the FBI to arrest him when he stepped from the plane at Kennedy Airport. Since JFK was in the Eastern District, and the FBI was the federal law enforcement agency with the most clout, I felt confident I'd recaptured my prize.

I was wrong. In the early morning hours of January 22, 1973, my arrest party, headed by FBI agents, arrived at the nearly empty Pan Am terminal at Kennedy. I say nearly empty because there was a second arrest party on the scene. Assistant U.S. attorney Wally Phillips, assistant U.S. attorney Wally Higgins, and two U.S. marshals from the Southern District were there on the same mission. The FBI agents immediately realized what was happening, but there was nothing in the FBI's copious regulations that covered a rival raiding party of federal law enforcement officials.

It was every lawman for himself. Phillips and Higgins seized the moment by bolting from the terminal and racing across the road to the control tower at JFK. They barged into the nerve center of air traffic at one of the world's greatest international airports. The two prosecutors demanded that the FAA supervisor on duty send a message to flight 202. The supervisor must have believed the plane was carrying the World's Most Dangerous Criminal. Still, he refused to send the message. Phillips and Higgins were undaunted. They found the Pan Am radio dis-.

patcher and demanded that he transmit a message directing James Coleman, a BNDD agent aboard the plane, to arrest Buschetta immediately. The dispatcher, who obviously knew nothing of federal law enforcement, sensibly suggested that Buschetta be arrested after the plane landed. Needless to say, Phillips and Higgins rejected this proposal out of hand. The message was dispatched. Moments later, a bewildered Buschetta was arrested and handcuffed in flight by Coleman. The Southern District completed its triumph perhaps an hour later when Buschetta—who was handcuffed to Coleman—emerged from the plane. A U.S. marshal raced forward and handcuffed himself to Buschetta, using the astounded drug dealer's remaining free wrist. Buschetta was then bundled into a black car and whisked off to a federal jail on the island of Manhattan.

I was upset about the abduction of my witness, but the FBI was truly embarrassed. They hadn't gotten their man. They were outmaneuvered by a couple of young punk lawyers—something that would never have happened to Efrem Zimbalist, Jr. Acting FBI Director L. Patrick Gray lodged a protest with Attorney General Richard Kleindeist. The upshot of all this was that Bob Morse, the U.S. attorney for the Eastern District, and Whitney North Seymour, Jr., the U.S. attorney for the Southern District, were summoned to Washington for a sit-down in same way two wayward Mafia bosses might be hauled before the Commission. Assistant Attorney General Henry Petersen told both men to behave themselves.

The feuding continued.

I learned a valuable lesson from this encounter. All my drug probes became joint investigations. A man from the BNDD and a Customs agent were involved at each stage of the investigation. Both agencies were kept fully informed of every move I made. I did not want interagency rivalry to destroy what I was doing, and to a large extent I succeeded.

The incident at JFK illuminates a hard truth of law enforcement. During my career as a prosecutor, I locked horns with powerful politicians, vicious drug dealers, Mafia bosses, clever con men, and corrupt, ruthless police officers. None of these formidable foes, however, caused me as much difficulty as bureaucratic rivals within the Justice Department. The crook-catching end of the business is pure pleasure compared to the bureaucratic maneuvering necessary for survival and success.

There was also a second, more sinister kind of internal warfare. Not all my rivals in law enforcement were working the same side of the street. My activities soon brought me face-to-face with an iron clad law of narcotics enforcement: A widespread investigation of drug trafficking inevitably puts you on the trail of police corruption. There was a theory that police officers willing to look the other way for "harmless" vices like gambling would never dream of protecting drug dealers. Unfortunately, greed can't be compartmentalized, and police corruption increases in proportion to the amount of money available.

The modern history of police corruption in New York began with Frank Serpico, the cop who refused to take part in the bribe-taking rituals of the NYPD in the late 1960s. Corruption had been an integral part of police life for decades and was so pervasive that any cop who attempted to do an honest job became the target of suspicion from his fellow officers. Serpico, just such an honest cop, complained about widespread graft in the department. When police brass ignored his story, he and another officer went to *The New York Times.* The resulting exposé prompted Mayor John Lindsay to establish the Knapp Commission in the spring of 1970, chaired by Whitman Knapp, a sixty-two-year-old attorney. The committee quietly conducted an investigation of police corruption that was capped by public hearings in October 1971.

New York was exposed to a stomach-turning catalogue of police greed and corruption. Cops would race to the scene of a reported death to search the corpse for cash and jewelry. And race they did—the first cops to arrive got the loot. The graft was so institutionalized that commission exhibits included a neatly typed interoffice memo from the Statler Hilton naming twenty-seven police officers who got cash payments from the hotel at Christmas. Undercover agents told eyewitness tales of bribery and payoffs.

Even with this sordid prelude, many New Yorkers were not prepared for what was to come. On December 14, 1972, the police department held a news conference. Stunned reporters were told fifty-seven pounds of heroin—the drugs seized in the celebrated French Connection case—had been stolen from the police property room. It would be difficult to exaggerate the impact of this announcement. Despite the tales of police corruption that emerged from the Knapp Commission, it was hard to accept that police officers were depraved enough to become heroin wholesalers. Almost anything else was believable, but selling heroin? As the weeks unfolded, the amount of heroin and cocaine discovered stolen from the property room rose to an astonishing four hundred pounds. The drugs had a street value of $73 million.

The movie version of the French Connection story had been a tremendous hit only a year earlier and the winner of the Academy Award as the best film of 1971. A pair of rugged, fearless, and nearly penniless New York City narcotics detectives smash a gigantic drug transaction engineered by a wealthy, arrogant French heroin dealer called Frog 1. The cops grab a huge shipment of Frog 1's heroin and arrest his Italian-American mob confederates and the rich Jewish businessman bankrolling the deal. (The detective heroes also manage to abuse numerous blacks and to shoot an obnoxious FBI agent to death before the film ends with their transfer out of narcotics.) The public loved it. New York City narcotics detectives, it was clear, would stop at nothing to protect the people from the curse of heroin.

Box office receipts would have plummeted drastically if Gene Hackman and Roy Scheider, who played the colorful detective Popeye Doyle and his loyal partner Cloudy, had acted the part of real New York City narcotics detectives, circa 1970. In that case, they might have extorted a huge cash bribe from Frog 1 to ignore the whole transaction. Or the detectives might have smashed their way into Frog 1's hotel room with guns drawn if their illegal wiretap disclosed that he was stupid enough to keep large amounts of cash or drugs there. They would find the contraband and steal it for themselves. The happy ending would find the detectives buying lavish homes, expensive cars, and businesses that they would operate after they retired from the police department.

The theft of the French Connection heroin added new weight to the anticop sentiments of a hostile citizenry. While no one had been formally accused of the thefts, even the most credulous New Yorker assumed that corrupt police officers had simply checked the narcotics out of the property room and become millionaire drug wholesalers.

The public perception was very close to the truth, though no one outside of a few people in law enforcement knew just how bold the police officers responsible for the thefts had been. The cops had removed drugs from the property room on six occasions between March 1969 and January 1972. On each occasion, flour was substituted for the narcotics and returned to the property room.

Only once had there been a hitch. On August 12, 1970, a man who identified himself as "Detective Nunziata" requested a suitcase containing thirty-one pounds of heroin. But this time, the heroin thieves ran up against a brick wall. A note was attached to the suitcase: "This evidence is not to be released without the permission of the commanding officer, Narcotics Division."

"Detective Nunziata" was duly informed the drugs were off-limits. Now, thirty-one pounds of heroin was a relatively small amount of drugs, given the appetite of the officers who were doing the stealing. A more cautious gang of thieves would have backed off and chosen another target. But "Detective Nunziata" returned to the property room the very next day and presented the clerk with a neatly typed letter on police department stationery. It authorized the bearer to remove the heroin. The letter was signed by John M. McCahey, the commanding officer of the Narcotics Division. The large, clear, sweeping letters with which McCahey signed his name suggested that he was a man of great self-confidence. Of course, the signature on the letter looked nothing like the handwriting of the real McCahey. The thieves made no effort whatsoever to make it look genuine. Any impressive-looking signature would do. "Detective Nunziata" walked out of the property room lugging a suitcase filled with heroin that would soon find its way back into New York's black neighborhoods.

The search for the police officers who committed what was

arguably the greatest theft in U.S. history would consume more than three years of my life, even though I entered the investigation at a late stage. The solution to this case was a kind of Holy Grail to criminal prosecutors, and naturally everybody had to be involved. The first of many turf fights over the case was decided in favor of Maurice Nadjari, a New York City native who had risen to fame as a prosecutor in the office of Manhattan district attorney Frank Hogan. Nadjari was a terror when it came to official corruption. He had personally tried Queens district attorney Thomas Mackell for misconduct in failing to investigate crooked prosecutors in his own office. He later went to the Suffolk County district attorney's office, where corrupt Republicans on Long Island felt his wrath. The disturbing revelations of police corruption in New York City made him seem a logical choice to clean things up.

Three months before the theft of the French Connection heroin was discovered, New York's governor, Nelson Rockefeller, had appointed Nadjari as a special state prosecutor, responsible for going after the corruption exposed by the Knapp Commission. Nadjari and the city's five local prosecutors (one for each borough) all leaped for the property room case. Nadjari won the prize by persuading Rockefeller to issue an executive order giving the special state prosecutor exclusive jurisdiction.

His subsequent effort to solve the case ended in failure, though no one who read the newspapers, including me, could have guessed that at the beginning. Nadjari publicly boasted he knew the names of the police officers involved in the crime and how they had removed the narcotics from the property room. Indictments, he said, would be forthcoming when sufficient evidence had been obtained. These kinds of statements, although they may have had a legitimate law enforcement purpose, came back to haunt Nadjari later on.

Rockefeller's executive order on the French Connection case did not apply to federal agencies, but I did not get involved in the property room investigation until 1974. There didn't seem to be a need. Nadjari, after all, was going great guns. But after more than a year passed, it became increasingly clear that a solution to the case was nowhere in sight.

During that time, my own work with drug dealers insured that the case was never far from my mind. The dealers complained to me about being ripped off by police officers who stole their money and their drugs. The biggest thieves, by far, were often members of the police department's elite Special Investigating Unit. The SIU was made up of the department's top narcotics detectives. Its jurisdiction took in the whole city. SIU only investigated major drug dealers, and, occasionally, these dealers were arrested and sent to prison. But since some SIU detectives regarded each investigation as an opportunity to make money rather than to enforce the law, their greatest exploits went unpublicized. An SIU investigation often began with an illegal wiretap on the phone of a suspected drug dealer. Once the wire had produced enough information about the dealer's operation, a raid would take place. If the raid did not yield enough booty for the detectives, the dealer would be given a chance to buy his way out of the case. The dealer might be taken to a bar, where negotiations between him and the detectives would establish a price, typically $10,000. This was only one way of earning money. Tipping off drug dealers about confidential state or federal investigations was another lucrative source of income. Stealing money from the evidence safe in the office of a federal prosecutor was still another.

This kind of activity occasionally moved the police department brass to action. In 1968, for example, $1,700 intended for the widows of two detectives killed in the line of duty was stolen from a petty cash fund in the Narcotics Division. A police captain crying in the wilderness said the 350-member Narcotics Division was "riddled with corruption." The result was an "investigation" that resulted in a raft of transfers. A group of supervisors and detectives in Narcotics was sent off to do penance in precincts in the wilds of the Bronx and Staten Island. End investigation. The brass would then wait for things to quiet down, as things always did.

Not everyone in the PD was crooked, of course. They were many fine officers, though not nearly enough of them. They tended to be outsiders in their own departments. It took some effort to remain honest, and those officers who did developed their own bag of tricks. Joe Comperiati, the veteran police officer who investigated the French Connection theft for the department, scheduled his vacations at Christmastime, since the payoffs to New York's Finest reached a crescendo during the holidays.

With this history in mind, when I did decide to take a crack at the property room thefts, the crucial investigative question I asked myself and others was moral rather than factual: Who possessed the kind of towering arrogance and greed it would take to pull off a crime of this magnitude? The answer, in general terms, was obvious. The thieves were SIU detectives.

I was gradually—but steadily—drawn into the French Connection investigation by events unfolding inside and outside the United States. Any lingering doubts I might have had about the dishonesty of SIU detectives were quickly erased by a major international upheaval, the 1974 overthrow of Chilean president Salvador Allende. The military junta that seized power was naturally chummy with our CIA people there: Would the junta mind turning over some drug dealers wanted by U.S. authorities? No problem. The fugitive Chileans were rounded up by the police, tortured, and kicked out of the country. They were treated in the same fashion as their counterparts in Brazil, and I can tell you that the dealers were as happy to see the soil of the good old United States as any long-suffering American POW. About a dozen of the Chileans quickly agreed to cooperate and began identifying SIU detectives who had ripped them off. A drug dealer named Coco Torres, for example, told me he had $400,000 in cash when he was grabbed by SIU detectives. But only $25,000 had been turned in. I hoped these episodes would be useful in putting pressure on SIU detectives who might be persuaded to tell the truth.

The difficulties of the French Connection theft were well illustrated by the difficulties I encountered in establishing exactly how the crime was carried out. We knew that there were six withdrawals from 1969 to 1972, and that in each case, the narcotics had been checked out by someone who signed the name of a real-life SIU detective named Joe Nunziata. The drugs were replaced with flour and returned to the property clerk's office the same day. The handwriting expert used by the police concluded that the same man had written Nunziata's signature on all six occasions. The expert was unable to match the handwriting on the ledger with that of any other suspect in the case, including Nunziata. But handwriting analysis is inherently unreliable. To me, it was tantamount to tea leaf reading. The very fact that handwriting analysis had been an important aspect of the investigation was a tribute to the poor quality of evidence in the case.

To further complicate matters, Nunziata died, an apparent suicide, eight months before the French Connection thefts were accidently discovered by personnel at the property clerk's office. Nunziata shot himself in the head in April 1972, three months after the French Connection thieves had removed 220 pounds of cocaine and heroin from the property room. He had been caught accepting a bribe from a federal informer posing as an international drug dealer and was under pressure to cooperate in an investigation of other corrupt police officers. Shortly after his suicide, two police officers who emerged as key suspects in the case retired from the department. And the thefts stopped. There were no more withdrawals after Nunziata's death.

I spent hundreds of hours trying to figure out why Nunziata's name was used. If Nunziata was part of the crew that stole the drugs, why would he draw suspicion to himself by using his own name? Was he arrogant enough to believe the thefts would never be detected? The answer to that question may have been yes. Security and record-keeping at the property clerk's office were appalling. Police officers and detectives showed up at the office and routinely checked out drugs, jewelry, furs, weapons, and a hundred and one other items that became evidence in criminal cases. A detective might be asked to produce some identification. On the other hand, he might not. As a general rule, the property clerk pursued a policy of no questions asked. To the shrewd, tough, and unscrupulous detectives who stole the dope, it must have been the world's largest candy store. (The property clerk's office was actually located in a former candy factory on Broome Street in lower Manhattan.) To make the situation even sweeter, the thieves knew that someday the department would overcome its normal state of bureaucratic inertia and burn the drugs. Evidence of their crime would literally go up in smoke.

One fascinating story about SIU detectives and the property clerk's office came from writer Robin Moore, the author of the novel *The French Connection*. Moore said he invited Eddie Eagan and Sonny Grosso, the detectives who made the real-life seizure of the French Connection heroin, to Jamaica in 1967 for help in finishing the screenplay for the movie. Grosso and Eagan brought along a friend: Joe Nunziata.

During a boozy evening at a bar owned by Moore, Nunziata came up with a great idea for a new book and movie: the theft of the French Connection heroin from the property room. Eagan and Grosso expressed enthusiasm for the idea, though neither detective matched Nunziata's ardor.

"What a piece of cake," Moore later quoted Nunziata as saying. "It's worth at least fourteen million dollars wholesale. More if a panic gets going."

"Maybe we could make a fiction book on a caper where they steal the shit," Grosso added.

In the world of law enforcement, Nunziata theories flew fast and thick. Some investigators believed he never would have used his own name if he was involved in the thefts. Others thought his suicide was a sure sign that Nunziata feared his role in the French Connection caper would be uncovered. Some thought another detective signed his name—or that the detectives who stole the heroin used a confederate who was not a police officer to sign Nunziata's name. Still others thought that Nunziata—a gregarious, popular, and well-known detective—would have had to sign for heroin if he went to the property clerk's office, since he was so recognizable. There were those who believed the dead detective may have signed the log book with his right hand (he was left-handed).

The permutations seemed limitless.

There was also a long, tortured search for an inside man who helped the detectives. The office was staffed by police officers who were unfit for regular duty. They might have mental, physical, or emotional problems that prevented them from working the streets. Collectively, they were known as the "rubber gun squad." Needless to say, neither morale nor expertise was particularly high in this group. Would the tough, shrewd detectives who stole the heroin have a drink with these men, much less make one a member of the gang?

Nadjari and the police department had already searched long and hard for an inside man. One clerk had been involved in four of the six removals. Nadjari worked on the guy forever, threatening him with all kinds of dire consequences. They did a background investigation on the clerk and found out that the clerk, who was married, had a girlfriend. To put extra pressure on him, Nadjari subpoenaed him, his wife, and the girlfriend to testify before a grand jury on the same day. Nadjari then had them all sit together in the waiting room outside the grand jury for hours.

I, too, thought that there may well have been an inside man. When you take out the French Connection heroin, which was the basis for a best-selling book and Academy Award–winning movie, it's like somebody saying: "We're checking out the Hope diamond, we're bringing it to court." Someone in the office should have remembered something, but no one remembered anything. Yet no credible evidence emerged that would have linked any of them to the theft. I went back to the property clerk's office repeatedly and tried to visualize how the detectives came in, requested the drugs, and then hauled them away to a car that would have been waiting outside. They then would have driven to an apartment where the narcotics were replaced with flour. The heroin (or cocaine) would go to a major drug dealer, and the detective-partners would split up the money from the sale.

But my vision was always shadowy, always hazy.

The struggle to make that vision clear led me to Bob Leuci, the former SIU detective who had become an informant and the darling of the Southern District. The whole nation eventually came to know Leuci—or at least a sanitized version of him—through the book *Prince of the City,* which later became a popular motion picture of the same name. The movie is still in all the video stores. Rent it sometime and you'll see actor Treat Williams playing the handsome, noble, tormented detective Leuci—kind to pathetic junkies, loyal to his friends, determined to help weed out corruption in the police department.

I'm in the movie, too. Look for the incredibly mean balding prosecutor who tries to do him in.

The real Leuci was very charming, articulate, and manipulative. He was also often as phony as a four-dollar bill. Some said you'd have to completely replace his blood with sodium pentathol to have any hope he might tell the truth. He'd been an SIU detective for three years when he agreed to cooperate with the Knapp Commission's probe into police corruption in 1971. Leuci was not the target of a corruption investigation. Nicholas Scopetta, a Knapp Commission attorney, had called the detective in for routine questioning when Leuci volunteered his services as an undercover agent. Did a tormented conscience or the fear of future exposure as a corrupt cop prompt Leuci to cooperate? The answer to that question depends largely on whether you choose to believe Leuci the book, Leuci the major motion picture, or Puccio the prosecutor.

Naturally, Scopetta wanted to know about his new recruit's previous corruption track record. Leuci swore he had committed only three minor illegal acts in his entire police career. In retrospect, it's hard to believe that smart New York prosecutors would swallow that "three little things" story, given what we knew about the depth of corruption in SIU, and the unpleasant new revelations we were receiving every week. The fact that Leuci could sell that story, and keep it sold, was partly a tribute to his own talent for manipulation. But it also showed how desperate all of us in law enforcement were to believe that most corrupt city cops were only *slightly* corrupt—willing to pocket a little extra cash, maybe, but still genuinely concerned about enforcing the law when things got really serious.

Anyway, Leuci began working as an undercover agent, first for Scopetta and later, when the Southern District took over the corruption probe, for Southern District attorney Mike Shaw. His sixteen-month stint undercover hooked only one big fish— Edward Rosner, a well-known lawyer who represented a lot of major drug dealers. But Leuci couldn't have picked a better target from the point of view of Southern District prosecutors. Rosner had been adept at obtaining acquittals for drug dealers arrested in the Southern District, and his conviction on bribery charges was regarded as a huge victory. And Leuci, who had pretended to accept the bribe while the hidden tape recorders whirred, became a full-fledged hero—a star in the Southern District firmament.

Leuci's cover was blown in January of 1972, but he remained on at the Southern District as a kind of police corruption expert in residence. His family was moved to a comfortable home in Virginia, and Leuci commuted there on weekends while spending his work week in New York, preparing to testify at more trials based on his undercover work. Meanwhile, lionizing Leuci became a Southern District cottage industry. "The U.S. attorney's staff kept assuring the detective that he was performing a hero's role in helping to bring an end to corruption in the administration of justice," wrote Southern District U.S. attorney Whitney North Seymour, a charter member of what came to be known as the "I Love Leuci" club.

Eventually, this internal back-slapping was not enough. Seymour wanted to let the public in on the wonder that was Leuci, and he approved a plan to memorialize the detective's activities by giving his story to *Life* magazine in order to "show the world that he had done courageous things in the interest of justice." Even before that story came out, *The New York Times* publicly disclosed Leuci's role as a federal undercover agent. He became a *Times* "Man in the News." The newspaper quoted friends of the tough young detective as saying he had become even tougher after entering narcotics work "by refusing to accept the corruption that he saw around him on the force." These unidentified "friends" could only have been Southern District prosecutors. Leuci, by then, had no other friends.

I had been eager to meet this paragon of informers myself, figuring he was bound to know everything about corruption in the police department. Naturally, I wanted to question him about the French Connection theft. But I had been hearing some disturbing things about Leuci, too. Most of them came from Carl Aguiluz, another SIU detective who had agreed to cooperate with the government.

Aguiluz was a cop who admitted he had sold heroin. This was

a genuinely shocking revelation. To be sure, the French Connection theft had established that *somebody* in the force was trafficking in heroin. But the case remained unsolved, and the idea of drug-dealing cops was still an abstraction until Carl Aguiluz came along—a flesh-and-blood detective who readily admitted he and his partners peddled dope.

This incredible betrayal of everything the police department was supposed to stand for began with a big, well-publicized arrest. Aguiluz and his partners made a fantastic law enforcement score, seizing 105 kilograms of heroin—the most ever confiscated at one time, bigger even than the original French Connection seizure in 1962. There were triumphant newspaper headlines. But Aguiluz and his partners regarded the whole matter as a terrible disappointment. They had seized a lot of drugs, but no money. The detectives were used to pocketing at least $4,000 to $5,000 per arrest. Sometimes a collar might net as much as $10,000 or $12,000. To make this particular seizure pay off, the detectives decided to hold out five kilos. Over the next several months, they used their drug informers to sell the heroin for $40,000 to $45,000 per kilo.

Aguiluz went on to recount eighteen or twenty thefts of cash from drug dealers, and numerous other crimes. Every investigation the detectives undertook was regarded as an opportunity to make money—the hallmark of SIU. And although he had never been one of Leuci's partners, he had no hesitation about insisting the darling of the Southern District was no different from any other SIU detective.

"That fucking Leuci," Aguiluz would tell me. "Speak to Leuci. He's got to know a lot."

Yet when I finally got Leuci into my office, I was amazed that he seemed to know nothing.

"Wait a minute," I said to Leuci. "You're cooperating with the government. What did you say you'd been involved in?"

"Well, I've only been involved in two or three corrupt deals for a total of about seventy-five hundred dollars."

Then he rattled off an account of his transgressions.

"I find that very, very hard to believe," I said.

Uneasiness about Leuci's credibility had also crystallized in the Southern District, where Aguiluz had originally been arrested and turned into an informant. Leuci had lied convincingly at the Rosner trial when he told the jury about his relatively blameless past. But now Rosner was appealing, and the defense had obtained an affidavit from a drug dealer who had been one of Leuci's informers. The dealer claimed, among other things, to have purchased drugs from Leuci on a number of occasions.

The drug dealer plus Aguiluz made it very hard to continue believing Leuci's "three little things" tale. And the issue of his honesty was no little matter. Rosner's conviction, of course, was on the line. So were the string of future convictions prosecutors had hoped to make using Leuci as a witness. So, of course, was the credibility of the Southern District, which had made such an effort to promote Leuci to the press.

Paul Curran, who replaced Seymour as the U.S. attorney in the Southern District, chose an aggressive young prosecutor named Rudy Giuliani to cooperate with me in getting to the bottom of things. Rivalry between the two law enforcement districts was still a major problem, and I think Curran regarded the two of us as a promising team that could bridge the animosity between Brooklyn and Manhattan. Giuliani, at twenty-nine, was my age, and came from a similar middle-class Italian upbringing in New York. He was a no-bullshit guy who really knew how to conduct an investigation, and our cooperation worked out tremendously. Like me, Rudy believed there was simply no way Leuci was guilty of only a few acts of minor misconduct. The strategy we devised to make him tell the truth was a simple version of the old good cop–bad cop routine. We agreed that it made sense for Rudy to play the good cop, since he was from the Southern District, where the "I Love Leuci" club still had a lot of members. I got to be the bad cop.

Leuci's chief vulnerability was his desperate desire to make other people like him. He had a very fragile personality. And though he was an astonishingly brazen liar, he was the soul of sensitivity when it came to how other people viewed him. If even a flicker of displeasure glinted in your eye while Bob was going through his "love me" routine, it was enough to ruin his weekend.

Leuci's status as a weekend commuter to Virginia turned out to be a great advantage here. I used to summon Leuci to my office in Brooklyn on Fridays and ask him three or four questions, usually about the allegations and complaints from drug dealers who said they had purchased narcotics from Leuci or had their money stolen by him. After patiently listening to his denials, I'd have him sit outside my office for a couple of hours to let the pressure mount.

Then I'd call him back into the office to express my total displeasure with his answers.

"Bob, you're full of shit."

These harsh words would produce a veritable torrent of denials and special pleading.

"Look, Tom, there's no way I would have anything to do with the scumbags you're talking about," Bob would tell me.

He did not want to leave my office until he'd convinced me he was telling the truth and was a great guy to boot. In fact, it became nearly impossible to shut Leuci up.

"Bob, I really don't want to talk to you anymore because I don't believe a word you're saying" was my conversation closer.

That line was Leuci's weekend ruiner. He would sadly board the Eastern shuttle for the trip to see his family at their government-provided home in a wooded area of Virginia outside Washington. Then he would call Rudy at home and start crying on the phone.

Bob would have to return to New York on Monday for a new round of coaxing from Rudy and his dreaded session with me at the end of the work week. Rudy and I repeated this procedure for about five weeks, with Rudy always providing a more sympathetic ear for Leuci's laments about the guy from the Eastern District. Finally, I called Bob over on a Friday and had a drug dealer named Freddy Avilez sitting in the waiting room outside my office when Leuci arrived. A few days earlier, Avilez had told me what had become a very familiar story: Detective Leuci had stolen his money. The only new twist Avilez could provide was the fact that Leuci had also stolen the watch off his wrist.

I had Freddy sit outside with Leuci for about half an hour. The two men did not exchange a single word, but both were no doubt meditating on their old times together. I then called Leuci into my office and came straight to the point.

"Bob, I'm going to indict you on the basis of Avilez's testimony," I said.

The threat had the desired effect. Leuci's expression betrayed fear and wonder. Could it really be that this strange man who refused to like him was about to shatter his world? He immediately went into his please-believe-me act, but his heart didn't seem to be in it. I think he sensed correctly that I wasn't bluffing.

If you've seen the movie, you know that Leuci turned all this into a morality tale. The brave detective fibbed about his past transgressions but only to protect his former SIU partners from prosecution. Those decent men were his friends—if Leuci talked, it would ruin their lives! The ruthless prosecutors (present company definitely included) were ready to destroy Leuci and his friends, just out of the selfish desire to advance their careers by making convictions against police officers.

The truth was that Leuci never cared about his partners and never expressed any concern about them—to me or anyone else in law enforcement. Bob Leuci was a bad cop who had followed the traditional SIU route of turning law enforcement into a personal graft-making machine. He lied only to protect himself.

The Leuci mythology has him returning to his home in Virginia in a suicidal state. He has an emotional telephone conversation with Rudy, who leaps onto the shuttle and flies to Washington. Once at Leuci's side in the woods of Virginia, Rudy listens compassionately as a distraught Leuci confesses all his sins. The truth, I regret to report, was much more prosaic. Several days after I had threatened Leuci with indictment, he called early in the morning, from his mother's house in Brooklyn.

"I've got to come over! I've got to come over!" he said.

"Look, Bob, I've got a very busy day ahead of me," I replied. "Let's do it some other time." My coldness was partly bad cop role playing, but partly genuine. I *did* have a busy day, and he was not all that high on my list of priorities. From my Eastern District perspective, Leuci was just one small part of an intense investigation aimed at cracking the French Connection case.

"I've got to talk to you!" Leuci wailed again.

I relented.

"Well, come over and see me at five o'clock," I said.

Several hours passed, and Leuci made his way from his mother's house to the Eastern District.

The phone rang. It was Rudy.

"You've played with this guy's mind for weeks and you've turned him into a total basket case," Rudy said, while the target of our Pavlovian experiment listened intently to Giuliani's end of the conversation.

"He's dying to come over to confess and you're telling him, 'Come at five o'clock,' " Rudy complained. "The guy might kill himself."

Well, we couldn't let that happen.

"Look," Rudy said. "We'll catch a cab."

What followed in my office was Bob's "confession," a long and utterly depressing catalog of medium-size scores and rip-offs Leuci had pulled with his SIU partners. It was almost always impossible to know when Leuci was telling the truth, but it seemed abundantly clear to me that he was being honest about the only thing that really mattered to me: Bob Leuci was not involved in the French Connection theft and did not know anything about it.

Leuci's confession, of course, made a lot of people in the Southern District very, very depressed. And it exposed Leuci to some legal danger. Paul Curran could, if he chose, decide to charge the ex-detective with perjury for his testimony in the Rosner case. The movie version of Leuci's life shows his fate indeed hanging in the balance as prosecutors gather in front of a wise-looking Curran to debate the brave detective's fate. Naturally, the demonic Puccio character calls for Leuci's destruction while the saintly Giuliani character threatens to resign from the U.S. attorney's office if the poor man is indicted.

Such a meeting, of course, never took place. Rudy never threatened to resign. There was no controversy. The Southern District was not about to embarrass itself by indicting a man who had been its corruption expert-in-residence. And once I was satisfied Leuci knew nothing about the French Connection theft, I completely lost interest in him.

People often used to ask me how I felt about the way I was depicted by Leuci. I always tell them there are three stories about Bob: the book, the movie, and the truth. The only thing I regret about my role in the Leuci affair was that I didn't pay more attention to what was going on. If I had known the whole saga was soon to be a major motion picture, I'd have taken better notes.

I watched *Prince of the City* at a special screening, and I was surprised at how little emotion I felt at seeing myself portrayed as a demonlike figure intent on destroying a good man's life to satisfy his own ambition. (At one point the character actor who plays me is slugged by another aggrieved SIU detective. Generally, I'm told, the audience bursts into cheers.) I did feel sorry for the actor, who received much rougher treatment in the movie than I ever did in real life. But I partially regarded the whole tale as a tribute to my efforts at playing bad cop. And the movie, I figured, was certainly faithful to Leuci's view of the world and my place in it.

Rudy Giuliani, now the mayor of New York City, emerges in the movie as the epitome of justice and compassion. But that isn't the real story.

I've been told that to this day Leuci—now retired from the force and writing crime novels—refuses to believe that Rudy was just a prosecutor playing a role and not his true friend. I guess for once the star manipulator got manipulated himself.

3

MAKING THE FRENCH
CONNECTION

THERE WAS one thing Leuci said that did stand out in my mind. It was during a conversation about New York's seemingly endless ranks of crooked cops. Which ones, I asked him, were the biggest outlaws? Which ones were capable, say, of stealing the French Connection heroin?

"Frank King, Pat Intrieri, and Vinnie Albano," Leuci responded.

All three were on my short list of suspects in the French Connection theft.

Frank King was a big, beefy, brutish narcotics detective who, I believed, had arranged for the sale of the stolen heroin to a major New York drug dealer named Vinnie Papa. I had first heard of him in 1972 from Tom Dugan, who thought Detective King would be able to help us by testifying in a big upcoming narcotics conspiracy case.

"We've got to call King," Dugan kept saying to me. "He's going to be a corroborating witness."

The trouble with Frank King was that no one ever seemed able to find him. Dugan went through a whole two-month trial without ever being able to locate the detective. When we'd call to inquire about him, the police department would say he was traveling. Or retired. We got all kinds of funny answers. The only thing I knew then about King was that he was never around when you needed him.

Eventually, I learned much, much more. The most striking thing about King was the kind of fear he instilled in criminals. This was not because they believed he would bring them to justice. They regarded King as the kind of cop capable of blowing their brains out—always a big respect builder in the underworld. King was also perceived—correctly—as a police officer who was tight with really powerful mobsters. He thought and acted like a hood, holding court at Vincent's Clam House in Little Italy.

King grew up in the Bronx and joined the police department in 1955. After a stint as a patrolman in Harlem, he moved into the police department's School for Thieves: plainclothes. Plainclothesmen enriched themselves mainly by taking payoffs from gamblers, but no form of graft or corruption was too small or too petty for most of them. After a few years as a plainclothesman in the Bronx, King was ready for the big time. He moved into the Narcotics Division and became an SIU detective.

King had already been publicly identified as the key suspect in the French Connection thefts by the time I became involved in the investigation. Nadjari's chief assistant, Joe Phillips, had publicly boasted that his boss was closing in on the detective who masterminded the theft. At a press conference, Phillips referred to this detective, with great emphasis, as the "kingpin." This none-too-subtle ploy had the desired effect: New Yorkers were soon reading about Frank King, the chief suspect in the French Connection theft.

I never completely trusted Nadjari. He was a very driven guy, also very publicity-conscious. He was a great prosecutor, but he lived by the press and he died by the press. The press built him up and then tore him down—and it tore him down because he couldn't deliver. After his fall, the big rap on Nadjari became that he was an enemy of constitutional rights, suspending civil liberties and putting the Constitution on ice to chase innocent people. But that is simply not true. Nadjari often had the right crooks, and he often indicted the right people. He wasn't exactly hounding the innocent. Like a lot of professional law enforcement people, I was not an admirer of Nadjari because too often he could not put away the people he was investigating. King was a perfect example. Nadjari indicted him twice on charges that weren't directly related to the French Connection case. The idea, of course, was to put enough pressure on King to force him to talk. But King kept his mouth shut, both indictments collapsed, and so did Nadjari's power and prestige.

Not that this did anything to diminish suspicions about King. If anything, it made the rest of us more obsessed with trying to get him.

Police investigators discovered that King had been a member of an SIU team that placed legal wiretaps on the home and business of a high-level drug dealer from Queens named Vincent Papa. This was a very interesting connection. Papa was a career criminal who was quite capable of moving the large quantity of drugs stolen from the police property room. On the night of February 3, 1972, a month after the last and biggest withdrawal of narcotics from the property room, federal and local police pulled over a car carrying Papa and a Bronx drug dealer named Joseph DiNapoli. In a suitcase in the trunk of the car, the police and agents found a million dollars in cash. Papa, through his lawyer, said he and DiNapoli found the money and were on their way to the police to turn it in when they were intercepted. The New York papers found this story amusing in the extreme. But only after the police learned ten months later about the missing property room drugs did they begin to suspect where the cash might have been headed.

Not surprisingly, the SIU investigation of Papa was a complete failure. The wiretaps produced no information of any value. One night, King and Julie Tucker, an attractive SIU detective, were monitoring the King wire in the basement of a school near the drug dealer's home. King made a pass at Tucker, which she rebuffed by ignoring him and busying herself with some paperwork.

"You're wasting your time," King told her.

"What are you talking about?" Tucker asked.

King then boastfully informed Tucker that he had "sold" the wire to Papa. Other members of the SIU team probing Papa were Joe Nunziata and Detective John McClean. After the operation ended in failure, Nunziata gave McClean $1,500. The money, he explained, was his share of the $7,000 Papa had given to King for telling the drug dealer about the wiretaps and the investigation.

John McClean was outraged.

He did not believe a drug dealer with the stature of Vincent Papa had paid only $7,000.

A CLOSE associate of King was Pasquale Intrieri, a police lieutenant who had spent many years in the Narcotics Division. King and Intrieri formed a private detective agency following King's abrupt retirement from the police department in 1972. (They retired shortly after the apparent suicide of a good friend: Joe Nunziata.) An early client was none other than Vinnie Papa. At the time, a gang of kidnappers was making things difficult for the city's leading drug dealers by abducting the dealers' relatives and holding them for ransom. King and Intrieri became bodyguards for Vincent Papa's children.

The third man on my list was a detective named Vincent Albano. Weeks after the withdrawal of the French Connection heroin from the property room, Albano was gunned down in front of a nightspot in the Bronx called Chez Joey. Albano, who was hit five times in the chest, was rushed to a nearby hospital. Men in such a position generally want the support and comfort of their families. But Albano, however, did not only reach out for his wife or parents. The first call of the gravely wounded detective was to Frank King and Pat Intrieri. The three men spent an hour alone in Albano's hospital room in whispered conversation.

My task in putting together a solution to the French Connection was based on a simple principle: Follow the money. We conducted so-called net worth investigations on more than sixty SIU detectives. These were painstaking analyses of their yearly income. If, for example, an SIU detective with a salary of $12,000 spends $100,000 in a given year, you have the makings of a federal income tax case and he has a lot of explaining to do.

These investigations turned up many examples of unexplained income. However, it was generally the kind of money that could be attributed to the run-of-the-mill activity of SIU detectives: ripping off drug dealers. During our investigation only three suspects had income that went off the scale—income that would suggest the kind of money to be made by wholesaling four hundred pounds of cocaine and heroin. The three were were King, Intrieri, and Albano.

They were clever and resourceful men, but none had a grasp of international finance or the convenience of owning a numbered Swiss bank account. Their cash went into the wall at home, and occasionally into a local bank. Pat Intrieri, in particular, was an excellent example of a cop who was bad at concealing.

Intrieri was very tough and very shrewd. Once Nadjari's investigators started crawling all over Frank King, Intrieri made himself very scarce. He stopped showing up at the offices of Statewide Investigations, the private detective agency he ran with King, and seldom even phoned in. On the few occasions he did call, Intrieri would always identify himself as "Pat O'Leary." O'Leary, of course, was the police commissioner. It was Intrieri's way of mocking the police officers monitoring the wiretap on the phone.

This Bronx-born cop was a protégé of Mario Biaggi, the former police officer and U.S. congressman later convicted of corruption in New York's Wedtech scandal. Intrieri remained comfortably in the shadows throughout his police career.

Intrieri had worked in Narcotics from 1960 to 1968, where he met and befriended Frank King. He was kicked out of Narcotics in one of the periodic shakeups that followed allegations of corruption. He later worked as the commander of a precinct detective squad in the Washington Heights section of Manhattan.

By the time I entered the hunt for the French Connection thieves, it was impossible to use any of the time-honored investigative techniques on Intrieri. His telephone savvy was superb. He never said anything of interest over the phone and never blurted anything out, which sometimes happens even when a suspect has good reason to believe his phone is tapped. And we quickly discovered that Intrieri was almost surveillance-proof. He spotted and shook any tail we put on him.

It was then that Tony Valente and Roy Weinstein, the superb IRS investigators looking into Intrieri's finances, proposed a "garbage cover." Rummaging through the trash of criminal suspects (or celebrities) has received some publicity in recent years, but in 1974 it was still considered very unusual. (There had been some previous cases. The IRS, for example, obtained evidence on New York mobster Frank Costello by searching his garbage.)

There were even some legal questions about the technique. Did rummaging through somebody's trash can constitute an illegal search and seizure? Since Intrieri's trash was put out on the sidewalk, I decided it was in the public domain. With a completely straight face, I approved the "garbage cover."

Valente and Weinstein persuaded the sanitation men who had Intrieri's house on their route to put his trash into plastic bags. The investigators got together with the sanitation men a few blocks from Intrieri's home and carried off their haul.

The garbage cover was very productive. Mysteriously, it must have seemed to Intrieri, we began to question the people he was meeting with. Indeed, despite all his precautions, we seemed to know his every move. Intrieri had a desk calender he used to jot down the details of the meetings he was going to. He'd rip off the page each day and toss it into a wastepaper basket. As a result, we would learn—a day or two days later—where he was going and who he was meeting with. I also found I could order up needed documents through the cover. I would, for example, subpoena Intrieri's financial records and then sit back and wait for them to show up in his garbage. Other goodies, like $10,000 bank money wrappers, also showed up in the Intrieri trash.

(I had a reputation in the Eastern District for refusing to accept copies of documents. "Get me originals!" I would shout at the agents unlucky enough to enter my office with photocopies. When Valente and Weinstein showed up to give me what I wanted from the garbage cover, I took one whiff and changed my policy. "Give me copies!" I told them.)

Thanks in part to their arrangement with the Sanitation Department, Valente and Weinstein conducted a very thorough investigation of Intrieri's finances. It showed Intrieri was concealing thousands of dollars in illegal income by laundering it through a battalion of relatives. His mother-in-law, for example, was driving a Mercedes-Benz Intrieri had purchased in Connecticut. Other relatives had houses and metal boxes overflowing with cash.

I decided it was time for a chat. Intrieri showed up at my office on a chilly day in February 1975 with his lawyer, Jonathan Rosner, a bright, burly guy who had once been a federal prosecutor himself. Valente and Weinstein also attended the session. I decided against beating around the bush:

"The reason we're here is because we think you stole the French Connection heroin," I told Intrieri.

He angrily denied any involvement in the theft. I then gave him some details of our tax case against him and pointedly told him that his mother, brother, mother-in-law, and other relatives would be called to testify before a grand jury.

"You little piece of shit!" Intrieri cried out. With that he lunged over my desk at me.

Intrieri was then in his early forties. He was about five foot ten and had a slender but lithe build. He had straight black hair with a touch of gray and an intelligent face. What I most remembered, though, were Intrieri's cold, hard, dark eyes. They were the eyes of a killer.

Rosner and Valente hauled the enraged ex-cop away from my desk before any damage was done. The interview was less than a smashing success, particularly from Intrieri's point of view. But he remained firm in his denial of any involvement with the French Connection theft.

"I'll take a polygraph anytime," he said.

Fine, I thought. As I've said, I have little faith in the polygraph, but a suspect's willingness or reluctance to submit to the test can sometimes tell you a lot. This was certainly the case with Intrieri.

We set February 28, 1975, as the date for Intrieri's session with a private polygraph examiner in Manhattan. A few days before the test was to take place, the garbage cover revealed an intriguing fact.

Intrieri had flown to the airport in Miami for a two-hour meeting with a retired federal agent, a former associate from New York. Intrieri did not linger in Miami. He stepped on a plane and roared back to New York as soon as the meeting was completed. The agent, we quickly discovered, was working as Broward County's polygraph expert. (Florida police departments, by the way, were a major resting place for crooked federal agents and cops from New York. After a long career of thievery in the North, they would go off and become the chief of police of a small town in Florida.)

The agent was terrified when we contacted him. He was afraid he'd lose his job if it became known he was under investigation. He offered to cooperate with us in any way and quickly told us the purpose of his meeting with Intrieri: The agent had given Intrieri what amounted to a crash course on ways to beat a lie detector. With this backdrop, I was intensely curious to learn how pupil Intrieri would fare on his test. A day later, the retired police lieutenant and his lawyer showed up at the offices of the polygraph examiner, where he was given a list of the questions he'd be asked. This, by the way, is standard procedure. No surprises are wanted.

I had picked out five pithy questions for Pat Intrieri:

1. Are you the person who masterminded the theft of the French Connection heroin?
2. Did you ever knowingly get any money from the French Connection heroin?
3. Did you ever have in your hands any of the French Connection heroin?
4. Did you ever see Vincent Papa?
5. Did you ever talk to Vincent Papa?

After reviewing the questions, Intrieri made a decision.
"I'm getting the fuck out of here," he announced.
And he did.

Intrieri later caught on to our garbage cover and signaled his displeasure with our tactics by depositing a rat in his trash. That was the last thing we heard from Pat.

I indicted him for income tax evasion. Intrieri's task at trial was to explain where he had gotten more than $100,000 in cash. The defense said the money was left to the Intrieri family by deceased relatives who put the money in tin boxes because they did not trust banks. One of the defense exhibits was a photograph of a tin box. This was like saying you had dinner with a ghost and offering a photo of the plate as proof.

I called practically his entire family as hostile witnesses. It was a parade of tin boxes—money provided by dead relatives who didn't trust banks because of their bitter experiences in the Great Depression. Mysteriously, the family members said they either spent this money on Intrieri or gave it to him.

A major source of the cash, family members testified, was Intrieri's late stepfather. The man just never trusted banks, they said.

In a magnificent piece of investigative work, Tony Valente was able to locate a number of bank accounts held by Intrieri's stepfather. Even during the Great Depression, when many lost faith in the banking system, the stepfather made regular deposits.

That revelation pretty much blew the defense out of the water. On January 17, 1976, Intrieri was convicted of four counts of income tax evasion. He went off to jail without a word. His prosecution, it seemed, had brought me no closer to a solution to the French Connection case.

Neither did the prosecution of Vinnie Albano.

Our net worth investigation of Albano turned up a tremendous amount of cash he couldn't explain. In addition to various bank deposits and a liquor store he was operating in lower Manhattan, we discovered that Albano was holding a $150,000 certificate of deposit that he purchased with cash from a bank on the Lower East Side.

Albano had worked for Intrieri during his stint as a narcotics detective. He'd been out of the police department for a long time by the time my investigation started. Among the cops, he'd had a reputation of being sort of crazy. I didn't detect any signs of disturbance, but I did discover he was a man who believed in going directly to the top.

One day I got a phone call.

"I'm the guy with the CD," the caller said.

"What do you want?" I asked.

"I want to talk with you."

"Fine. Come into my office."

"No way," Albano replied. He gave me the name of a coffee shop in one of the hotels at Kennedy Airport.

I decided to go, much to the displeasure of the federal agents working on the case. Albano, they said, was not known as a well-adjusted citizen. And I was just a prosecutor, not Gene Hackman.

But I decided to go ahead. The coffee shop meeting was memorable mostly for the clientele. There were about fifty customers in the place, and it seemed like forty-six of them were federal agents.

Albano wanted to make a deal. All by himself, with no lawyers or agents as intermediaries, he wanted to negotiate.

"Leave me alone and I'll cooperate," he said.

I tested his information for a while. Albano seemed to be a veritable storehouse of detail—all of it about people we had no interest in. He denied knowing anything about the French Connection theft.

I told Albano we had nothing to discuss, went back to the office, and indicted him on tax evasion charges. He pled guilty shortly after the indictment and, like Intrieri, went off to jail without a word. Five years after he was released from prison, his body was found in the back of a car at Kennedy Airport. He had been bound, gagged, and shot in the head.

Like Nadjari before me, I focused most of my energy on Frank King.

In his desperation to break the retired detective, Nadjari planted enough bugs and wiretaps to start a Frank King Memorial Library with the transcripts. This was at a time when there were perhaps twenty wiretaps authorized by the federal government across the nation. But Nadjari had them all over the place. One interesting set of tapes came from Vincent Papa's lawyer, Frank Lopez. While Papa was in the federal penitentiary in Atlanta, serving a five-year sentence on narcotics charges, Lopez was coordinating a defense strategy to counter Nadjari's furious efforts. Naturally, Lopez's office wound up with both a bug and a telephone wiretap.

King would occasionally drop in at Lopez's office. One discussion was an attempt to smooth King's feelings after Papa's children had identified him and Intrieri as their bodyguards in testimony before a Nadjari grand jury. Another topic of interest was the pending grand jury testimony of a top Papa lieutenant. Lopez assured King he had nothing to worry about on that count, then got around to a matter that was obviously of deep concern to Papa.

"Do we have anything to worry about the handwriting?" the lawyer asked King. "Vinnie has not been able to sleep because of this."

Vincent Papa obviously had more faith in handwriting analysis than I did. A massive effort to match the handwriting of the person who signed Nunziata's name on the property clerk's logbook to that of the suspects in the case had been a failure. But Papa had no way of knowing this.

I couldn't wait to hear King's response. But there was no answer on the tape! Only silence. King, presumably, had answered Lopez's with a shake of his head.

This was grist for another round of endless speculation. It was reasonable to assume that King's answer was "no," since a "yes" would have prompted Lopez to demand an explanation.

And if the answer was no, did that mean the person who signed out the narcotics was dead, not under any suspicion, or simply not the kind of person Frank King believed would talk? If the deceased Nunziata had signed his own name to the logbooks, the answer would certainly be "no."

But, of course, we could never even be absolutely certain that King's answer was "no." Maybe he had made a gesture, indicating he wanted to discuss the matter later. Hell, maybe he held up a sign.

It was maddening.

I redoubled my efforts with Frank King. I was proceeding on two tracks. The illegal wiretaps and shakedowns King had engaged in as an SIU detective would form the basis of a federal civil rights case. And the net worth investigation was turning up lots of unexplained income.

I got copies of the files in every narcotics case that King worked on during his career in the police department. I then went out and interviewed every single person King had ever arrested. There were more than a hundred of them. I also combed the case folder and then immediately ordered current rap sheets on all of the people King had investigated. A very clear pattern emerged. All of King's investigations of top mob narcotics dealers like Vincent Papa were huge failures. None of them ever went anywhere. King would install a wiretap on the phone of the dealer. That was the extent of his investigation. Unfortunately, it was beyond my power to get these high-level mob dealers to cooperate with me.

I had to go down lower in the narcotics feeding chain to get anybody to open up. One of King's investigations involved a Chinese drug dealer named José Loo. King's José Loo folder showed a lot of surveillances and then the case was abruptly closed without any action. I tracked Loo down and got him to cooperate. He told us, of course, that King had shaken him down instead of arresting him. Loo also said that a few weeks after one of the thefts from the property clerk's office King asked him if he was interested in purchasing narcotics. But they were never able to get together on a deal.

King's modus operandi was vintage SIU. He would put in an illegal wiretap, and when enough information was gathered, he would rip off the drug dealer. I went to many, many basements in the Bronx to have a look at the place where the taps were installed. We actually found one of them, still intact. I eventually became an expert on illegal wiretaps. King would go to a telephone box in the basement of the building where the dealer lived and locate a pair of screws that went to the dealer's phone. It was a simple matter of attaching a pair of wires to the screws. If you followed the pair of wires coming out of the box, they would lead you to another room, where you would find a voice-activated tape recorder. These crude but effective taps were sometimes discovered. But in the unlikely event that they were reported, the phone company would conduct a perfunctory investigation and then drop the matter, reluctant to press a case against a cop.

Regrettably, the witnesses we turned up on this end of the investigation were mostly drug dealers unlikely to make much of an impression on a middle-class jury. Still, it was absolutely essential to find out exactly how King and his SIU bretheren operated if we were going to get to the bottom of the French Connection case.

When I wasn't interrogating King's former targets, I was interviewing his fellow detectives. I talked to just about every SIU detective before I was through. I concluded there was very little difference between them and the guys they were chasing. They came from the same background as the wise guys, had the same mental processes, and took the same attitude toward life. Taking money was like getting up in the morning and going to work. About half of the eighty-odd detectives in SIU were greedy guys who initiated the ripoffs. The other half were followers who went along with the program. The popular wisdom was that there was not a single detective in SIU who didn't take money. (By then, the SIU's days were numbered. Our work, taken together with Nadjari's effort and Southern District prosecution, literally destroyed this "elite" unit.)

When we could make cases against these detectives, I prosecuted them. I indicted an SIU detective named John McClean and his partners for violating the civil rights of the drug dealers they were extorting money from. McClean was found guilty and sentenced to nine years in jail. He subsequently agreed to cooperate with me. McClean, of course, was the guy who had worked with Frank King on the Vincent Papa wiretap. I now knew enough about SIU mentality to understand McClean's anger when he received only $1,500 from King for the "sale" of the Papa wire.

This, of course, strengthened the civil rights case I was building against King. The jury would hear not only from drug dealers but also from one of King's former partners.

The net worth investigation was also going very well. We quickly learned that King had lots of unexplained income. We also discovered he loved to gamble. On one occasion, he went to Las Vegas and checked into the Sands Hotel under the name James Harris. On one of his tax returns, he had listed gambling winnings of $50,000, which is an ancient way of explaining extra income. I actually brought the pit boss, who had left the Sands, back from Africa. He identified James Harris as Frank King and said King had actually lost thousands of dollars.

King was a married man with four children. He and his wife, Catherine, lived for a while in a modest, middle-class home on Long Island. But King's conventional lifestyle changed dramatically in the early 1970s. In 1972, King and his wife were divorced. In 1973, he married Ann King, another SIU detective who had the same last name. King purchased a $110,000 five-bedroom home for his new wife in Chappaqua, a posh Westchester County suburb of New York. At the time, $110,000 was still regarded as an enormous amount of money to pay for a home. King gave the seller $30,000 in cash under the table to make the purchase price appear lower than it was. He paid $12,000 for a boat, and thousands more to furnish his new home. He also had the expense of maintaining three apartments he was renting and the Cadillac he was driving. All in all, not a bad life for a former narcotics detective.

But those who should have been closest to King weren't doing nearly as well. My IRS investigators, Tony Valente and Roy Weinstein, went to King's home on Long Island on a bitterly cold night in the winter of 1975 to interview his first wife, Catherine. The house had a run-down look and was almost completely dark. Mrs. King, bundled up in two heavy sweaters, opened the door and invited them in. Tony and Roy were astonished at how cold the house was. As they passed through the living room, Tony saw King's two small sons wearing winter jackets as they did their homework by the light of a dim lamp. The interview took place in the kitchen, which was somewhat warmer than the rest of the house. Mrs. King told Tony that her former husband had not given her any alimony or child support payments in a year. Her voice was tinged with bitterness, but she doggedly refused to give Tony any information that might have helped our investigation.

It was easy to juxtapose King's gambling trips and lavish outlays with the plight of his children. So this was the great Frank King, detective extraordinaire with his fancy house in Chappaqua and new wife. It would be a pleasure to put this guy in jail.

I WASN'T the only prosecutor pursuing the French Connection case now that Maurice Nadjari had faded from the scene. The Southern District was making its own attempt to solve the mystery, and its method was brutal and direct. Vincent Papa and his son, Vincent Jr., were both arrested on narcotics charges. The Southern District prosecutors figured if the old man would not talk to save his own skin, perhaps he would cooperate to help his son. The strategy failed. Vincent Papa was convicted and sentenced to twenty years in jail, but his son was acquitted. And there was no way Vincent Papa would cooperate with the men who tried to harm his son.

By now, the French Connection case had created an enormous amount of misery for the people involved in the theft and their families. Vincent Papa had been jailed for twenty years. SIU had been disbanded, with most of its members headed for jail. Frank King had been placed under relentless scrutiny, first by Nadjari, and then by me. His second wife, Ann King, had cracked under the pressure. She now lived a sheltered existence with her mother in Poughkeepsie, unable to face the world.

The most intense fire had been aimed at the police, but it was the mobsters, to my surprise, who cracked. Members of Vinnie Papa's organization were feeling the heat. Everyone from the lowliest gofer to Papa himself had been hounded by federal, state, and local law enforcement officials. Our informers began to tell us that members of Papa's organization believed they were doing a disproportionate amount of the suffering. The detectives involved in the French Connection thefts, they thought, should "share the weight." This was in mid-1975, before Intrieri, Albano, or King had been indicted.

Two lawyers, Frank Lopez and Ivan Fisher, who defended Papa and his son at the trial that resulted in Papa's imprisonment for twenty years, came to me with a deal:

I would be given the story of the French Connection thefts. Members of the Papa organization already in jail would be given no more prison time for their role in selling the stolen drugs. And those still free would be sentenced to no more than five years in jail. And the heat would end.

I was intrigued by the idea of finally learning exactly how the drugs were stolen and who was involved. It was also clear that Papa himself had dispatched Lopez and Fisher to meet with me to work out a deal that would take the pressure off his drug organization. I decided to take a wait-and-see attitude.

A few days later, Fisher and Lopez went to Frank King's home in Chappaqua in an effort to persuade him to talk. I remained at my office in Brooklyn on standby alert. The lawyers gave King a message from Papa: The imprisoned drug boss wanted an end to the French Connection case. A deal would be worked out in which everybody, including Frank King, would "share the weight."

I waited in my office until early in the morning. The news from Lopez and Fisher was bad: Frank King was not going to cooperate with anyone. It was becoming increasingly clear to me that Frank King and the other cops were tougher than the hardened criminals supposedly bound by a code of silence.

I pressed on by indicting King and his partners on civil rights and illegal wiretapping charges in December 1975. It was a tough case in more ways than one. I naturally hoped a conviction would make King talk. During the trial, King offered to plead guilty if I would drop the charges against his partners. It was the kind of grand gesture the wise guys so admired by King would have appreciated. I turned the deal down because I wanted the solution to the French Connection case much more than I wanted Frank King. The jury acquitted King and his partners on all counts. The charges were old, many of the witnesses were drug dealers, and King's lawyer, Barry Slotnick, did an effective job of impeaching the credibility of my star witness, the less-than-angelic John McClean. Frank King had slipped through my fingers twice in a single trial!

With no one to blame but myself, I went back to work on the tax evasion case against King. But I was very soon confronted with a double deadline. The last theft of drugs from the property clerk's office had occurred on January 4, 1972. The five-year statute of limitations would expire on January 4, 1977. I had also been appointed chief of the Organized Crime Strike Force. I'd be taking on a new role in 1977—one that wouldn't include the French Connection case.

I decided to make one last-ditch effort to crack the case by talking to Vincent Papa. I used an intermediary to arrange a meeting with Papa in New York around Chistmastime. The understanding was that we would talk. There was no obligation on either side. Papa was brought from the penitentiary in Atlanta to a federal jail in Manhattan and then to my office in Brooklyn.

I had, of course, seen photographs of Papa, but I guess over the years he'd become larger than life. I was surprised to see that he was just a little old Italian man who looked like all the other little old Italian men in my neighborhood in Brooklyn.

"Congratulations on your new job," Papa said in greeting me. Our conversation quickly turned to the French Connection case. Up until this time, no one had admitted involvement in the drug thefts and no one had been actually charged in the case. Now Papa was telling me that he'd gotten to know Frank King well after paying off the SIU detective for disclosing that his phones were being tapped and that he was the target of an investigation.

"We've got some stuff coming from the factory," Papa quoted King as telling him. Papa said he had paid King $300,000 for thirty kilos of heroin stolen from the property clerk's office in 1971.

Papa also described a meeting in which King was accompanied by another police officer, but he wasn't able to furnish me with enough information about the second officer to make an identification.

"Can you tell me who signed the stuff out?" I asked.

"I don't know that," Papa replied.

It soon became clear that Papa would tell me no more. He had given me a small piece of the story, and now the ball was in my court. His admission brought me great personal satisfaction, but it would be truly useful only if Papa agreed to become a wit-

ness and tell the whole story. And in order to obtain his cooperation, I would have to offer him a deal. But what kind of a deal? It
would take time to work out an agreement, and I was fast running out of time. And I wasn't at all sure I'd be able to come up
with an offer that would satisfy Papa.

Vincent Papa returned to Atlanta in January 1977, the same
month I put Frank King on trial for tax evasion in Brooklyn federal court. By then, King had twice been indicted by Maurice
Nadjari. Both indictments had been dismissed. I had tried and
failed to convict him for illegal wiretapping and civil rights violations. This was the last time around for everybody involved.

I was pleased by the way the case unfolded. I had former SIU
detectives testify how they had shared the money from the
shakedown of various drug dealers, but the case was more about
expenditures than income. There were gambling trips to Las
Vegas and Puerto Rico. I brought the former pit boss at the
Sands Hotel back from his home in Africa to testify that King,
posing as James Harris, dropped at least $10,000 at the tables.
There was also testimony about his under-the-table payments
for the Chappaqua house. Throughout the trial, King remained
calm and impassive. It was a demeanor he had managed to maintain through more than four years of tremendous pressure. The
pressure had been intense enough to make a hardened career
criminal like Vincent Papa admit his own role in the French
Connection and point a finger at King and his second wife.

King was an incredibly cool character, or so I thought.

One of the witnesses I called was King's first wife, Catherine.
She was a reluctant witness and a very minor figure in the case,
but there were a few things we were interested in, including
some child-support payments King had made to her and the
purchase of the car she was driving. She had married Frank in
1954, about eighteen months before he became a police officer.
They lived in the Bronx before moving into a modest home in
Commack, Long Island, in 1962. Frank and Catherine had four
children. They separated in 1970 and divorced in 1972.

A nagging legal element of the case involved jurisdiction. We
maintained that King continued to live with his wife on Long
Island—which was part of the Eastern District—even after the

couple separated. One obvious proof of this was the fact that Mrs. King had become pregnant with the couple's fourth child during the period of separation.

The defense, I discovered, was not necessarily willing to concede this point. While Mrs. King was on the stand, there was a "sidebar" to discuss this and other matters with Judge Jack Weinstein.

A sidebar is just that. The judge and lawyers stand to one side of the judge's bench to discuss in hushed tones matters that should not be heard by the jury. Such discussions are not secret. They are, in fact, taken down by the court reporter and become part of the official court record. Regrettably, portions of the sidebar conversations can easily be heard by all in the courtroom if one of the parties inadvertently raises his voice to a normal conversational level.

That was how Mrs. King, seated in the witness box a few feet from the sidebar, heard King's lawyer say this: "Well, Your Honor, there seems to be some question about whether Frank King is the father of this baby. Yes, out of the goodness of his heart, he supported this child . . ."

The lawyer for Frank King, detective extraordinaire, had struck for his client one of those horrible personal blows that only people who are intimate can inflict on one another.

The unflappable Frank King had heard it too. He was on his feet, shouting, "Who said that? You have no authority to say that or even hint at it!" he bellowed.

I presume that King discussed disavowing the child with his lawyer but never conceived it would come up in open court. Now, he was out of control. Judge Weinstein declared a recess. No words can describe the hatred in Catherine King's eyes as she passed her former husband on the way out of the courtroom.

When I stepped outside the courtroom, King turned his anger on me.

"You goddamn son of a bitch, I'm going to get you . . ."

"Motherfucking little bastard, if I get my hands on you . . ."

King's lawyer tried to restrain him as I headed for my office, where Mrs. King was trying to compose herself, and groping for a method of revenge.

"You want to know about the car? I'll tell you about the car," she said bitterly.

Catherine King drove a 1971 Ford Maverick, and we had been curious about how she paid for it, since it was purchased while she and her husband were separated.

Sitting in my office, trembling with rage, Mrs. King explained that after the separation she was forced to badger King for a car—an absolute necessity in suburban Long Island.

King finally arrived at their home one night, she said, to fill her request.

"You want a car?" he snarled angrily. "Here's your fuckin' car!"

With that, King contemptuously threw $10,000 in cash onto the kitchen table.

Catherine King had never seen so much money in her life.

"Frank, where did you get this money?" she asked.

"I stole it!" King shouted angrily. "I stole it for you, you bitch. Here's your fuckin' car. Now leave me the fuck alone!"

Catherine King's angry story did not become part of the evidence against her ex-husband. It was never recorded in any official proceeding or document. But her devastating confirmation of King's slimy character and Vincent Papa's admissions to me—which would also never see the light of day—solved a big chunk of the French Connection mystery, at least to my satisfaction.

The rest of the trial was almost anticlimactic. On January 20, 1977, Frank King was convicted of income tax evasion. A few weeks later, Judge Weinstein sentenced Frank King to five years in jail.

The statute of limitations expired, and the investigation ended. No one ever found out who signed Detective Nunziata's name in the property office log, or how all that heroin got removed from the office without attracting attention. But at least I had administered a form of rough justice by sending three of the detectives I believed responsible for the thefts to prison.

4

THE SICILIAN FEUD

THE FIRST FAVOR I ever did for the FBI was to wipe out one-fifth of the Mafia hierarchy with a single telephone call.

It was in January 1977, during my first few weeks as the new head of the Organized Crime Strike Force in Brooklyn. The strike force was an elite group of federal prosecutors who reported directly to the Justice Department in Washington and thereby remained insulated from political pressures that might make local prosecutors think twice about tangling with influential criminals. However, the main task of the strike force was to make criminal cases against the nation's most powerful and dangerous mobsters.

We had a bright young intelligence analyst named Helen Ceglia who kept track of the mob. One of the first things I did after taking over was to call her into my office.

"Helen, I'd like to see the FBI's list of Mafia members," I told her.

"We don't have the FBI list," she said.

"That's impossible," I replied.

New York, after all, was the hometown of the American Mafia. The city's five families were the most potent criminal organizations in the country.

"Well, we have some old things that we've put together from information we've gotten from the New York City Police Department over the years, and bits and pieces from congressional investigations," she said.

The police department material was hardly classified information. You could read most of it in the *New York Daily News*.

Anybody could attend a congressional hearing. I thought the situation was totally ridiculous. I summoned the FBI's "liaison" to the strike force, an agent named Stanley. In theory, the FBI would provide the bulk of the manpower and resources needed to carry out important strike force investigations, but that wasn't happening when I took control. When our liaison arrived, I came right to the point.

"Stanley," I said, "I want a copy of the FBI's Mafia membership list."

Stanley stared at me in complete astonishment. I might as well have demanded the blueprints to the War Room at the Pentagon.

"Well, let me see. I don't know," Special Agent Stanley mumbled. (There are no ordinary agents in the Bureau. Every agent is called a "Special Agent.")

My request touched off several days of bureaucratic wrangling. Calls went back and forth between me and the Bureau. I was told I would have to discuss the matter with the "assistant director" and make a specific request. (Because of the importance of the FBI's New York operations, Bureau chief J. Wallace LaPrade was given the title of assistant director.)

The Bureau had promised me full support when I was appointed the new strike force chief. I knew their pledge was somewhat insincere, but it made it harder for them to turn down my request, especially when I said, "Hey, look, it's my job to investigate these guys. At the very least I ought to know who the hell they are."

About a week later, an agent was dispatched from Washington to personally hand me a copy of the secret list. I half expected him to walk through the door of my office with a briefcase chained to his wrist. The emissary from FBI headquarters cautioned me about the highly sensitive and confidential nature of the information that I was being given: I should be extremely careful, and I shouldn't show the list to anyone.

"Don't worry," I assured him, "Nobody will see it."

As soon as the agent left, I summoned Helen Ceglia.

"Look, Helen, these are the names of the members of the five families," I said. "Forget about the soldiers. Take the bosses, the underbosses, the consiglieres and the capos. Search our files and give me everything we have on them."

There were about eighty people in leadership positions in the five crime families, according to the FBI. Helen only took about a day and a half to finish the job. She informed me that fifteen of the eighty people supposedly running the Mafia in New York were dead, some of them for many years.

I immediately picked up the phone and called J. Wallace La-Prade.

"Wally, I want you to know that I've been on the job for about two weeks, and I have already eliminated twenty percent of the Mafia leadership in New York," I cheerfully reported.

LaPrade was not amused.

The second favor I ever did for the FBI was to prosecute one of its agents for corruption. Until I came along, no one in the Bureau had ever been convicted of a crime—any crime. Naturally the FBI was extremely pleased that I had ferreted out an evildoer from its ranks. To this day, FBI officials constantly come up to me on the street to remind me of the story and thank me for exposing their faults to the bright light of public scrutiny.

Just kidding.

Whenever I become involved in something new, I immerse myself in every conceivable detail of the new activity. So after taking over the strike force, I ordered the files on every investigation piled high in a conference room in our offices. Thousands of documents were stuffed into the bulging, reddish brown folders holding the case files. Beginning on a weekend, I sat alone in that conference room and attacked a pile of more than a hundred files. Stopping only to munch on sandwiches and sip coffee that was brought in, I eventually read my way through every investigative report and legal document.

Not long after I began my marathon review, I came across a file marked *United States* v. *Joseph Doe.* Its contents were disturbing, to say the least. An FBI agent named Joseph Stabile had been accused of taking a $10,000 bribe from a Mafia hoodlum named John Caputo to fix a gambling case.

Now FBI agents had been accused of various kinds of misconduct in the overzealous pursuit of left-wing and radical groups, but this kind of corruption was unheard of. Incorruptibility was a mainstay of the Bureau's public image. What made the case even more extraordinary was the fact that Stabile's principal accusers were two other FBI agents.

The case was an old one. Stabile was accused of taking the payoff in 1971, but an internal FBI inquiry had cleared the agent of any wrongdoing. My strike force predecessor, Denis Dillon, had apparently been unsatisfied with the results, since he opened his own investigation in 1973. Dillon was a very honest guy and a strong supporter of the FBI. The fact that he had dug into the case suggested to me that there might well be some merit to the charges. Still, it was now 1977, and the statute of limitations had practically run out.

The file contained an angry memorandum Dillon had written to the head of the Justice Department's Organized Crime Section in Washington. After a nightmarish runaround from FBI investigators, Dillon realized that the only agents the Bureau was interested in making a case against were George Moresco and Anthony Villano—the men who had made the accusation against Stabile.

"The incredible incompetence demonstrated during this whole investigation, and the Bureau's placing priority on the punishment of Moresco and Villano lead me to that conclusion," he wrote.

Dillon asked the Justice Department to assume complete control of the investigation and to compel the FBI to cooperate. I had to laugh when I read that one. Although the Justice Department's table of organization shows the FBI is under the direction and supervision of the attorney general, nobody tells the Bureau what to do. (I later learned that the FBI wanted to open an obstruction of justice investigation of *Dillon,* who had wisely refused to give the Bureau the name of an informer in the case.)

I read the Stabile file with fascination, but I was quickly brought back to earth by my own ambition. This is crazy, I thought. I'm just taking over this office. I'm trying to rejuvenate it and get things rolling again. I want to make a reputation for myself as a great strike force chief. The last thing I wanted to do is alienate the FBI. I might as well go home if that happens. No prosecutor, from the humblest country district attorney to the most high-powered Justice Department lawyer, can hope to be effective without the support and cooperation of the law enforcement agency assigned to conduct criminal investigations for him. I slipped the file back into the back of a drawer in my desk and moved on to less dangerous matters, like murderers and racketeers.

The Organized Crime Strike Force was built on the ideal of a multiagency approach to fighting crime. Each federal law enforcement agency had a representative assigned to work with us, frequently on a full-time basis. If, for example, the Mafia was importing heroin into the United States, agents from the Drug Enforcement Administrations, Customs, Immigration, and the IRS could bring their special skills to bear on the case.

But the FBI, the most famous and powerful law enforcement agency in the United States, wanted nothing to do with this kind of approach. J. Edgar Hoover had never believed that his agents should idle away their hours in an organization run by prosecutors. The agents, and everybody employed by the Bureau, worked for him, and him alone.

The Bureau's man at the strike force was called a liaison. Like agents from other federal organizations, the FBI liaison had an office at the strike force, but he never used it. He would stop by to see what was going on, but he was always afraid of being too close to us and spending too much time with us. His real job was to find out exactly what we were doing and report back to the Bureau, to make sure the FBI wasn't taken by surprise or embarrassed by what was happening at the strike force. Hoover had set this pattern—he was fearful that another law enforcement agency would investigate a case that was technically under his jurisdiction. Normally, the Bureau would send an empty-suit kind of guy to be the liaison.

As my experience with the Mafia membership list suggests, the FBI was an agency beset with serious problems. Hoover had died in 1972, but the organization he built over nearly five decades did not change quickly or easily. The FBI had been credited with great achievements under the old man, but a lot of them were statistical accomplishments that Hoover was a master at presenting to Congress. He would announce that the FBI had recovered nine thousand stolen cars in a given year. If ten thousand recoveries were made the next year, it was interpreted as a sign of significant "progress." It was the triumph of quantity over quality. As a result, the FBI was very slow to get into such important areas as organized crime and political corruption. At the time I joined the strike force, the Bureau had about 1,000 agents in New York, but it seemed to me that only about 75 of them were working with federal prosecutors on criminal matters. The other 925 seemed to be watching members of the American Communist party empty their garbage or chasing Soviet spies.

Despite its many failings, the FBI was still the finest law enforcement agency in the United States. The Bureau's personnel and vast resources were unmatched, and it was capable of doing magnificent work under the right circumstances. (More than 3,000 agents had fanned out in the search for the man who killed Hoover's old enemy, Martin Luther King, Jr. The Bureau soon tracked down James Earl Ray in London.) I regarded cultivating a solid relationship with the FBI as the key to the entire strike force operation. Without the Bureau's backing, we were never really going to get off the ground. The FBI would provide the engine I needed to power great strike force investigations.

The strike force was located on the third floor of an office building attached to the federal courthouse in downtown Brooklyn. The courthouse is a sterile six-story concrete rectangle faced with buff-gray marble. A passageway connected the court to the office building, which was known as the IRS wing because the tax people took up the bulk of the space. The complex, built in the early 1960s, is located across from a small park where the towers of the Brooklyn Bridge can be admired through a haze of automobile emissions.

The IRS wing swarmed with clerical workers who all seemed to wear short-sleeve shirts with white plastic pen pouches stuffed into their shirt pocket. Visitors entered our area through a small, windowless reception room with a forbidding metal door that was always locked. Staff and visitors alike had to be buzzed in by our receptionist-gatekeeper, a plump, thirtyish woman who was positioned at a desk next to the metal door. The reception room was furnished with chairs and a couch that might have been lifted from the lobby of one of New York's finer hot-sheet hotels. I'm sure there were more inviting drop-in centers for the homeless, but there was nothing at all unusual about this brand of hospitality in federal law enforcement. Later, in fact, we slashed the comfort level still further by moving the chairs from the reception room to the hallway outside. We didn't want a waiting visitor to overhear the receptionist putting through telephone calls to the staff.

Anyone who made it through the metal door entered a suite of offices best described as Spartan. Things weren't bad enough to make you want to head back to the reception room, but visitors quickly realized that we weren't exactly living it up while they waited uncomfortably outside. The metal walls were painted a sort of off-white shade that eluded precise color classification. The floors were covered with drab gray carpeting. The harsh fluorescent lighting was bright enough to have enabled us to administer the third degree just about anywhere, if we were so inclined.

At a desk outside my office sat the world's greatest secretary, Lilly Grant. Lilly was a young, clever, and incredibly funny woman who was federal law enforcement's answer to Whoopi Goldberg. Her implacable cheerfulness buoyed my visitors on more than one occasion, since finally making it to my office was no guarantee anyone would actually get to see me. Frequently, a visitor with an appointment still had to wait several hours (some swore it was several days).

I had a large corner office with windows that looked out on the small park across the street from the courthouse. The place was big enough to hold an old leather couch where I could stretch out and a conference table and chairs for meetings. Most of the time, the table was laden with recording equipment and other electronic goodies. I had a huge wooden desk of the kind that the federal government issues to its "executives." It had been lovingly made by federal prisoners on the road to rehabilitation and good citizenship. The office was to be my command post for six hectic and exciting years.

The months rolled by. I pursued ongoing investigations that seemed promising, closed out those that weren't, and opened new investigations. I hired new attorneys and built bridges to the FBI and other federal agencies. The strike force provided me with independence. It was a little like running my own law firm. I liked managing the budget and doing all the hiring. I felt I was building the strike force into a formidable law enforcement organization.

Still, the Stabile case just sat there and looked at me. I finally decided to give the file to my new deputy, Joel Cohen, one of a group of superb attorneys I had hired in my first nine months as strike force chief. Joel was a Brooklyn boy who had once put in a stint as a public school teacher in the Brooklyn ghetto of Ocean Hill–Brownsville. When I was chief of the Criminal Division for the Eastern District of New York, I had worked with him on the fabled French Connection drug theft case. I knew Joel was a very skillful criminal prosecutor.

We discussed the case in great detail. It stretched back to 1971, when the FBI and the strike force were conducting an investigation of a gambling ring run by the Joe Columbo crime family. Columbo's operation was based in Brooklyn, but the ring subcontracted some of its business to a Lucchese family bookie from lower Manhattan named John Caputo. When the FBI moved in on the ring, Caputo was among thirty-four hoodlums arrested.

It was one of many worthless roundups of mobsters that attracted widespread publicity but made no real impact on the Mafia. Such cases would frequently result only in fines, if they were not dismissed altogether. Occasionally a high-level mobster did get sent to prison, but those isolated triumphs did little more than create vacancies in the Mafia hierarchy for younger hoodlums. As Tom Sheer, one of the shrewdest FBI men I have ever known, ruefully remarked, "We were running a career development program for the mob."

The Columbo roundup, however, very much angered a balding forty-three-year-old FBI agent named Joseph Stabile. Stabile was born and bred in Brooklyn, and he had worked as a New York City police officer for nine years before joining the Bureau in 1962. He was a street-smart guy with a wiry build and a big nose that seemed to have been glued to the center of his face. He was popular with other agents, who enjoyed his flair for storytelling and his talents as a mimic. (Stabile drew chuckles with his imitation of FBI supervisors, but the routine most loved by his fellow agents was an imitation of a swishy homosexual.) Although he had enough ambition to get a B.A. and a master's degree in business administration while working as a patrolman, Stabile had shown no drive or energy during an undistinguished career with the Bureau. He spoke Sicilian but had been unable to develop any informers within the mob or to make any cases.

As an agent, the most noticeable thing about Stabile was probably the fact that he was Italian. The FBI was still largely a Wasp/Irish-Catholic organization in the early 1970s. One of the reasons the Bureau had done so poorly on organized crime was its inability to infiltrate the mob with undercover agents. As things stood, the Irish Republican Army was one of the few groups the Bureau was well positioned to penetrate. Indeed, as I was to discover, some Bureau officials seemed to regard the FBI's handful of Italian agents as exotic creatures.

Stabile was something of a history buff. While working in Organized Crime for the Bureau, he struck up a friendship with Anthony Villano, another Italian agent who was also a history lover. (The two men quarreled heatedly about whether Alexander the Great was a homosexual, and eventually had a falling out.) George Moresco, a third Italian agent, was casually friendly with Stabile and Villano.

The three agents were to become the cast of characters in what a high-ranking Bureau official described to me as a "Sicilian feud." My family came to this country from Sicily, but the official evidently didn't consider that I might be "Sicilian" or that I might take offense at his remark. He certainly had a broad view of geography. George Moresco's "Sicilian" family came from Genoa.

Three or four days after the Columbo roundup, Stabile confronted John McGinley, the agent who was in charge of the investigation. He demanded to know why he hadn't been informed of Caputo's arrest. Stabile implied that the arrest had damaged his efforts to turn Caputo into an informer for the Bureau. He complained that it was highly embarrassing to learn of Caputo's arrest from Caputo himself.

McGinley was apologetic about the breakdown in communications. The FBI's Organized Crime Division was then divided into seven squads. A squad was assigned to each of the five families, and two others tracked traditional mob enterprises: gambling and hijacking. Coordination among the squads was not always ruthlessly efficient.

"The case against Caputo is very weak," McGinley assured Stabile. "It's going to be dismissed."

The matter was forgotten until January 1973, when agent George Moresco ran into a boyhood friend, New York City police detective Joseph Schiaffino.

"I hear that one of your guys, Stabile with a *b,* made a fifteen-thousand-dollar score with one of our guys, Statile with a *t,*" Schiaffino told his friend. Schiaffino said agent Stabile and Sergeant Eugene Statile had received the cash for fixing a gambling case.

Sergeant Statile was a New York City police sergeant with a reputation for greed impressive even within the corrupt confines of the NYPD. He was the kind of man who would have carted away the Chrysler Building on a flatbed truck if he thought he could get away with it. He was a member of a group of corrupt officers known as the "sergeants' club," who systematically extorted payoffs from peddlers on Manhattan's Lower East Side.

Moresco knew Stabile and Statile liked to play the stock market and were members of a stock club run by the money-hungry police sergeant. But he was not overly concerned by Schiaffino's accusation. This kind of "ribbing" was not uncommon among FBI agents and city cops. Moreover, the Bureau's reputation for incorruptibility was more than a myth foisted on television audiences by Efrem Zimbalist, Jr. Moresco and his Bureau colleagues across the country believed it as an article of faith. Nevertheless, the "sergeants' club" had come under intense scrutiny from state prosecutors, and Moresco was concerned about Stabile's relationship with the corrupt cop. He decided to warn Stabile with a *b* to stay away from Statile with a *t*.

Moresco took Stabile to a coffee shop near Bureau headquarters on Sixty-ninth Street in Manhattan, where he decided to mention the allegation about the payoff.

"Look, I'm telling you this as a friend," Moresco began. "It's being said that you and Statile got fifteen thousand dollars to fix a gambling case downtown."

Stabile held up ten fingers and told Moresco that his share of the payoff was ten thousand dollars. He said Statile had received five thousand for setting up a meeting with Caputo, but that neither man had to lift a finger to earn the money.

"It was a sting," Stabile boasted. "The case was getting dismissed anyway, and I beat the guy."

Moresco was astonished, but he managed to draw Stabile out by reacting skeptically.

"It's hard to believe you got fifteen thousand for a lousy gambling case," he said. (In 1971, fifteen thousand dollars in cash was a very large bribe.)

"These guys are really afraid of the Feds," Stabile replied. "They'd pay three or four thousand dollars just to find out what kind of bullets we're shooting at them."

Warming up to the subject, Stabile also told Moresco that he was angry at his former friend, agent Anthony Villano. Villano had cultivated a high-level informer in the mob who had given the FBI damaging information about Caputo. He called Villano's informer a "rat bastard."

Now, FBI agents do not refer to the Bureau's confidential informants as "rat bastards." The deeper implications of Stabile's corruption began to dawn on Moresco. The identity of informants was supposed to be a closely held secret, even within the Bureau, but agents could and did learn the identities of one another's sources. Stabile was capable of inflicting enormous damage on Bureau operations, not to mention the danger to the lives of its informers.

I don't know to this day why Stabile decided to make these damaging admissions to Moresco. He may have believed—accurately, as it turned out—that if Moresco ever did say anything, no one in the Bureau would want to believe him.

I do think Moresco's talent as an investigator played a role in getting Stabile to open up. George was a real-life Columbo. When he wanted to, *d'ese, d'ems,* and *d'ose* fell freely from his lips and tended to conceal his lively intelligence. He had attended Notre Dame on an athletic scholarship, breezed through Fordham Law School, and fulfilled his lifelong ambition of joining the FBI. (The Bureau liked to create the impression that most of its agents were lawyers or accountants, but in fact only a minority had the kind of professional credentials George did.)

Moresco was a skillful undercover operative who had posed as everything from a crooked lawyer to a hard-nosed truck driver. Such assignments were always nerve-racking. On one occasion, Moresco the shady lawyer had to appear at a meeting with a group of cutthroats. The meeting was held at a house on Staten Island within walking distance of his mother's home. George literally knew hundreds of people on Staten Island, but he betrayed no nervousness, and the meeting went off without a hitch.

Now Moresco was facing a problem unlike any other he had encountered as an agent. He was deeply troubled by Stabile's admissions and decided to tell Villano about the situation. George wanted Villano to speak with his informers to see if he could develop any more information about Stabile's relationship with the mob. But Tony Villano had grander ideas.

The tall, dark, and handsome Villano was an unusual agent, and not just because he was one of the Bureau's rare "Sicilians." The average FBI agent dressed much like an insurance adjuster or a Catholic elementary school teacher. But Villano dressed fashionably. In the argot of the times, other agents called him "mod." He was also very good at his job.

Villano had entered the FBI as a stenotypist and attended college at night until he got a degree and qualified to become an agent. While he was still a clerical employee he was part of a team that had been secretly installed in two cells on death row at Sing Sing prison next to convicted atomic spies Julius and Ethel Rosenberg, ready to take down the Rosenbergs' confessions if they broke down and admitted their crimes. Instead, Villano sat in his cell on the night of June 19, 1953, while Julius and Ethel were electrocuted. (He said later that contrary to movie legend, the lights never flickered.) Villano left the prison sick to his stomach and permanently opposed to capital punishment.

Tony Villano was slick, articulate, and very persuasive. He was also a dreamer. Within hours of his conversation with Moresco, Villano had worked out a fantastic finish to the Stabile problem: Villano would wire himself with a body microphone and then confront Stabile at three o'clock in the morning. He would force Stabile to confess and then relieve the wayward agent of his gun and "creds" (credentials).

It was a great plan. So great, in fact, that Villano couldn't wait to put it into action. He immediately informed his supervisor, an FBI veteran named Sean McWeeney, about the corrupt agent in their midst. McWeeney's reaction was entirely appropriate.

He fainted.

J. Edgar Hoover's Stalinesque approach to running the FBI included the belief that the presence of a bad agent must mean there were serious management lapses by the Bureau. This judgment was not confined to the poor creature with the misfortune to be the offending agent's immediate supervisor. Who was the Special Agent in Charge of the office? And where else had the evildoer worked? How was it that the men in charge of those offices had failed to detect the character flaws in this agent? Who, indeed, was responsible for hiring this man in the first place? A bad agent could wipe out a whole layer of FBI management. Men with long, solid careers could be demoted and shipped off to Butte, Montana, in a twinkling of the director's eye. Hoover, of course, was dead, but his philosophy lived on in the men he had handpicked to run the Bureau. Having a delinquent agent under your command was almost as bad as being delinquent yourself. And this wasn't a guy who had romanced the office secretary or embarrassed the Bureau by getting arrested for drunk driving. This was an agent accused of taking a large cash bribe from a made member of the Lucchese crime family.

Little wonder that Sean McWeeney collapsed.

What followed might have wound up on the cutting room floor of the *Police Academy* movies. Hours after Villano blew the whistle, Stabile was summoned to a meeting with John Malone, the head of the New York office, and Bob Franck, Special Agent in Charge of the Organized Crime Division. They asked Stabile if he had taken a bribe from a known mobster.

Stabile said no, and everyone said they were glad to hear it. End of story.

The most generous thing I can say about this approach is that it was an example of rank amateurism. If a similar accusation was made against a federal prosecutor, the FBI would have put fifty agents on the case and investigated the prosecutor for six months. Then, only after putting all the pieces together, would they have approached him for an interview.

Moresco, who knew very well that what Villano had done was suicidal, was hauled in to make a statement. George was then working as the Bureau's resident agent on Staten Island. After giving a statement to his superiors, he was taken into another room at FBI headquarters for a face-to-face confrontation with Stabile. The accused agent repeated his denial. Moresco was then given his marching orders by Bob Franck: "I want you to go back to Staten Island, and don't do one thing to actively assist this investigation."

The Bureau also interviewed mobster John Caputo and Sergeant Statile. Both men weighed in with denials. It was now time to wrap things up. The investigation would have a happy ending, just like all the "Untouchables" episodes. The Bureau administered lie detector tests to Stabile, Moresco, and Villano and was pleased to discover that, like the good honest agents they were supposed to be, all three men passed the test. The Bureau managed to ignore the fact that they told contradictory stories.

Only one more touch of magic was needed. Villano was transferred to Philadelphia, Stabile was shipped to Boston, and Moresco was banished to Baltimore. There, George was restricted to conducting background checks and other menial work. (I later got access to his personnel file and discovered that George had been banned from doing criminal investigations because "his name is on the street." I had no idea whatsoever what this snatch of B-movie dialogue was supposed to mean. Neither did George.)

The FBI's problem had not only been solved, it was made to disappear. After all, it was only a "Sicilian feud."

But the Stabile investigation wouldn't die. Villano was injured in an automobile accident and remained off duty until he eventually decided to retire on a disability pension. That made it much easier for him to do the unthinkable. He went to strike force chief Denis Dillon and told him the entire story.

Going outside the Bureau was the worst sin imaginable for an agent. It created the conditions under which the FBI might be subjected to negative publicity and embarrassment. When Dillon opened his own investigation, the Bureau really closed ranks.

On August 27, 1973, Dillon was visited by two FBI inspectors. He thought that they were in charge of the Bureau's investigation of the allegations against Stabile, but they quickly made it clear they were only interested in agents Villano and Moresco. They repeatedly mentioned the seriousness of taking such a matter to someone outside the Bureau. They asked Dillon not to interview Moresco, and promised the strike force chief that they would notify him before they approached the agent themselves. Dillon demurred—he wanted the first crack at Moresco and assumed that the Justice Department in Washington would make the final decision.

But as George later told me, the inspectors left Dillon's office and went straight to Baltimore, where they confronted Moresco, accusing him of inventing the bribery allegation against Stabile. Moresco, they charged, belonged to the same stock club as agent Stabile and Sergeant Statile, lost a great deal of money, and blamed Stabile for his misfortune. The bribery allegation, they claimed, was Moresco's way of retaliating. The inspectors made it clear to Moresco that it would be most desirable if he fell on his own sword. But Moresco stood his ground. He denied the stock club lie and angrily told the inspectors that they would have to fire him to get him out of the Bureau.

Dillon pressed forward and opened a grand jury investigation that took testimony from most of the principals, including agent Stabile. But Dillon was unable to develop any conclusive evidence, and the probe sputtered to an end in the fall of 1973.

That was the can of worms I was considering reopening—not a very promising project for a young federal prosecutor who hoped to do great things with the help of the FBI. Nevertheless, as I reviewed all the facts in my mind, I became more and more convinced that Stabile was guilty. My decision to look into the case again was closely held, even within my office. Joel Cohen and I would carry out the entire probe, including all of the interviews and legwork that needed to be done. I had no intention of repeating the mistake of letting the Bureau gain control of the investigation.

Nevertheless, I was obliged to inform the FBI as well as my superiors in the Justice Department of my decision to reinvestigate the Stabile allegations. First I called Lee Laster, the special agent in charge of the Bureau's Brooklyn-Queens office, where Stabile had been reassigned. Lee was brand-new in the job, having just come to New York from Hawaii. (I remembered someone asking Lee if the Bureau had taken his gun away when it informed him he was being transferred from Honolulu to Queens.) Laster was less than happy about the news I brought him, but he reacted professionally.

High-ranking FBI officials in Washington were another matter. At the time, the FBI had an Office of Professional Responsibility. The OPR was supposed to investigate wrongdoing by Bureau personnel. The head of the office, an FBI veteran, was outraged by what we were doing. His attitude was that there never was and never would be a corrupt agent in the FBI. Period. And this was the man who was supposed to ferret out corruption in the Bureau.

Joel and I flew to a meeting in Washington to discuss the case with top officials from Justice and the FBI. There was a great deal of talk on the FBI side about the purity of the Bureau and the utter impossibility of a corrupt agent existing within its ranks.

"Do you really believe there's never been a corrupt agent in the fifty-year history of the Bureau?" one of the Justice officials asked the FBI group.

"Well, I guess with so many more minorities in the Bureau

now, it is a possibility," an FBI official replied. He was referring to black and Hispanic agents, who had begun joining the FBI. His remark was a good measure of what we were up against. I should add here that my own superiors in the Justice Department backed me up completely from beginning to end.

Back in New York, there was more flak from the FBI rank and file. The case was closed. It was a dead issue. There was a lot of ugly speculation about my motives: I was trying to build a big name for myself on the back of an innocent agent.

The investigation did not get into high gear until the summer of 1978. In addition to all the other complications of the case, we were faced with a serious time problem. Stabile had allegedly accepted the payoff in 1971, and the five-year statute of limitations on the crime of bribery had long since come and gone. If Stabile was to be prosecuted at all, he would have to be charged with perjury for his testimony before the grand jury impaneled by Denis Dillon. Stabile had denied taking a payoff from John Caputo on September 17, 1973. If we were unable to build a case against Stabile by September 17, the five-year statute of limitations on perjury would run out as well, and any chance of bringing him to justice would slip away. Joel and I were going to be slowed down by working alone, but there was no other choice.

The key to a good investigation is painstaking effort and minutiae. There is no such thing as too much investigation. I was very compulsive and aggressive. If I was told that there might be a valuable piece of evidence in a warehouse filled with documents, but that the search would take twenty days and the odds against finding what we wanted were a hundred to one, I would do it. There would never be a stone unturned.

Joel and I went over all the ground covered by Denis Dillon in 1973. We reinterviewed all of the witnesses in the case, and then we interviewed all the FBI officials who had originally interviewed the witnesses. If possible, this last step made me even more unpopular with the FBI. I was not only saying that I suspected an agent of being corrupt, I was also saying that the Bureau had conducted a slipshod investigation.

Now if the agents who did the original investigation were able to forcefully argue the case for Stabile's innocence, it would have made an enormous impact on me. But the Bureau people were unimpressive—resentful, suspicious, and nervous about what I was up to.

Stabile himself repeated to me the story he had given under oath to the grand jury, and I quickly decided he was lying like crazy. I had a lot of experience with crooked cops. During my investigation of the French Connection heroin theft from the NYPD property room, I had confronted tough, slick narcotics detectives who were able to look me straight in the eye and repeat bald-faced lies with complete conviction. Compared to them, Stabile was a bumbling amateur. He was belligerent and denied taking the bribe in a tone of voice that I found much too emphatic and emotional. Indeed, it was almost theatrical.

The first important step in advancing our investigation would be obtaining the cooperation of Statile "with a *t.*" He had been dismissed from the police department for corruption by the time I reopened the investigation. The ex-cop was represented by a notorious mob lawyer named Gino Gallina, with whom I already had a passing acquaintance. I was pleasantly surprised by the fact that Gallina offered very little resistance to my efforts to recruit his client. The strike force had a very weak income tax case pending against Statile, and I used a promise to drop the case as the bargaining chip in our negotiations.

I worked very hard to gain Statile's confidence. To win over someone like Statile, you simultaneously had to make him afraid of you, make him respect you, and make him recognize that you were savvy enough to reject outright lies. When working with criminals, I liked to have them taken out of jail on a Saturday morning and then spend the whole day talking to them. My style was very laid back. I might talk to a guy for two hours about matters that had nothing to do with the case I was interested in. I have a natural sense of curiosity, and I think these guys correctly sensed that I was genuinely interested in them and the kind of lives they led. I also delivered on my promises to criminals who cooperated, whether it was dropping a tax case or persuading a judge to show leniency. My reputation was such that on one occasion, a major drug dealer who had been arrested asked to see me before talking to his own lawyer.

Things were going well with Statile when I received an early morning phone call from Joel Cohen. "Gino Gallina has been murdered in Greenwich Village," Joel said.

Great, I thought. So much for setting Statile at ease. The lawyer's death only temporarily sidetracked my effort to get Statile's testimony, but such misfortunes were a constant reminder that I was not practicing maritime law.

As the investigation unfolded, I racked my brain for a way to turn around the FBI. Stabile, of course, had been loudly declaring he'd cooperate in any way to prove his innocence.

Well, why not?, I thought. I decided to invite Stabile to take another lie detector test. It was a big gamble on my part, particularly in view of my own feelings about the polygraph. First of all, the field is full of charlatans who will tell you what you want to hear. A lot of defense attorneys use polygraph results for this very reason. They get what they pay for. And polygraphs can be beaten. The biggest advantage to requesting someone to take a polygraph is the information you get when they tell you whether they're willing to take it. If someone refuses to take it, it's an indication he may be lying.

I had already interviewed the FBI agent who had done the original polygraph of Stabile and come away deeply suspicious of the test results. Nevertheless, I decided to take the plunge. Law enforcement agencies tend to believe in the validity of lie detector tests as an article of faith, and I might be able to change the Bureau's hostile attitude if Stabile flunked an honestly administered test.

At the time, the FBI had a new polygraph examiner named Paul Minor, a tall, taciturn Southerner. I insisted on personally conducting a long interview with Minor. His professional credentials were very impressive, and I decided he was too new to the Bureau to have absorbed the FBI's circle-the-wagons mentality.

Stabile was in no position to turn down my invitation. He had offered to cooperate fully, and his FBI superiors might well reach unpleasant conclusions about his innocence if he refused. In utmost secrecy, we made arrangements to give him the test at the Sheraton Hotel near La Guardia Airport. The moment of truth, so to speak, came on a hot Saturday afternoon in July 1978. Lee Laster, his deputy, Terry Knowles, and Minor appeared, for the FBI. Stabile arrived with his lawyer, and, of course, Joel Cohen and I were there.

We waited in the hotel lobby while Minor and Stabile went to a room upstairs where Minor's equipment was set up. I was very nervous. It was a high-stakes game of investigative chicken.

Minor came downstairs about an hour later and announced that Stabile had flunked the polygraph.

It was a major turning point in the investigation. The test had no standing in a court of law, but I was enmeshed in a bureaucratic struggle as much as a criminal investigation, and the test would have plenty of standing in FBI circles.

Laster, Knowles, Cohen, Minor, and I went into the hotel restaurant to eat. Over lunch, Laster and Knowles went back and forth with me about the reasons why Stabile may have flunked. Was he nervous? Sick? Overtired?

Paul Minor looked up from his plate. "He flunked because he's a goddamned liar!"

There was complete silence around the table. Then Minor added the coup de grace.

"Not only did he flunk the polygraph I just gave him, but I reviewed the charts of the polygraph he took in 1973, and he flunked that one too."

With the test results in hand, I decided it was the right moment to open our own grand jury investigation of Stabile. Our grand jury investigation would bring the Stabile case to an end, one way or another. In my days as a young lawyer, I'd been impressed by the mystery and secrecy surrounding the grand jury. But from the inside, the reality is much more prosaic. The twenty-three citizens of our grand jury met in a plain, low-ceilinged room in the courthouse building. They sat in padded leather swivel chairs bolted to the floor. A judge's bench at the front of the room had a witness box and seats for the grand jury foreman, deputy foreman, and secretary.

Tom Sheer, my old friend in the FBI, told me in the late 1960s that a grand jury, properly led, would indict a ham sandwich. I liked the line so much I began using it myself in speeches. Much later, Sol Wachtler, who was then New York state's chief judge, made his own ham sandwich speech and became widely known as the inventor of the metaphor. The ham sandwich mantle, however, brought its own burdens. Wachtler was angrily denounced in some quarters.

But it's perfectly true. The panel of twenty-three citizens is supposed to protect the target of criminal investigation from arbitrary and unjust treatment by government prosecutors. But by and large, the grand jury is the private tool of the prosecutor. The citizens don't contribute anything more than an audience. Normally, the prosecutor won't present any evidence that tends to support the innocence of his quarry. The grand jurors, therefore, don't get any information that would enable them to dispute the government's version of events. Grand juries also have a cinema verité quality. The prosecutor sits in the director's chair and spins out a gritty, real-life crime story in front of men and women who lead ordinary lives. This process tends to leave the grand jurors eating out of the prosecutor's hand. Dissenters rarely appear, and if one does, well, you only need twelve of the twenty-three grand jurors to get an indictment.

Some prosecutors use the grand jury as a dodge. They will claim that the grand jury was responsible for indicting or not indicting an individual. That is a very dangerous practice. A responsible prosecutor won't shift the burden of responsibility to the grand jury. You have to be able to prove your case in court, whatever a grand jury may do.

Denis Dillon had obtained the cooperation of detective Joseph Schiaffino, who had originally told agent Moresco about the Stabile payoff. He repeated his story for us: Schiaffino's father owned a dive on the Lower East Side called the Paris Bar. A craps game could be found at the Paris at noontime, and it attracted a cast of crooked characters that would have made it the perfect setting for a grade B gangster movie. Detective Schiaffino admitted making a phone call to help in setting up a meeting between Caputo and Sergeant Statile. Statile later gave

Schiaffino $200 for his work. He said Statile bragged that he and an FBI agent named Stabile had "shaken down" Caputo for $15,000 on a gambling case that was going to be dismissed anyway.

Then came Sergeant Statile, who testified that agent Stabile was a member of his stock club, and that the two men occasionally got together for drinks. He said Stabile told him he was "closing out a case" on John Caputo and asked the sergeant to set up a meeting with the mobster. Statile knew that "closing out a case" was police slang for taking a bribe to kill an investigation. He later met Caputo at the bar and passed along the message from agent Stabile. Subsequently, he was paid $5,000, and gave $200 to Schiaffino.

Unfortunately, both men made poor witnesses, evasive and unconvincing on the stand. This would be a problem if I decided to indict Stabile. I also subpoenaed John Caputo. Not surprisingly, the mobster refused to testify and was jailed for contempt.

Agent Stabile's promises of total cooperation had gone up in smoke after he flunked the polygraph. He now had no interest in appearing before my grand jury. Nevertheless, I decided to put before the grand jury evidence that might tend to show Stabile was innocent. Prosecutors seldom go this route, but I thought it essential to be absolutely evenhanded in view of the Bureau's suspicions.

As part of my effort to give Stabile's side of the story to the grand jury, I presented a witness named Frank Ruotolo. He was Stabile's cousin, and Stabile had used him to account for the bulk of the extra income he'd gotten from the Caputo payoff. Ruotolo testified that he'd loaned Stabile $7,000 in 1971, and he brought in two canceled checks to back up his story. I really hammered away at Ruotolo in the grand jury, getting him to deny again and again and again that he was lying to protect his cousin.

I was somewhat puzzled as to why Stabile had bothered to drag his relative into his crooked game. Ten thousand dollars was a lot of money, but not so large it needed to be disguised in this fashion. But Stabile was a former New York City policeman, and my own experiences with the NYPD in the 1970s suggested there was so much corruption in the department that ordinary police officers had become rather sophisticated. Cops would sit around and talk about the best ways to conceal bribe money in the same way New York football fans might talk about the Giants or the Jets. I guessed that Stabile was being fancy—trying to cover every conceivable base by getting Ruotolo to lie for him.

Our star witness would be George Moresco. Agent Anthony Villano had brought the bribe allegation to the attention of the Bureau and Denis Dillon, but he had no firsthand knowledge of the case. He had simply reported what Moresco told him about Stabile's admissions. I made sure that Villano was kept in the background. Bureau officials regarded him as a devil figure for having gone outside the organization, and I had no intention of antagonizing them unnecessarily. (Villano had even written a book about his career in the FBI that was filled with stinging criticisms of the Bureau. The last thing I wanted was to seem to be associated with a publicity-seeking renegade agent!)

Moresco was understandably reluctant to testify. His cooperation the first time around had earned him an unwanted trip to Baltimore and a ban on what he did best—criminal work. Stabile, as I've said, had been brought back to New York by the Bureau. But Moresco was still working in the hinterlands, though the Bureau had shifted him from Baltimore to Newark. I decided to write a letter to the Bureau's new director, William Webster, asking Webster for a pledge that Moresco's cooperation with our investigation would not subject him to any disciplinary action. Webster's letter to me was cordial and polite, but his answer was very clear: Forget it.

Moresco voluntarily appeared before the grand jury anyway. I carefully led him through the story of how Stabile had admitted getting a $10,000 share of the bribe for fixing the gambling case against Caputo. As usual, I positioned myself at the back of the grand jury room. I like to stand as far away from a witness as possible so that the jury is between me and the witness. That forces me to keep my voice up so the jurors can hear everything. If you stand very close to a witness, as some lawyers do, your examination can turn into what amounts to a private conversation. I was elated by Moresco's forceful testimony. I had a strong feeling the grand jurors believed he was telling the truth. I felt the same way.

It was now time to make a final decision on the case. The pressure was tremendous, if only because the September 17 deadline for indictment was just two weeks away. I was very uncomfortable. Prosecuting a police officer or an FBI agent is one of the toughest cases you can take on. Ordinary citizens feel these guys are risking their lives to protect the public. They don't like to convict law enforcement officials of anything. You have to prove them guiltier than the run-of-the-mill defendant. We very much needed a strong case, but we didn't have one.

It seemed to be a no-win situation. If I lost the case I could see my whole career with the Justice Department going up in flames. And if I won, convicting an FBI agent wouldn't exactly make me wildly popular. But I couldn't quite bring myself to close the books on the case because I was so convinced of Stabile's guilt.

I flip-flopped. One day I would firmly decide to go forward, and the next day I would just as firmly decide to drop the case. Joel Cohen was aggressively pressing me to do the right thing and indict Stabile. He had even enlisted two other strike force lawyers, Larry Sharf and Ed McDonald, to lobby me for an indictment. But Joel was one of the Indians, and I thought he was incredibly naive about the implications of losing this case.

I always believed that in any case destined to get public attention, not losing is more important than winning. Winning a big case takes you a few steps forward. But losing a big case takes you many giant steps backward. You can really get creamed by losing an important case. It erodes the confidence placed in you by your colleagues in the Justice Department and the public. Everybody loves a winner, and law enforcement is no different. If you lose a big case, you'll find that investigative agencies like the FBI aren't eager to trust you with another one. The government is expected to win, and people tend to come down on you like a ton of bricks if you lose.

I was discovering for the first time that there really was a major difference between the people who make decisions and those who play the role of adviser.

I had even worked out a little speech, which I delivered to

Joel, rationalizing a decision to drop the case. Pressing a case we might very well lose in court was irresponsible, I told Joel (and myself). We might inflict long-term damage on the strike force. We'd go down fighting the very agency we needed for success. I argued that putting away one supposedly corrupt agent wouldn't exactly remake the law enforcement landscape. Besides, I said, Stabile was no longer involved in sensitive Bureau investigations. He'd finish out his career somewhere on Long Island handling stolen car cases. Yes, I conceded, George Moresco had been unfairly punished, but he hadn't been hurt that badly.

It was one great argument, but it failed to convince the main audience: me. Despite all the solid reasons I'd come up with to drop the case, I couldn't shake my belief that Stabile was corrupt and deserved to go to jail.

Two days before the statute of limitations expired, I presented the grand jury with an indictment charging Stabile with two counts of perjury for denying that he took a bribe from Caputo. The grand jurors quickly voted a "true bill." With a feeling of relief and accomplishment, I walked from the grand jury room on the fourth floor of the courthouse to the courtroom where Judge Charles Sifton was sitting. I completed the legal formalities by handing up the indictment to Sifton.

The glow didn't last long. Stabile was not a respected investigator within the Bureau, but he was well liked, and many agents reacted with outrage to news of the indictment. A defense committee was quickly established, and agents began collecting money for his legal defense.

Interestingly enough, the case never attracted much publicity outside law enforcement circles, despite the unprecedented nature of the charges against Stabile. I can remember reading a brief Associated Press dispatch that quoted Attorney General Griffin Bell as saying the FBI had cooperated fully in my investigation.

Good grief.

The judge in the case was Thomas Platt, who had a well-deserved reputation as a tough, law-and-order jurist who didn't hesitate to mete out long prison sentences. That seemed a promising development, but Platt was also a former federal prosecutor with tremendous admiration for the FBI. It became all too apparent that he was antagonistic toward the prosecution. I don't mean to suggest that his rulings were unfairly slanted toward Stabile. They weren't. But his hostile tone and manner made it very clear he had little sympathy with the case I was bringing. The ink on the indictment was hardly dry before I began to believe many of my worst fears were being realized.

A week after the indictment was returned, I had to fly to Washington to brief FBI Director William Webster on the case. Ed McDonald, one of my top assistants, accompanied me. For young federal prosecutors, a personal meeting with the head of the FBI was a very big deal. Ed and I took a cab to FBI headquarters and went through an elaborate security routine because we were there to meet the director.

Webster was a former federal judge and a very formidable figure. He was articulate and radiated an aura of polish and class. I firmly believed that Webster was the right man to bring the Bureau out of the Hoover days and into the late twentieth century. But he was new, and I think he had been co-opted by high-level Bureau officials. I was already very familiar with the message he must have been given: This guy Puccio is a lawyer from Brooklyn who's trying to make a name for himself.

We discussed the case for about thirty minutes, and Webster delivered his assessment of its merits.

"I don't believe this case will ever reach a jury," he said.

Well, I certainly couldn't accuse the director of holding back. His parting words didn't exactly send me cartwheeling back to the airport either.

"Good luck," he said. And then after a long pause he added: "I think."

We flew back to New York, and I took my place at the end of the limb I had climbed out on. People had been pawing over the Stabile case for more than six years now, and I had taken it as far as it could go. It was time to prepare for trial.

I was sitting in my office with Joel Cohen on a chilly morning in early November when my secretary, Lilly, interrupted.

"A Mr. Frank Ruotolo is at the front desk, and he'd like to see you," she said.

Stabile's cousin! Joel and I looked at each other. I instantly recognized something miraculous was about to happen.

"Joel, let's get this guy in here right now," I said. Joel brought Ruotolo into my office and sat him down in a chair in front of my desk. Ruotolo was a tall, slender candy manufacturer with a pompadour haircut.

"I had to see you," he said. "I feel terrible about what I've done. I lied. I haven't been able to sleep a night since my grand jury testimony."

With that, Ruotolo began to sob. Joel had already rushed out of my office to phone the clerk in charge of grand juries. We wanted to "lock in" Ruotolo's confession as quickly as possible.

Now, this kind of break happens to prosecutors a lot—on TV. I've put several thousand scoundrels and ordinary citizens through grand juries over the years, and Ruotolo was the only person who ever recanted because his conscience was bothering him.

Ruotolo was a devout Catholic, and he told me his feelings of guilt had been tormenting him. I got up from behind my desk and walked around to where he was sitting. I wanted to look a little less like an interrogator and a little more like someone he could talk to.

His story poured forth. Stabile had come to him in 1971 to ask for a favor. The FBI agent told his cousin he'd won a great deal of money gambling, and because of Bureau regulations, he needed a way to account for the cash that wouldn't let his bosses know he'd been gambling.

He wrote checks totaling $7,000 to Stabile, and the FBI agent immediately handed Ruotolo the same amount in cash. It was a simple and rudimentary way of "laundering" the bulk of the bribe money. And, I had thought all along, totally unnecessary. Stabile really had outsmarted himself.

We obtained a sworn affidavit from Ruotolo, but we weren't able to get the cousin before a grand jury that day. Joel and I both spent a nervous night. Ruotolo had said that he'd talked with Stabile on the night before his first grand jury appearance, and we were afraid Stabile might call his cousin and discover what had happened. But he returned the next day and repeated his story to a grand jury. It was well that we moved as quickly as possible. Ruotolo's attorney soon called me to say he never would have permitted Ruotolo to testify if he'd known what was going on.

I was overjoyed. We immediately obtained another indictment charging Stabile with obstruction of justice. For years, Stabile had fiercely protested his innocence and portrayed himself as the innocent victim of a witch hunt. Now he collapsed overnight. I began plea negotiations with his lawyer. But the talks soon became very strange.

"Look, I'm thinking of taking a plea and I'd like to talk to you about it," Stabile said. He asked to speak with me alone in my office.

Criminal defendants do not ask their tormentors for legal advice. It was an incredible development.

"Do you think entering a plea is a good move for me?" he asked.

"If you really want to know if I think we have you, I think we do and here's why," I said. I went on to lay out the facts of the case in a very clinical way.

On November 9, 1978, Stabile appeared before Judge Platt and became the first FBI agent in history to plead guilty to a crime. He received a year and a day in jail, a sentence I thought to be incredibly lenient. The case involved straight-out corruption. There was no way you could put a good face on it. But I didn't complain. I was too relieved by the outcome.

Stabile came back to see me after the sentencing to ask me where the federal Bureau of Prisons might send him. As we chatted about the possibilities, I noted the extraordinary change in his demeanor. The belligerence was gone. So was the proud, injured tone of a man unjustly accused. He was utterly servile—a pathetic figure.

I believe that even the most crooked cops and law enforcement officials have a moral sensibility that makes it difficult for them to lead two lives. The courageous, honest guardian of the law that their friends and family see clashes with the reality of the hypocrite who is extorting payoffs from a cast of sleazy characters. Young men don't go into law enforcement with the idea of making dirty money. They become corrupted on the job. I think Stabile was greatly relieved to drop the pretense, and his visits to me were perhaps a way of affirming in his own mind that he was back on the right team.

The case was an important turning point in my career. It earned me the respect of William Webster and of my own superiors in the Justice Department. The confidence they were now willing to place in me was very important to my later investigations, especially Abscam.

Stabile's voluntary guilty plea convinced his most die-hard supporters in the Bureau that I'd done the right thing. A few people from the FBI came by to congratulate me, but by and large, I never again heard anything about this case from people in the Bureau. It was just something that was never discussed.

About two weeks after Stabile pled guilty, I ran into FBI Director Webster at a luncheon at the Waldorf-Astoria in Manhattan. He greeted me warmly, but I couldn't resist.

"You were right about the Stabile case," I told him. "It never did reach a jury."

5

ABSCAM

WHEN I TOOK over the Organized Crime Strike Force in 1977, I naturally envisioned myself spending the next few years hauling in major-league Mafiosi. It didn't work out that way. My biggest haul was a net full of crooked politicians—incredibly greedy congressmen and local officials, some of whom practically chased the undercover men down the street, demanding a bribe or kickback.

The investigation was called Abscam, and it wound up convicting more members of Congress of corruption than any investigation in American history. Nothing like it had ever happened before, and I can definitely guarantee you nothing like it will ever happen again. There's only one reason, in fact, that my office managed to get away with it at the time: Abscam was all an accident. Nobody planned it. Nobody had any idea, when it began, that it would turn into the most successful investigation into congressional corruption ever. Nobody was thinking about congressmen at all. In the beginning, I thought of Abscam—when I thought about it at all—as a cut-rate sting operation that might net us a few wise guys selling stolen art or bogus securities. And to be truthful, I didn't even expect that part to work.

The idea, when it was proposed, seemed crazy to me. Mel Weinberg was a short, squat, balding Jewish guy with a thick Bronx accent. He was a veteran con man who had moonlighted in the past as an FBI informer. Jack McCarthy was a straight-arrow FBI agent who looked like the grand marshal of the St. Patrick's Day Parade. Weinberg and McCarthy were to pose as the personal representatives of a wealthy Arab sheik with hundreds of millions of dollars to invest in the United States.

The scheme called for the FBI to buy stolen art for the "sheik" by setting up something called Abdul Enterprises. (The term Abscam is a combination of *Abdul* and *scam.*) I had very good reasons for doubting it could ever work. Undercover operations were not exactly the FBI's forte. As Meyer Lansky said, you can always tell an FBI agent by the cheap watch and college ring. The Bureau was largely composed of Irish Catholics with some Wasps at the top.

But by the late 1970s, the FBI was experimenting with undercover techniques and had begun investigating white-collar crime. And although Abscam did not seem very promising, I was inclined to give it a shot. The man promoting the idea was John Good, a marvelous FBI agent who tended to ignore many of the Bureau's stifling bureaucratic imperatives. John's talent far exceeded his station at the Bureau. He was in charge of the FBI office in Hauppauge, Long Island. I had worked with Good on a number of cases in the past, and I regarded him as a first-rate investigator.

John must have felt the same way about me. I was the only prosecutor lucky enough to be offered Abscam. Good, with Weinberg and McCarthy in tow, came to my office in the spring of 1977.

"I think we can pull it off," Good said, radiating enthusiasm.

I looked at the extremely Jewish Weinberg and the deeply Irish McCarthy dubiously. Typical Arab sheik retinue if I ever saw one.

"Well, give it a shot," I said, not wanting to throw cold water on an agent as enterprising as Good.

Abscam did have one overriding virtue, besides Good's energy. It was incredibly cheap. The budget for the entire operation was only $30,000. I was already involved in several expensive undercover operations. One, on which I was pinning great expectations, involved establishing our own trucking company at Kennedy Airport with the hope that the mob would quickly move in on our operation. Compared to that project, Abscam was like a low-budget, grade B movie with unknown actors.

I assigned one of my deputies, John Jacobs, to work with

Good on the operation and went back to more important matters—like assembling a new staff, battling government red tape, and overseeing my airport trucking company. (The Kennedy Airport production, by the way, would turn out to be a complete failure.)

I fully intended to ignore Abscam as much as possible. But Abscam wouldn't go away.

Weinberg, an accomplished thief, quickly attracted an army of hustlers, chiselers, and scam artists to Abdul Enterprises. It was becoming evident that the cover story was working. I couldn't for the life of me understand why. Even though the newspapers were filled with stories about OPEC and Arab oil wealth, even a credulous kindergartener should have been able to see through the Abscam cover.

Weinberg set up "Abdul Enterprises" in a vast room formerly occupied by a bank, in the same Hauppauge office that housed the FBI. This coincidence did not seem to trouble Weinberg's visitors. No one asked why the personal representative of an incredibly wealthy Arab sheik was headquartered in a place called Hauppauge. No one seemed to wonder why he had only managed to furnish his big office with only one desk and three chairs. No one was puzzled by the fact that a presumably conservative Arab sheik had entrusted his fortune to a shady American Jew. No one apparently thought it odd that the sheik's other U.S. deputy—a red-faced Irishman—looked a hell of a lot like a cop.

And no one questioned the sheik's apparently limitless appetite for stolen goods and illegal services. Hot paintings? Why, the sheik was an art lover! Pornography? The sheik was crazy about pornography but couldn't get it in his own country. Machine guns? Thank God. The sheik needs weapons to placate the PLO militants in his emirate. He'll buy the machine guns and present them as gifts to the PLO firebrands. Forged, stolen, or counterfeit certificates of deposit? Just what the sheik desperately needs! Because of Islamic laws against usury, the sheik cannot earn any interest on the money he keeps in Arab banks. He'll give the certificates of deposit to his Arab bankers in exchange for cash. Then he can invest the money elsewhere.

Abscam's initial success was not only bewildering—it was irritating for those of us who had to follow through. The cases that emerged during the first eighteen months of the operation tended to be troublesome and schlocky. Weinberg nailed a pair of low-level Long Island swindlers, but if I indicted them, Weinberg's role as an FBI operative would become known. Could I postpone the indictments, Good asked? Of course I would postpone the indictments. Delighted, in fact.

Weinberg also arranged to purchase $200 million in bogus certificates of deposit in exchange for $17 million in cash from the grateful sheik. The FBI burst in on the exchange and arrested the swindlers. To make things look good, the Bureau also pretended to arrest Weinberg, McCarthy, and another FBI agent involved in the sting. Again, I agreed to postpone the indictments. My deputy, John Jacobs, did some playacting in court, and Weinberg complained bitterly to the swindlers that one of them must have betrayed the deal to the FBI. He moaned about the loss of the $17 million. (The "money" was telephone books that had been cut up and stuffed into suitcases.)

But this time, I received an unpleasant shock. The swindlers filed a federal civil suit contending that the transaction was perfectly legitimate. They demanded the return of the $17 million. We were being sued for our chopped-up telephone books! The con men were setting a world record for chutzpah, but their loony suit created serious headaches for me. I secretly submitted a sworn affidavit to Jacob Mishler, the judge in the case, explaining the Abscam operation. Mishler cooperated by putting the case on a back burner, but I was eventually obliged to drop the indictment against the swindlers in order to keep the undercover operation confidential. As 1978 drew to a close, Abscam equaled civil lawsuits, secret meetings with judges, and worthless cases as far as I was concerned.

Thus began what was later described as a diabolical plot to ensnare congressmen. Later, Abscam's critics would charge that each meeting with a politician was carefully worked out in advance, with an elaborate "scenario" designed to lure into crime unsuspecting representatives of the people. The simple fact of the matter was that John Good and I never discussed a politician. We certainly never imagined that this shoestring operation would take us into the halls of Congress.

But Abscam was filled with surprises. Late in 1978, a hustler named Bill Rosenberg urged Weinberg to persuade the sheik to invest his money in an exciting new industry then being launched in Atlantic City: casino gambling. New Jersey's so-called Casino Control Commission appeared to have erected a daunting series of barriers for potential casino operators. For one thing, the commission insisted that casino operators receive their approval before beginning construction and again after casino construction was completed. Banks were understandably reluctant to lend large amounts of money to a casino operator who might be refused permission to open after construction was completed. At the time, Resorts International was struggling to obtain commission approval. Weinberg expressed enthusiasm for the casino idea but wanted to know about the license.

"Look at the problems Resorts is having," he said.

Rosenberg assured Weinberg there was a way to eliminate the uncertainty of getting a license. He had a friend. The kind of man who would take a hot stove: Angelo Errichetti, the mayor of Camden, New Jersey. Rosenberg offered to set up a meeting between Weinberg and Errichetti.

Camden, New Jersey, is best known as the home of Campbell's soup, but by the late 1970s, it had taken on a reputation far removed from the Campbell kids. Mainly black, extraordinarily poor, it had begun to lose even the most basic amenities—movie theaters, department stores, and supermarkets. Meeting Errichetti, you got the instant suspicion that Camden's slide into oblivion might be due to something besides simple bad luck. The mayor looked, acted, and talked like a hood who had stepped right out central casting. As we later learned, Errichetti's idea of economic development was to use the port of Camden to import narcotics and firearms.

But Errichetti, who doubled as a state senator, was also one of the most influential politicians in New Jersey. We all sensed he might provide an important turning point in the investigation. In his honor, we decided to add a new technical flourish to our routine tape recordings. The meeting would be videotaped.

Videotapes had been used in criminal cases prior to Abscam, but few people, even in law enforcement, comprehended the tremendous power this kind of evidence would have before juries. The tapes were also tremendous tools for supervisors. I no longer had to rely on a standard briefing from agents for information on what took place at a meeting. The videotape would be brought to my office, where I could see everything that happened firsthand.

By now, Abdul Enterprises had moved to swanker offices in Holbrook, Long Island. It was here that Errichetti first met with Weinberg and Jack McCarthy on December 1, 1978. The mayor looked, talked, and acted exactly the way we'd imagined. It was almost as if a director had called out, "OK. Send in the guy with the black shirt and white tie." Unfortunately, our technicians failed to capture Errichetti's Abscam debut for posterity. The videotape machine was not ready, and our regular taping system broke down. Still, the mayor established himself as totally corrupt within the first fifteen minutes of the meeting. His message was loud and clear: "I can give you fuckin' Atlantic City."

In subsequent meetings, Errichetti became more specific. It would take $400,000 in bribes to guarantee a casino license. The mayor said that he "owned" Kenneth MacDonald, the vice chairman of the Casino Control Commission. Through MacDonald, Errichetti said he controlled three other votes on the five-member commission, including the vote of chairman, Joseph Lordi. (This was untrue.)

By the way, the mayor said, he would need $25,000 in cash immediately to get things rolling. There was no question in my mind about coming up with the $25,000 needed to cement our relationship.

The mayor had provided another Abscam surprise by mentioning that he was friendly with Alexander Feinberg, a New Jersey lawyer Errichetti matter-of-factly described as the bagman for Senator Harrison Williams. (A bagman is a person who collects bribe money intended for another.) Harrison Williams—now *there* was a name we hadn't expected to be hearing. Williams, the chairman of the Senate Labor Committee, was a powerful figure on Capitol Hill. The senator had a courtly, aristocratic bearing and an excellent reputation as a statesmanlike champion of progressive causes. Would such a man have anything to do with riffraff like Angelo Errichetti?

The mayor offered to arrange a meeting with bagman Feinberg. We immediately accepted the invitation. McCarthy and Weinberg heard the lawyer spin out a bizarre story. Senator Williams, Feinberg, and two other men, including a New Jersey garbage contractor named George Katz, were partners in a titanium mine located in Virginia. Titanium was a rare metal desperately needed by the government for various weapons systems. If the sheik would provide the funding, the titanium venture would produce millions in profits from government contracts.

Good Lord, titanium. What was next—a kryptonite contract? I was left to ponder who was scamming who. Was the Virginia titanium mine a Beltway version of selling the Brooklyn Bridge? And would a distinguished United States senator become mixed up with a garbage contractor and various other sleazy characters in such a dubious deal?

We hooked Errichetti with a $25,000 bribe at Abdul's Holbrook office on January 29, 1979. This was a key moment in the investigation. Errichetti became the first public official in Abscam to commit a crime as our video camera rolled.

Needless to say, I eagerly looked forward to viewing the dramatic videotape of Errichetti's wrongdoing. Unfortunately, cinematography was not yet an FBI strong suit. The camera hidden in the Holbrook office was focused on the table where the bribe money was placed. I watched the tape intently as a hand reached out to take the bribe money. The hand then scooted away with the cash. Regrettably, the owner of the hand, Angelo Errichetti, was not in the picture. The FBI agents on the scene could, of course, testify that Errichetti had taken the money, but this was not at all what we had in mind.

Had Martin Scorsese started out like this?

MARCH 1979 was a pivotal point in the development of Abscam—we made our second big score, with the payment of a

$100,000 bribe to Kenneth MacDonald, the vice chairman of the Casino Control Commission. Even more memorable, for Abscam aficionados, was our great yacht party—the first and last time we trotted our sheik into society. In terms of criminal justice, the results were mixed. But you had to admit the sheik was one hell of an interesting host.

Let me be the first to admit we got a bit carried away. The idea was to impress Williams and other potential Abscam targets with the sheik's fabulous wealth by throwing a party aboard a sixty-five-foot yacht that had been seized by the government for drug smuggling. The party would be held in Del Ray Beach, Florida, where the boat was berthed. Mel Weinberg was placed in charge of issuing invitations, with results that proved all too predictable. The boat overflowed with con men, hustlers, counterfeiters, drug dealers, professional gamblers, thugs, crooked lawyers, and a host of other unsavory characters.

In honor of the occasion, we actually decided to produce the mythical sheik, Yassir Habib, to be played by Richard Farhardt, an FBI agent from Cleveland. For once, we had found an operative who at least had Middle Eastern genes—Farhardt was of Lebanese extraction. Unfortunately he spoke not a word of Arabic.

The party also featured the debut of a new key employee in the sheik's entourage. Jack McCarthy had proved to be just too much of a Boy Scout for the operation, and John Good had decided to phase him out slowly. His replacement at Abdul Enterprises was an FBI agent named Anthony Amoroso, the casting coup of the entire Abscam production. Amoroso, the son of a tailor, had grown up in poverty on the mean streets of the South Bronx. He affected the kind of shirt-open-to-the-navel-and-enough-gold-chains-to-blow-up-a-metal-detector look necessary to deceive people like Angelo Errichetti.

Tony initially posed as the sheik's "project engineer." Needless to say, Amoroso had no background or experience in construction or any field remotely related to engineering. At one point early on, one of Weinberg's invitees asked innocently where Tony had studied engineering.

"None of your fuckin' business," Amoroso shot back.

We knew right then we had a potential Oscar winner in our midst. Such an answer would have immediately aroused deep suspicion in polite circles, but it was absolutely perfect in the company Amoroso was keeping. Nobody batted an eye.

Still, we didn't want to encourage any further technical inquiries about Amoroso's background in construction. So Tony—without explanation—switched jobs and became the chairman of the board of Abdul Enterprises a week or two after being introduced as Abdul's "project engineer." Amoroso was also given a rather murky background as a former CIA/military intelligence operative

None of our sting targets batted an eye, but this sort of disregard for consistency drove people on the other end of the investigation crazy. One of my deputies, Larry Sharf, was reviewing tapes of Abscam meetings and phone calls to insure the operation was being carried out legally and in accordance with Justice Department guidelines. Larry has an orderly mind, and he went nuts listening to conversations in which the same sheik would wind up coming from a different country every week. Sharf pleaded with Weinberg and Amoroso to do a little reading about the Arab Emirates in order to make their pitch somewhat more authentic. Mel and Tony nodded agreeably and totally ignored Larry's suggestions.

I allowed John Good, Mel, and Tony a great deal of latitude in carrying out the operation. Getting a working knowledge of the Arab Emirates was perfectly logical, but Abscam was not a "logical" undertaking. It was built on smoke and mirrors. Weinberg and Amoroso instinctively knew what to say and do. They were tuned in to the mind-set of Abscam's swindlers and crooked politicians in a way we prosecutors could never hope to match.

The big boat party was held March 24, 1979. I half-expected Harrison Williams to flee the yacht in terror when he first cast eyes on his fellow guests. But, in fact, Williams seemed quite at home, greeting the "sheik" and chatting with the other partygoers. And nobody, of course, wondered why Yassir Habib seemed to understand English but not speak it. As a social event, the whole evening was something to remember—sort of a

"Miami Vice" version of that famous bar scene in *Star Wars* where weird aliens from every part of the galaxy sit around together, hoisting a few and exchanging pleasantries.

But as a criminal justice operation, the party proved to be a bad idea all-around. An undercover meeting should focus on one person. But there were simply too many crooked people aboard the boat to keep track properly of all that was going on. We did obtain one taped conversation in which the senator announced his interest in the titanium mine but warned that anything involving the mine would be handled by lawyer Feinberg. This was interesting, but it was the kind of information we could have gotten in another setting. And, we would discover later, the boat party resulted in an extraordinary breach of security—one that should have blown the operation before any congressmen were caught in its web.

A much more important, though slightly less colorful, event was unfolding during the same month in New Jersey. By now, the obliging sheik was eager to open his own casino in Atlantic City. (The sheik has always wanted to be in the gambling business!) The whole deal, of course, hinged on the proviso that a license could be guaranteed.

Errichetti assured Weinberg that a $100,000 bribe would do the trick. The mayor would pass the cash to Macdonald and three other commissioners.

There were two problems with the mayor's proposal. I did not want the money passed to MacDonald through a middleman like Errichetti. It would be too easy for MacDonald to later claim he never received a penny. If we were to build a solid criminal case against the commissioner, he would have to take the money. Weinberg and Amoroso pressed Errichetti for a face-to-face meeting with MacDonald at which the bribe would be paid.

"You couldn't hand [the commissioners] anything," the mayor protested. "Because that would be the end of it. I'm their bagman. They're gonna deal with me. I'm gonna deal with you."

This made perfect sense. It would be foolhardy for Mac-Donald to accept personally a large cash bribe from a couple of decidedly shady characters who claimed to represent a wealthy Arab. Moreover, dealing through a middleman was the customary way of conducting this kind of business. The Abdul team's insistence that Macdonald personally take the bribe should have raised an enormous red flag. But Abscam was an operation that had more red flags than the Indianapolis 500. Like all the rest, this one didn't seem to attract any notice.

Errichetti eventually agreed to set up a meeting with Macdonald. The mayor still insisted on taking the suitcase with the cash himself, but I decided MacDonald's presence in the room when he did so would be sufficient.

So far, so good. Now, how to get the money? We couldn't pay MacDonald off with sliced-up phone books. There appeared to be no way the Bureau would authorize the expenditure of this much cash for such a low-priority undertaking. The mayor's interest in Abdul Enterprises was a promising development, but from the FBI's point of view, Abscam was still very much a shoestring operation. If Errichetti and MacDonald walked out the door with $100,000 in FBI money, there was no assurance that the Bureau would see the cash again. And we could not even guarantee that an important criminal case might result.

John Good was despairing. He believed coming up with $100,000 in cash was crucial to establishing Weinberg and Amoroso as "serious" people. But there seemed to be no way his request for the money would survive the FBI bureaucracy in Washington. I decided to circumvent the red tape by picking up the phone and calling FBI Director William Webster. Now, a middle-level federal prosecutor in Brooklyn doesn't ordinarily call to chat with someone like the director of the FBI. The Justice Department is a regulation-encrusted bureaucracy driven by paperwork. My phone call broke no rules, but it was something that just wasn't done.

Nevertheless, when I explained the situation to Webster, he immediately agreed to authorize the expenditure of $100,000 for the bribe. I like to think Webster's action was a kind of reward for doing the right thing in the Stabile case. Webster had gotten to know me during that investigation, and he had developed trust in my ability and judgment.

Abscam was still on track.

The meeting with MacDonald and Errichetti took place at

Abdul's office in Long Island exactly one week after the Florida boat party. One of my assistants, John Jacobs, and several FBI officials watched the meeting in an adjoining room. The video camera was concealed in a file cabinet. And this time, it was focused to film more than hands. Once again, however, Abscam failed to produce an Academy Award winner. The camera worked properly, but the acting was less than compelling.

Jack McCarthy was making his final appearance as an Abdul Enterprise operative, and it was his job to pass the bribe to Mac-Donald and Errichetti. The mayor, good to his word, insisted on taking the money himself. McCarthy, giving it the old college try, wanted to hand the cash to MacDonald. He flipped open the briefcase to display the money in all its glory. Errichetti reached for the handle. McCarthy pulled it back. Thereafter, the mayor and the undercover FBI agent nearly wound up in a wrestling match over the bribe money. The mayor finally seized control of the briefcase.

MacDonald, a Republican, was the former mayor of Haddonfield, New Jersey, a posh suburb of Philadelphia. His appointment to the Casino Control Commission by Democratic Governor Brendan Byrne had supposedly angered Camden County Democrats, though Angelo Errichetti was clearly not among the aggrieved. Compared to his friend the mayor, this graduate of the Wharton School of Business looked like a somberly dressed Mr. Clean.

While McCarthy and the mayor played musical briefcase, MacDonald looked on with an expression of haughty disdain that the lord of the manor might have cast at two brawling peasants.

There was more in store. MacDonald and Errichetti met with Weinberg and Amoroso at a nearby Holiday Inn immediately after the payoff was made. MacDonald, who died before he could be brought to trial on corruption charges, angrily denounced McCarthy's crude behavior.

"What's wrong with that clown?" MacDonald sputtered.

I couldn't believe it. We were getting a lecture in crook ethics.

As a final "bonus" on this memorable day, Errichetti presented Weinberg and Amoroso with a long list of local, state, and federal officials in New Jersey who could be bribed. With our $100,000 payoff locked safely in the trunk of his car, the mayor must have been swept up in the spirit of giving. My initial reaction was that we had our hands on an intelligence bonanza, but surveying the list, I rapidly began to lose interest. One of the alleged felons in Errichetti's gallery of rogues was none other than Millicent Fenwick, an elderly Republican congresswoman who epitomized patrician virtue. Fenwick, who has since passed away, was the model for the adorable Congresswoman Lacey Davenport in the Doonesbury cartoons. The mayor might as well have added Mother Teresa to his list. Since Errichetti did not have a well-developed sense of irony, I can only guess that in his eagerness to impress us, he threw in Fenwick's name.

Overall, the quality of the MacDonald tapes made me feel we were making some progress in our effort to become documentary filmmakers. The only real problem was McCarthy's poor performance. Jack was subsequently given a nonacting role in Abscam. The crooks were simply told McCarthy had taken another job in Abdul's vast empire. They believed this, just as they believed everything we told them.

Indeed, it seemed nothing could arouse their suspicion. The sheik could have left a message on his door directing bribe takers to pick up their money at the FBI office upstairs, and I suspect some of them would have trotted right up, with their hand out.

Abdul Enterprises had a "secretary" played by FBI agent Margo Denedy. Margo, who only worked on the sting part-time, was summoned to Kennedy Airport one day to participate in the arrest of a female skyjacker. The next morning, Margo's picture appeared in *Newsday,* the Long Island newspaper.

Bill Rosenberg, the swindler who introduced Mayor Errichetti to Weinberg, immediately placed a phone call to the FBI con man. Rosenberg was understandably upset about the fact that Weinberg's secretary was apparently an FBI agent. Weinberg soothingly assured Rosenberg there was no way Margo could be an FBI agent. He had, after all, known her for years.

Rosenberg believed him.

An even more egregious security breach involved the fabled yacht party. Unknown to me and John Good, the FBI's Miami office slipped one of its informers, a small-time criminal, aboard the boat party in Del Ray Beach. The informer was not told much, but he knew the party was part of an FBI undercover operation and that Tony Amoroso was one of the key players.

In the summer of 1979, the informer passed this information along to a friend of Errichetti's, who quickly informed the mayor.

Weinberg soothingly assured the worried mayor that it could not be so. Errichetti was convinced.

Abscam seemed to be operating under a lucky star, impervious to ordinary disasters. About the same time the informer was ratting on us to Errichetti, my deputy, Larry Sharf, received a phone call from a reporter from a New Jersey newspaper.

"We hear there is an investigation involving casino gambling and public figures in New Jersey, including Senator Williams," the reporter said.

Sharf was flabbergasted. Abscam's existence was a closely held secret, even within our office. Larry worked behind the scenes on the case, and few knew of his involvement in the investigation even after Abscam hit the headlines.

Sharf thought for a moment, and decided to lie.

"New Jersey?" he asked incredulously. "We don't have anything to do with New Jersey."

It was a pretty good lie. Why, indeed, would the Brooklyn-based Organized Crime Strike Force be investigating casino gambling and politicians in New Jersey?

"I don't know what you're talking about," Sharf added with finality.

We could only hold our breath. Clearly, there had been another serious security breach. But nothing appeared in print, and the targets of the investigation apparently never learned what the reporter was told. We were never able to determine the source of the leak.

So Abscam moved along nicely, though from day to day we were never quite certain where it was headed. Our star actors, Amoroso and Weinberg, composed the script as they went along. Even the "scenario" that resulted in the depressing parade of congressmen who scooped up satchels stuffed with cash in front of FBI cameras was solely the result of an idle conversation.

While Amoroso, Weinberg, Errichetti, and two other crooks were cruising aboard the sheik's yacht in July 1979, the "captain" of the ship, an FBI agent, pointed to a boat that belonged to deposed Nicaraguan dictator Anastasio Somoza. Somoza was then on the run, and Weinberg and Amoroso wistfully began to talk about how their boss, the sheik, might have to flee his emirate soon, since he was looting the national treasury. This was total improvisation. Weinberg and Amoroso might just as easily have been inspired to say that the emir was dearly loved by all his loyal subjects and would never encounter the problems Somoza was having. But they didn't, and their concern for their boss gave Mayor Errichetti a bright idea.

"I can introduce you to people who can take care of the sheik's problem," the mayor promised.

The "people" were congressmen. They could introduce special legislation that would guarantee the sheik permanent residence in the United States. Errichetti was as good as his word. He soon phoned Weinberg to report he was ready to arrange meetings with two Philadelphia congressmen, Raymond Lederer and Michael "Ozzie" Myers. As we learned a few weeks later, the congressmen had actually been brought in by a friend of the mayor's named Howard Criden. Criden was a Philadelphia lawyer with political connections that were even better than Errichetti's. Criden had already talked to Amoroso and Weinberg about a loan for a client who wanted to build a casino in Atlantic City. He would become more important to Abscam than the mayor in the months to come.

Later, critics of Abscam insisted that we had "targeted" these congressmen in an elaborate sting operation—supposedly working from voluminous FBI files. Let me explain how things really were. My "intelligence" file on the legislative branch of government was a little blue book we obtained from the government printing office. The book contained the names, photos, and party affiliations of members of the House and Senate. When the name of a congressman came up at a meeting, I would flip through my blue book. It is very hard to "target" people you've never heard of. (The one exception was Congressman John Murphy. At the time of Abscam, the FBI was conducting an unrelated criminal investigation of the Staten Island congressman.) None of us, of course, could fail to notice that most of the names cropping up on the tapes were Democrats. Given that the Democratic party controlled both Congress and the Carter White House, we all regretted there wasn't a better political balance in our rogues' gallery. During one of our strategy sessions, an FBI agent made the mistake of joking about it.

"Hey, can you bring us some Republicans?" he said pleadingly, looking at Mel Weinberg. "We want Republicans."

That got a big laugh. But Mel, like Angelo Errichetti, was not a big fan of irony. A week later, Larry Sharf was listening to the tape of a telephone call between Weinberg and one of his numerous swindler buddies.

"We need Republicans," Weinberg said. "Can you bring us some Republicans?"

We put a quick end to Mel's search for members of the Grand Old Party, but it was another reminder that Weinberg required special handling.

Besides being careful what we said around Mel, we tried to be constantly on the watch for any sign of free-lancing. Weinberg, we knew, was capable of initiating a sideline con of his own that could taint the entire probe. We never found any evidence, however, of serious wrongdoing. The worst charge leveled against him was when Mayor Errichetti later claimed that he had given Weinberg a VCR, a TV set, a microwave oven, and a stereo system. This was hardly earth shattering—the alleged payoffs were the kind of things a losing contestant on a TV quiz show might expect to collect. Still, Weinberg denied receiving anything from the mayor, and the controversy quickly died down. Personally, I found the charge plausible. Since Weinberg had been funneling bribe money to the mayor, crook ethics would have dictated that Errichetti show Weinberg his appreciation with a few "presents."

Certainly, Weinberg looked like an absolute paragon of civic virtue compared to the congressmen Errichetti was introducing us to. The first bribe taker was Ozzie Myers of Philadelphia, who agreed to meet the sheik's representatives at the Travel Lodge Hotel at Kennedy Airport on August 22, 1979. Myers was brought to the meeting by Mayor Errichetti and steered to a couch covered by our candid camera. Myers quickly agreed to introduce a bill in Congress that would give the sheik permanent residence in the United States in exchange for a $50,000 bribe. While the camera ran on, the representative from Philadelphia delivered his own personal interpretation of the subtleties of the legislative process:

"Tony, let me say this to you. You're going about this the right way . . . I'm gonna tell you something real simple and short. Money talks in this business and bullshit walks. It works the same way down in Washington."

The meeting was a complete success—legally and bureaucratically. Establishing jurisdiction was absolutely essential to maintaining our control of the case. That's why a Philadelphia congressman and a mayor from southern New Jersey were asked to come several hundred miles to an airport in Queens. In order to insure control of the case, I needed the crime to take place in the friendly confines of the Eastern District: Brooklyn, Queens, Staten Island, and Long Island.

This was the only aspect of Abscam that could fairly be said to be the product of deliberate manipulation. Others listening to the Abscam tapes might find the discussions of where a meeting would take place to be boring and inconsequential, but they were absolutely vital to me. There was no legal requirement that everything happen in the Eastern District, but at least some part of the crime had to take place there for me to keep the case.

When a meeting might logically take place in New Jersey, Weinberg would invent a reason for holding it at JFK or Abdul's Long Island headquarters. This approach sometimes worked to our advantage in other ways. When I was trying to convince FBI Director Webster to authorize the payment of a $100,000 bribe to Kenneth MacDonald, one of the things I pointed out was that it was strange indeed for the vice chairman of New Jersey's Casino Control Commission to be driving all the way to western Long Island for a meeting with representatives of "Sheik Yassir Habib."

Congressman Lederer was the next to take a bribe of $50,000 for the introduction of an immigration bill. The same script was followed. Lederer and Errichetti came to a hotel suite at Kennedy and departed with a suitcase stuffed with cash. During some postbribe chitchat, the congressman delivered an unnecessary assurance that he was "no Boy Scout."

At this point, Abscam unexpectedly turned comic again. Mayor Errichetti, who was taking a healthy cut of each bribe we doled out, came up with an extraordinary package deal. He would deliver Senator Herman Talmadge of Georgia, Georgia Congressman Wyche Fowler, and Mario Noto, the deputy commissioner of immigration. The mayor informed us that Talmadge would cost $100,000 and the apparently less important Fowler and Noto $50,000 each. I had to admit that it would be difficult even for the ever-willing Errichetti to assemble all these important people in the wilds of Long Island, or an airport motel. Philadelphia lawyer Criden was actually the man who put together the package.

We decided on a switch in locale. The FBI had an expensive Colonial town house in the posh Georgetown section of Washington. Use of the building would make it more difficult for me to retain jurisdiction, but the town house provided a perfect setting for meetings with crooked congressmen. The town house had been used in an unrelated undercover operation that had flopped. It was furnished with expensive antiques and contained a large wine cellar. Needless to say, it was also wired for sight and sound. The FBI adored this plan—it was a golden opportunity for the Bureau to justify the enormous amount of money it had poured into the failed undercover operation. (I think it's worth pointing out that Abscam was incredibly cheap by undercover standards. Apart from the salaries of the agents and prosecutors, which would have had to be paid anyway, the operation cost perhaps $500,000. Abscam's major expense was bribe money. And some of that money was later recovered by the government.)

It didn't seem to me that $200,000 was too much to pay for two of President Carter's political allies from Georgia and one of the highest ranking immigration officials in the United States.

Still, Angelo Errichetti was the same man who told us Millicent Fenwick was on the take. As usual, I could only wait to see who actually walked through the door. The bribe spectacular at the town house was set for September 19, 1979. But before the meeting took place, Criden called to say that Talmadge and Fowler would be unable to attend. Mario Noto, however, was still coming.

Maybe, I thought, we were being punished for going "upscale" with Abscam.

Mayor Errichetti and Commissioner Noto arrived on time and were ushered into the study, where a briefcase containing $50,000 was discreetly placed within the commissioner's reach. Amoroso and Weinberg looked intently at Noto and exchanged a quick glance. Prior to the meeting, they had studied a photograph of Noto, a routine part of the preparation for such a session. They both instantly realized that the Mario Noto sitting before them was an impostor. Errichetti and Criden were attempting to rip us off for $50,000 with a bogus immigration official!

Amoroso casually asked the commissioner for his business card. "Noto," unfortunately, did not have one.

Tony then asked Errichetti to step into another room.

Mel remained behind to entertain the "commissioner."

"I didn't get your name," Weinberg said.

"Nopo," the imposter replied. Then he helpfully spelled it out. "N-o-p-o."

Amoroso was in a difficult position—he didn't want to embarrass Errichetti by confronting him with the truth. But as always, Tony proved equal to the challenge. In conspiratorial tones, he informed the mayor that Noto was a fake. Errichetti, who said he did not know Noto personally, reacted with shock and outrage.

What if the imposter was an FBI agent? Amoroso worried. The two men agreed to end the meeting immediately by hustling Noto out of the town house. We later discovered that "Noto" was Ellis Cook—a law partner of Howard Criden.

Unfortunately, the "N-o-p-o" meeting marked the end of our relationship with Errichetti. He became distant and aloof after the fiasco at the town house. But I don't believe he ever became suspicious of our operation. I suspect that catching him in a crude attempt to rip us off was tremendously humiliating for him. Fortunately for us, Howard Criden remained willing and able to continue producing congressmen. Criden's law firm was a political powerhouse in Philadelphia, and the energetic lawyer seemed to have a million contacts in Washington and elsewhere.

Three weeks later, Criden walked through the door of the town house with Congressman Frank Thompson of New Jersey, one of the most senior Democrats in the House. The script followed the same route, but Thompson firmly declared he was not interested in money. This was really no surprise, since only the sloppiest and most dim-witted bribe taker would voluntarily announce his intention to break the law. Nobody at the meeting was supposed to believe a single word of what Thompson was saying. But the agents were under orders to extract a specific, concrete promise of wrongdoing by the congressmen.

Amoroso ended the meeting and hung on to the suitcase with the cash. Criden later returned to the town house alone, in a fury. The lawyer was so outraged that he actually began to weep. In effect, Criden argued that Weinberg and Amoroso weren't acting like good crooks. Amoroso should have handed him the briefcase at the end of the meeting. What the hell was going on?

Amoroso was a rock. Congressman Thompson would have to accept the cash personally and specifically acknowledge that he would use his office to help the sheik in exchange for the bribe money. These were preposterous conditions, and a veteran thief like Criden should have instantly become incredibly suspicious. But he didn't. Instead, he continued to negotiate with Amoroso. Tony finally agreed to a "compromise." Criden would be handed the briefcase with the cash but only if Thompson witnessed the payoff and agreed that the money was being paid for the private bill Thompson would introduce in the House on behalf of the sheik.

A few hours later, Thompson was back for his money. The grateful lawmaker promised to bring us other congressmen. This was another example of how Abscam grew. We had depended on middlemen like Errichetti and Criden to bring in politicians. Now Thompson, the chairman of influential House Administration Committee, had pledged to introduce us to other crooked House members. It was almost like putting Abscam on automatic pilot.

Senator Williams, three House members, and a cluster of lesser crooks had so far committed felonies in our presence. Who would come through the door next?

I am not a political junkie, and names like Williams, Thompson, Lederer, and Myers meant very little to me. Larry Sharf, who was much more interested in politics than I am, was often surprised by the calm, businesslike way I responded when he excitedly called me to report that this or that representative of the people had taken a bribe in front of our cameras.

But thanks to Congressman Thompson and Howard Criden, we were introduced to a man who got my own juices flowing. Thompson's friend was Congressman John Murphy of Staten Island. He was reported to have links to General Somoza and the shah of Iran. The congressman was a West Point graduate, a war hero in Korea. Up until now, we had been dealing with men who, despite their reputations and trappings of office, were amateur criminals. But Murphy was tough, shrewd, and gutsy—a wise guy in a business suit.

Weinberg and Amoroso performed the usual ritual. A meeting was set for October 20, 1979. It would take place in a hotel suite at my favorite airport. I had no intention of letting Murphy slip through my grasp because of a jurisdictional quarrel.

Murphy had a busy day. It began in Washington, where he went to the Justice Department and complained bitterly about news leaks emanating from the unrelated FBI investigation of his activities. A lesser man might have laid low with the FBI nipping at his heels and the press tipped to his possible wrongdoing. But that was not John Murphy's way. He boarded a plane for New York for the trip to pick up his $50,000 bribe.

The meeting, however, proved to be a bit disappointing. Mel and Tony did their now-familiar routine about the need for a private immigration bill for the sheik. Murphy agreed to assist, but he did so in an oblique manner that was somewhat inconclusive. He also made sure that Criden handled the briefcase with the $50,000.

Murphy was chairman of the Merchant Marine and Fisheries Committee, an obscure House panel. But there was plenty of money to be made in shipping and on the docks. The congressman, as it turned out, wanted much more than a one-time bribe. He was after millions. During the meeting, Murphy mentioned that he was interested in a shipping deal that some of his friends would discuss with Weinberg and Amoroso.

While the meeting made Murphy look very bad, to say the least, I decided more proof would be needed to build a strong criminal case against the congressman. We would simply have to wait and see what happened. Two weeks later, Criden produced a New Jersey shipping executive named Larry Buser. Buser told Amoroso he needed a $100 million loan from Abdul to buy a container shipping company. He suggested that Murphy would take care of the legislation needed to guarantee the success of the company. This was a promising development, but Murphy could always claim he knew nothing about the proposal.

Tony and Mel naturally pressed for a meeting with Murphy, but the congressman seemed unwilling to bite. Tony, as always, was adamant: There was no way he would recommend to the emir that the loan be made without specific assurances from Murphy that the needed legislation would be taken care of.

At long last, Murphy agreed to meet with us at the Washington town house in the company of Criden and Buser. The shipping deal was discussed in detail, but Murphy refused to acknowledge that he had any interest in the company despite Tony's best efforts to draw him out.

Instead, Murphy held forth on government, the law, and politics. His presentation was the exact opposite of Ozzie Myers's. In fact, Murphy's disquisition was so lofty that Bud Mullen, a top FBI official in Washington, was enormously impressed with the congressman after viewing the videotape.

"If I didn't know Murphy was a crook, I'd vote for him for president," Mullen told me.

Amoroso was also obliged to try to get the slippery Murphy to acknowledge he had received a $50,000 bribe at the previous airport meeting in New York. All efforts on this front seemed to end in a complete disaster. Tony maneuvered Murphy into the library at the town house, where they could talk alone.

AMOROSO: I was reluctant to give you the money, because you, you were, you were . . .
MURPHY: You didn't. You didn't give me any money.
AMOROSO: Well, OK then . . .
MURPHY: I never, I never received money from anyone . . . and would not accept anything . . . from you or Howard (Criden).

If this exchange had been tape-recorded only, I'm absolutely convinced Murphy would have been acquitted. But our video cameras saved the day. The look of knowing cynicism on Murphy's face when he uttered these words of denial was so obvious, so transparent that no juror could—or would—be fooled. In fact, I think Murphy's denial actually worked to our advantage at his trial. The jurors—who also saw the tape of Amoroso handing Criden the bribe money while Murphy looked on—simply didn't find the denial credible.

Murphy was in every way a tougher character than any of the sheik's other new-found friends. He was the only bribe taker who left the town house meeting suspicious enough to do some investigating on his own. The congressman hired a private detective named Joe Mullen to check out Abdul Enterprises. Mullen interviewed neighbors who lived near the town house, and he was able to put together a picture of the comings and goings of Mel, Tony, and other agents involved in the investigation. Mullen obtained no proof of our real identity, but he concluded fairly quickly that our people were government agents.

Murphy must have conveyed these suspicions to Criden, and perhaps to Thompson as well. Even without the detective's information, you'd have thought that they might have asked themselves why the sheik seemed to need the help of so many congressmen to enter the United States. But it seemed as if nothing could derail Abscam. Criden continued to be cooperative until the day Abscam ended, and congressmen continued to walk through the door.

The next two House members to take bribes were John Jenrette of South Carolina and Richard Kelly of Florida, the only Republican to accept a payoff. The same script was followed, with variations that might have depressed even the pluckiest good-government type. Jenrette's real estate dealings and suspected jury-tampering activities were the target of a federal investigation, and he told Tony Amoroso he would not take a bribe until his lawyer checked with Attorney General Civiletti to see if the Justice Department intended to end the investigation.

"I got larceny in my blood. I'd take it [the bribe] in a goddamned minute," Jenrette promised. And, good to his word, he later took the money with relish.

Kelly was, on every level, the stupidest congressman we encountered. We later learned that Kelly's performance as a state judge in Florida was so horrendous that he was talked into running for Congress as a means of removing him from the bench. Somehow, he won.

Kelly arrived at the town house accompanied by an out-and-out hoodlum named Gino Ciuzio. Usually, the middlemen were lawyers or at least pretended to be engaged in some kind of legal occupation. But Ciuzio made no bones about the fact that he was a mobster. Gino told us that the price for Kelly's cooperation was $250,000, of which the congressman was to get $100,000. He also insisted that the money be turned over to him rather than Kelly.

"You guys would like protection, too, from a fuckin' congressman who obviously ain't gonna go to jail for you and me," Ciuzio told Weinberg and Amoroso.

Gino was making a good point. Congressmen were not stand-up guys. If Kelly received the money directly from us and was later caught, he would surely give up Weinberg and Amoroso in an attempt to save his own skin. Had we been real crooks, we probably would have agreed to use Gino as the conduit for the cash. But I wanted Kelly to take the money, and so, as it turned out, did the congressman.

Kelly and Ciuzio had agreed to take a $25,000 "down payment" on the bribe to help the sheik. During the course of the meeting at the town house, the congressman patiently waited until Ciuzio left the room and then demanded that Amoroso immediately turn over the cash to him.

As Amoroso watched in stunned silence, Kelly quickly jammed the cash into his pockets. His intention, of course, was to stiff Ciuzio, but the scene produced Abscam's most memorable image: a greedy congressman literally stuffing his pockets with greenbacks.

The meeting with Kelly took place on January 8, 1980. It effectively marked the end of Abscam. It was hard to believe less than a year had passed since we bribed Angelo Errichetti. In that short period of time, we had assembled solid criminal cases against a U.S. senator, six House members, and a cast of lesser officials like the mayor of Camden.

And there were others, like Congressman John Murtha, who barely escaped criminal indictment. Murtha was brought to the town house by the ubiquitous Howard Criden. As it turned out, both Thompson and Murphy had put in a good word for us with the Pennsylvania lawmaker.

Murtha agreed to help the sheik, as did all the others. He also refused to take the money, but his motives may have been a tad less than noble. There was some discussion of getting paid at a later time, but the fact is Murtha walked out of the town house without the money. We later decided against indicting Murtha, partly because he had a good lawyer who immediately came in to see me after Abscam became public and pledged that Murtha would cooperate fully with the investigation. Also, since we thought Murtha's testimony would be useful in what might be a very tough trial involving Congressman Murphy, we gave him a pass.

In all, sixteen of the nineteen public officials who were offered bribes in Abscam accepted. The others, like Murtha, hardly covered themselves in glory.

The reasons for Abscam's success were both obvious and subtle. They say love is blind, but it can't hold a candle to greed. Time and time again, the congressmen and the middlemen should have figured out that there was something very fishy about Abdul Enterprises. But nothing of the sort ever happened, even in the face of major security lapses like the newspaper photo of Margo Denedy. The congressmen and the middlemen kept coming back for the cash. Seeing the money, it seemed, was all the reality that they needed.

In part, Abscam was a product of its time—a magnificent myth for an age when the public was obsessed with oil prices and wealthy Arabs. A scenario I originally regarded as preposterous obviously made a powerful impact on the greedy imagination of some of the nation's top politicians. The idea of an oil-rich Arab potentate recklessly throwing a few hundred million dollars of his limitless fortune around in the United States was something they all found perfectly plausible. They also believed without question that an Arab sheik fleeing his country would seek refuge in the good old United States, the greatest country on earth. Mel Weinberg and Tony Amoroso did a marvelous job of improvising, switching gears, and making things up on the spot to keep the illusion going.

Unfortunately, Abscam also produced powerful evidence of widespread corruption in Congress. After listening to hundreds of hours of taped conversations with these congressmen, the only reasonable conclusion one can reach is that bribe taking was an accepted feature of life for many in Congress. The politicians we caught were not only greedy but also careless because they believed what they were doing was part of an accepted routine. Arrogance also played a role in their downfall. There is no other way to explain how John Murphy could lodge a complaint at the Justice Department and then jump on a plane for New York to pick up a $50,000 bribe. Congress seemed to infuse its members with a feeling of invulnerability. Common sense told them federal agencies that needed their backing for legislation and budget allocations would not be systematically making criminal cases against them. But Abscam turned common sense on its head.

6

THE ENEMY WITHIN

For me the most depressing, disheartening part of the Abscam investigation had nothing to do with crooked politicians. As a New Yorker, I am capable of being pretty cynical at times, and I bore up well under the discovery that some of our congressmen were no more morally scrupulous than a New York City policeman on the take. And the discovery of widespread political corruption in New Jersey was, for anybody who knew New Jersey, about as shocking as the discovery that the sun comes up in the morning.

The awful part of Abscam, for me, was the infighting. I'd had my share of internal battles over control of a case or suspect before, but I'd never had anything like this. Fellow prosecutors attempted to wrest control of Abscam from me and the Organized Crime Strike Force. I discovered members of the Justice Department who apparently preferred to see crooked politicians go free than allow other federal prosecutors to convict them.

The hardest battle of Abscam had nothing to do with catching corrupt congressmen. It had to do with beating back New Jersey's federal law enforcement establishment.

Our "cooperation" with the office of Robert Del Tufo, the United States attorney in Newark, began early in 1979. Del Tufo was intelligent, cordial, and easygoing, a real glad-hander in fact. He had graduated from Princeton and Yale Law School, where he was editor of the prestigious *Law Review*. I didn't hold his Ivy League credentials against him. In fact, at the beginning of our association, he struck me as a straight shooter. Since our investigation involved important New Jersey officials, it was only proper and reasonable for my office to keep Del Tufo abreast of developments in the case.

I first went to Del Tufo's office in Newark early in 1979 to brief him about our contacts with Mayor Errichetti and the suggestions of corruption in the casino industry. In March, Del Tufo visited my office to view our early videotapes.

During this "honeymoon" period, two of Del Tufo's top aides, Edward Plaza and Robert Weir, began coming to our office in Brooklyn periodically for briefings on the operation.

Plaza and Weir never seemed satisfied with the briefings we gave them. At the outset, I believe, their concern stemmed from a fundamental misunderstanding of the way Abscam worked. The FBI was a bureaucracy that thrived on reports and paperwork, but John Good was an unconventional agent who always looked well beyond the "book" approach to law enforcement. If John had been a different kind of guy, Abscam never would have happened. There were very few people in the Bureau who would have welcomed new-fangled gadgets like video cameras in their investigations and fewer still who would have slapped a burnoose on an FBI agent from Cleveland and dubbed him "Emir Yassir Habib."

The bureaucratic downside to Good's approach was a healthy scorn for paperwork. As a result, the reams of documents Plaza and Weir apparently expected to collect simply did not exist. We were always falling behind administratively. The FBI, for example, was slow to make copies of the tapes of various meetings and conversations. Because of this, several weeks would often elapse between the time of a conversation and receipt of the tape for our review. These delays were annoying, but hardly sinister.

My deputies, John Jacobs and Larry Sharf, would turn over what we did have to Weir and Plaza, but they became increasingly suspicious.

"There must be more," was Plaza's repeated refrain. The New Jersey prosecutors would urge me to "lean" on John Good and the FBI to produce more paperwork on Abscam.

"I'll speak to them about it," I would promise. But I had no intention of becoming another bureaucrat. Good and Tony Amoroso were already busy fending off the second-guessing of some of their Bureau bosses, who frequently wanted to know why Amoroso had failed to ask this or that question during a meeting. It was sometimes difficult for Tony to explain why bringing up a bribe or another potential criminal act was not the "right" thing to do. Weinberg and Amoroso operated instinctively at these meetings, sizing up the people they were dealing with on the spot and deciding then and there what the best approach would be.

Following a script would have been fatal to Abscam. But—in effect—that was exactly what Plaza and Weir demanded. They began to criticize me, complaining that there was not enough control or supervision of Abscam. They were particularly harsh on our handling of Mel Weinberg—who they described (accurately enough) as deceitful and sloppy. They also wanted written FBI reports on every conceivable aspect of the operation and suggested that "the prosecutors" should call all the shots.

These complaints grew in volume and intensity in the summer of 1979. Indeed, they grew directly in proportion to the mounting evidence we were uncovering of corruption in New Jersey.

It quickly became absolutely clear to me that Del Tufo at the beginning was out to steal Abscam, although the New Jersey U.S. attorney would never have phrased it in such a bald way. I can tell you, in fact, exactly how he *would* have put it. Much later, after our relationship had soured, curdled, and generally gone to hell, I had a chance to suggest, in court, that Del Tufo was worried his office would look bad if someone else ran an investigation involving New Jersey public officials.

"Not exactly in those terms," he testified. "It was in the context of having the citizens of New Jersey expecting from its state and federal law enforcement a vigorous and fair participation in the criminal process, and that it certainly fosters public confidence if the office in which the officeholders were being pursued, the officials in that state participated in the course of the investigation, and quite obviously if it has impact on public officials in the state of New Jersey, we certainly wanted to be involved."

Rashly, perhaps, I took all this to mean "yes" and pressed my advantage by asking Del Tufo if he had ever complained to anyone in the Justice Department that he would be embarrassed if important criminal cases against New Jersey officials were handled by another (my) office.

"No, not that I would be embarrassed, but that if New Jersey was not involved in the course of the investigation involving New Jersey officials, public confidence and public expectations in what previously had been vigorous law enforcement by both federal and state officials might be damaged."

Right.

Early on in Abscam, I met with Del Tufo on several occasions at the World Trade Center in New York to discuss his ideas on the case. Del Tufo's thoughts began and ended with shifting the responsibility for the investigation to his office. But I had no intention of ceding control of Abscam to New Jersey. My position was self-serving, of course, but there were strong practical reasons for retaining control. I was familiar with every detail of the operation and I had an excellent working relationship with John Good, Mel Weinberg, and Tony Amoroso. Adding a new, second boss to the undercover operation would have slowed and perhaps even destroyed Abscam.

My refusal to budge prompted Del Tufo to turn to Washington. He, Plaza, and Weir complained bitterly that New Jersey was not being given a large enough role in Abscam, and that if their office was not given control of major aspects of the operation, the people of New Jersey would see it as a vote of no confidence in their own law enforcement officials. They also put pressure on FBI officials in New Jersey to put pressure on their Bureau counterparts in New York.

United States attorneys from important districts like New Jersey often exercise considerable clout within the Justice Department. But Del Tufo was relatively new—he had been appointed in 1977—and I was not without backing. The United States attorney in Brooklyn was Ed Korman, a close friend who was respected in Washington, where he had worked for the solicitor general. If Ed had been in any way hostile to me or Abscam, it's likely the operation would have quickly unraveled. But Korman provided me with strong support and political "protection" in Washington throughout the course of Abscam.

On July 18, 1979, Korman and I met in Washington with Del Tufo, Irv Nathan, the number two man in the Justice Department's Criminal Division, and other officials. A few days later, Phil Heymann, the chief of the Criminal Division, announced a compromise settlement: Del Tufo would be placed in charge of the investigation into Kenneth MacDonald and the state's Casino Control Commission. He was also given a case against a New Jersey state senator named Joe Maressa. Maressa, a political enemy of Mayor Errichetti's, had taken $25,000 in the sheik's money in exchange for helping Abdul get a casino license. The compromise left me a free hand with Errichetti and Senator Williams. Both offices were, of course, ordered to continue to "cooperate."

But the settlement settled nothing. Del Tufo had been cut out of the most important part of Abscam. So New Jersey responded by mounting a concerted attack on everything connected with the investigation. (Del Tufo, incidentally, did absolutely nothing with the MacDonald and Maressa cases. The Justice Department was ultimately forced to remove the investigations from his office and assign them to other prosecutors.)

From that point on, New Jersey's complaints about being cut off from the flow of information were right on the mark. I continued to "cooperate" with Del Tufo, but I always made sure his office was two or three steps behind us in terms of the flow of information. It's a cliche, but knowledge is power, and I had no intention of turning over a crucial weapon to my rivals. If New Jersey complained that some aspect of the investigation was moving slowly, I might shrug my shoulders and say it had already been completed. I kept some of my own superiors a little bit in the dark for the same reason. It always gave me an advantage. The only people who were completely up to speed were me, John Good, and Irv Nathan.

THESE BATTLES over turf were charged with tension because the stakes were so high. As Abscam uncovered wrongdoing by more and more congressmen, the price of failure became correspondingly higher. Congress controlled our budgets and had the power to pass laws that could change or restrict the way we operated. If Abscam somehow blew up in our faces, an aroused legislature might make fundamental changes in the way we operated.

It's for these reasons that I never expect to see another Abscam-style investigation into congressional corruption in my lifetime. Abscam made absolutely no sense in bureaucratic terms. It was foolhardy to provoke the very people who provided your budget. No high-level official at the FBI or Justice Department would have dreamed of approving—in advance—an undercover operation aimed at members of Congress. If anyone had been crazy enough to propose it, a hundred reasons why such an operation was a bad idea would have been put forward. The idea would have been talked and memoed to death.

But Abscam had grown serendipitously. Once congressmen came out of the woodwork seeking our sheik's bribes, bureaucratic timidity and caution actually became our ally. If it was true that getting advance approval for such an operation from high-level officials was a near impossibility, it was even more true that the same officials would be too frightened to kill such an investigation once it had started. In a town where news leaks are an important bureaucratic weapon, no one would want to be known as the person who let a U.S. senator and six House members off the hook by terminating a successful investigation.

I've always believed it takes more guts to kill an investigation than to authorize one, and that simple fact of bureaucratic life worked in our favor once Abscam gained momentum. Having said this, I think it's important to point out that I had very strong backing from my own superiors at Justice, including Dave Margolis, head of the Organized Crime Section, Irv Nathan and Phil Heymann. President Jimmy Carter's attorney general, Benjamin Civiletti, was briefed on Abscam, but he played no role in the day-to-day supervision of the operation. He never interfered in Abscam, even though all the congressmen but one were Democrats, and some, like Senator Williams, were well regarded by the White House.

I was never worried about Abscam being quashed from on high, but I was deathly afraid that it would be screwed up in a turf battle with other prosecutors. Our relationship with New Jersey was beginning to resemble that videotape of Jack McCarthy and Angelo Errichetti, wrestling over the suitcase full of money. After our victory in Washington, we felt more confident. But the cloud of New Jersey's hostility was always hovering over our heads, particularly in the investigation of the state's esteemed Senator Williams.

Harrison Williams and his three shady partners wanted the sheik to invest $100 million in their titanium mine. (By issuing stock in a paper company that controlled the mine, Williams stood to make a cool $17 million on the loan from the sheik. Williams's financial interest in the mine was, of course, to be kept secret.)

The enticement for the sheik was supposed to be that Williams would use his considerable clout on Capitol Hill to get government contracts for the mine. Using his office for personal gain was a federal crime. As usual, I insisted that Williams must personally promise to get contracts for the mine.

Weinberg set up a meeting in a suite at the Marriott Hotel in Arlington, Virginia. We installed our video cameras and set aside an adjoining room where my aide Larry Sharf and other officials could witness the meeting. Once again, Special Agent Farhardt was summoned from Cleveland to play the role of "Emir Yassir Habib."

Williams was told the sheik spoke no English, and that an interpreter would make the introduction. This never happened, of course, since no one, including the sheik and his "interpreter," spoke any Arabic. Weinberg, improvising as usual, advised the senator that while the sheik spoke no English, he understood the language perfectly. That was completely ridiculous, of course, but neither Williams nor Errichetti raised any questions about the supposed language barrier.

Williams would say things like "Hello my friend," and "We meet again," and "I recall how pleased we were to see you in Florida," and "This fellow Marriott. He owes me a lot of favors," to the Sphinx-like sheik, who sometime nodded. If you've seen any of the old cavalry movies in which John Wayne negotiates with the chief of the Indian tribe, you know exactly how

Senator Williams talked and acted around the "emir."
Williams assured the sheik he was well connected to virtually every important public figure in Washington from the president on down and would use his clout to get contracts for the mine.

"With great pleasure, I'll talk to the president of the United States about it and, you know, in a personal way, and get him as enthusiastic and excited, because we know what our country needs," Williams said.

In the other room, Larry Sharf had broken into a cold sweat. He was torn by a mixture of exhilaration and disbelief. The meeting was going very well by law enforcement standards, but Sharf, a liberal Democrat, had always admired and respected Senator Williams. It was a shock to watch a hero sell himself in this sleazy setting.

I later watched the videotape of the meeting in my Brooklyn office and was very pleased with how things had gone. But sometime later, when I was on Martha's Vineyard on vacation, I received a call from Ed McDonald, one of my deputies. Ed gave me the details on what was to become known as the "bullshit tape." It was an audio recording of a brief meeting between Weinberg, Williams, and Errichetti that took place at the hotel just prior to the session with the sheik.

As I mentioned, things moved slowly on the administrative end of Abscam, and it had taken nearly a month for a transcript of the "bullshit tape" to reach McDonald's desk. It was a pep talk in which Weinberg and Errichetti urged the senator to tell the sheik of his importance in the U.S. government. Like many Abscam meetings, it was a mixture of comedy and greed.

The senator, for example, asked for advice on how to address the emir, noting that he had heard him called both a "sheek" and a "shake."

WEINBERG: Call him "sheek."
ERRICHETTI: [Call him] my friend.
WEINBERG: [Call him] anything.
ERRICHETTI: I'm gonna say my friend, hello, my friend.
WILLIAMS: Very good. That's the way to do it, yeah.

Weinberg then urged Williams to be strong about his importance to the success of the mine.

"And you tell him [the sheik] in no uncertain terms without me there is no deal. I'm the man. I'm the man who's gonna open the doors. I'm the man who's gonna do this to use my influence and I guarantee this. Understand? . . . All bullshit," Weinberg told Williams. Weinberg also likened the senator's upcoming meeting with the sheik to being on stage for twenty minutes.

Now, unlike Larry Sharf, I had managed to listen to the evidence of Senator Williams's sleaziness with total equanimity. But the "bullshit tape" made *me* break out in a cold sweat. The meeting might have been viewed as an effort by Weinberg to coach the senator to make incriminating statements to the sheik. And the "bullshit" and "stage" remarks could be taken to mean Weinberg was signaling Williams that his meeting with the sheik was all an act.

With hindsight, I can see how inconsequential this was. Williams had on several occasions clearly stated that he would use his clout as a senator to get government contracts for the mine. He also understood perfectly well that his secret interest in the mine would give him millions of dollars.

But at the time, the "bullshit" tape was, for me, the bleakest moment in Abscam. It raised legal questions that would ultimately be resolved in our favor in the courts, but a more immediate problem was that it handed New Jersey fresh ammunition in our ongoing war. The struggle by then was taking an ominous turn. Del Tufo, et al., were no longer interested in gaining control of Abscam. They were intent on wrecking it.

As I expected, the instant the New Jersey prosecutors laid eyes on the transcript, they were on the phone, expressing deep shock and dismay. Plaza and Weir hammered away at Weinberg's performance during the "bullshit" meeting. Del Tufo phoned Phil Heymann, the chief of the Criminal Division, to complain. The episode was taken as further evidence of my inability to supervise the investigation properly. Weinberg was shifty, deceitful, manipulative, and, thanks to my incompetence, completely out of control. They said the case might well blow up in our faces, creating terrible embarrassment for the Justice Department and a reduced budget from a vengeful Congress. In August 1979, Del Tufo's office pulled out all the stops. Weinberg and Amoroso were invited to the apartment of the FBI's resident agent in Atlantic City, ostensibly to discuss a prospective casino developer. But waiting inside the agent's apartment was a surprise: Plaza and Weir. My undercover agents were about to be grilled by two Justice Department prosecutors! Plaza and Weir formed something of a good cop–bad cop team. Plaza was always loud and aggressive, while Weir came on as quiet and reasonable.

Armed with a transcript of the "bullshit" meeting, Plaza launched into a withering cross-examination of Weinberg. Basically, he accused the con man of leading Senator Williams into sin by putting words in his mouth. Plaza and Weir also demanded detailed information on Abscam's progress. Weinberg and Amoroso simply clammed up and walked out of the apartment.

From a law enforcement point of view, the Atlantic City ambush was bad Three Stooges. It was a desperation tactic, and one I found far more disconcerting than anything that Abscam's swindlers, shady lawyers, and crooked congressmen would ever throw at us. But New Jersey was far from discouraged. If anything, Del Tufo's office became even more vitriolic. Attorney General Civiletti had been sent a lengthy memo violently denouncing our handling of Abscam, and the Williams case in particular. Plaza and Weir continued to second-guess everything we did as quickly and as often as possible.

The battering from New Jersey helped convince me it was time to bring the Abscam investigation to a close. There were plenty of other practical reasons to call a halt. We had made criminal cases against congressmen from Pennsylvania and had bribed some of them in the District of Columbia. That meant the U.S. attorneys in Washington and Philadelphia had to be brought into the picture. The sheer number of congressmen we caught also guaranteed that the case was getting very close attention from top officials at the FBI and the Justice Department. The net result was that an enormous number of people had knowledge of the operation and something to say about it. Abscam had flourished on quick wits, flexibility, and ad-libbing. But now things grew slow and cumbersome, with monster meetings that accomplished nothing in terms of advancing the investigation.

And Abscam's nonpolitical cases were beginning to become more pressing. Over the course of two years, Mel Weinberg had made a score of crooked deals to purchase bogus certificates of deposit. He promised a small army of crooks and hustlers payment in cash for these certificates from the sheik. Then he proceeded to stall them on payment. But it was becoming more and more difficult to put off the impatient swindlers.

Besides, people were getting tired. Undercover work is exhausting. In Abscam, it was true, a chorus of sledge hammers would have failed to alert most of our targets, but we all had been working under great pressure for an extended period of time. (The exception, Tony Amoroso, still likes to describe his assignment as a piece of cake. This was because Tony had done undercover work for the FBI in the Detroit mob, where a slip might have quickly cost him his life.)

There were further arguments for calling a halt, like the fact that a number of newspaper and television reporters had gotten wind of the operation. It would only be a matter of time before one of them exposed Abscam. Some Justice Department officials even had philosophical reservations about extending the operation. One wondered aloud if permanent damage might be done to our democratic system if Abscam continued. Would the specter of dozens of corrupt congressmen shake the faith of the people in the system?

In the end, the decision to shut down the operation was an easy one. There was no dissent.

The finale to Abscam came on a cold, clear Saturday in February 1980. John Good and I had decided to dispatch teams of FBI agents to conduct simultaneous interviews with all of the congressmen and other suspects in the case. We set up a "war room" in my Brooklyn office where fifty agents and prosecutors set to work fielding phone calls, holding strategy sessions, and processing reports from agents in the field. The whole office hummed with excitement, and it occurred to me how wonderful it was to see everybody working together as a team after months of infighting and bureaucratic backbiting.

The rosy glow sweeping over me was, of course, illusory. At a morning briefing for prosecutors from other districts, Ed Plaza rose and delivered a violent speech denouncing me and Abscam. The prosecutors from the District of Columbia and Philadelphia were stunned. They stared at one another and shook their heads. It was another extraordinary moment in Abscam, with a federal prosecutor bitterly attacking a colleague in front of his peers on the very day a crucial criminal investigation was coming to a climax.

I waited patiently for Plaza to finish before responding. "I'm really sorry that you feel that way about me, Ed," I said. "I've always had the highest regard for you."

That was it for the meeting, but New Jersey's position on Abscam was now official. "I hope this whole thing blows up in your face," Plaza told one of my deputies.

Buoyed by those cheerful sentiments, we went back to planning the interviewing of the congressmen and other suspects. That was mainly a pro forma exercise that preceded their criminal indictment. We didn't expect anyone to break down and confess, though some of the statements the congressmen made to the FBI were helpful at trial.

Of much greater importance was our plan for Howard Criden. Criden had proved to be a fixer and middleman extraordinare. He had already produced four congressmen for us and often boasted he could bring in many more. We hoped to "turn" Criden and make him come work for us. To that end, before we closed in on the congressmen we set up a final meeting with Criden at the Hilton Hotel at Kennedy Airport.

In many ways, this last Abscam meeting was the most dramatic. I decided it would be desirable to have Criden make a videotape confession of all his wrongdoings from start to finish. Amoroso handled this beautifully by telling the Philadelphia lawyer that the sheik was on the way to the hotel room with more money for him. It would be important, Amoroso advised him, for the sheik to know all of the services Criden had rendered. The lawyer obligingly related every crooked act he had committed and promised to bring in five more congressmen. He also claimed Congressman Murtha was now ready to come in.

Their conversation was interrupted by a knock. Howard Criden perked up, expecting to see Santa Claus walk through the door in the form of Sheik Yassir Habib. Instead, Amoroso opened the door to let in another FBI agent and then flashed his credentials at Criden.

AMOROSO: Howie, my name is Tony Amoroso.
CRIDEN: It's OK.
AMOROSO: OK. Just so you know. [I'm] an FBI agent. Sorry, Howard.
CRIDEN: Yes, sir.

Criden was not arrested. In a state of shock, he was taken to my office, where he remained for hours while I attempted to "turn" him. The conditions were hardly the best. The office was a madhouse, with shouting, ringing phones, and gun-toting agents rushing back and forth. The scene must have appeared positively psychedelic to a veteran crook like Criden.

He sat on a couch opposite my desk while we chatted. Criden was actually quite cooperative, but he balked at the idea of becoming a government informer. I think he knew that the case against him was overwhelming even though—like all the others—he could not comprehend the power of the videotape evidence.

"I had a feeling something was wrong, but I could never really put my finger on it," Criden told me.

After a couple of hours of conversation, I could wait no longer. I gave the order for teams of FBI agents poised around the country to move in on the congressmen.

Throughout the afternoon and early evening, reports flowed into us, and we, in turn, reported developments to Washington. As all this unfolded, I made periodic stabs at enlisting Criden's cooperation. As the evening wore on, he seemed to weaken. But around 8 P.M., an FBI agent just outside my office mentioned that Abscam was on the front page of *The New York Times.* Criden and I both overheard the remark, and I could see in that instant that I had lost my chance to turn him. Criden, who had never been placed under arrest, simply got up and walked out of my office.

Abscam quickly mushroomed into the nation's number one news story. But I didn't have time to savor the headlines. I had to prepare for a series of high-profile criminal trials. And there was another little problem I had to contend with. I had become the number one target of a major internal investigation by the Justice Department.

The investigation involved a leak to the press. There were a number of news leaks when Abscam became public. Given the number of people who knew about the operation by the time we were ready to move on the congressmen, that was probably to be expected. But there was one leak in particular that my superiors in the Justice Department could not overlook. Leslie Maitland, a *New York Times* reporter, had been given access to the prosecution memo in Abscam. This memo was the central document in the investigation—eighty single-space typed pages of information on every aspect of the case, including legal strategy and possible weaknesses in our cases against the congressman. Its disclosure to a newspaper reporter—or any other outside source for that matter—was an astonishing breach of security. Maitland's story never mentioned the memo, but it was absolutely clear that she either had a copy of the document or had been permitted to read it. The memo had been completed in December 1979, before our still fast-moving investigation had reeled in Congressman Kelly. The memo, while rich in facts and details, was one congressman short. So was Leslie Maitland's story.

Dick Blumenthal, then the U.S. attorney in Connecticut, was chosen to find the source of the Abscam leak. Blumenthal was a sweet guy with Robert Redford–like good looks. Some in the Justice Department thought sending this clean-cut nice guy to New York to look for leakers was like dropping him into a shark tank.

Blumenthal's primary suspect was me. And he had very strong circumstantial evidence to justify his suspicions. The prosecution memo was, after all, my memo. And during my years as a prosecutor, I had become friendly with several journalists, including Leslie Maitland. Moreover, Maitland had been seen entering my office the day before her story appeared. It seemed only logical that I had given her the document. Indeed, even members of my own staff who had not been involved in the Abscam investigation believed I must have been responsible for the leak. (When *Absence of Malice,* a movie about a prosecutor who leaks a memo to a female reporter, was released later, some people assumed Maitland and I were the models for the characters.)

The Blumenthal investigation gave me an interesting, though not particularly welcome, opportunity to learn what it's like to be on the other side of a Justice Department probe. Blumenthal was so certain of my guilt that a written confession was prepared for my signature and sent to my office.

An FBI official from Washington who interrogated me repeatedly was also absolutely convinced I was the leaker (Ironically, he was one of the FBI officials involved in the Stabile investigation a few years earlier.) He urged me to come clean— again and again. Sometimes, he would phone me from Washington: "I just called to see if you're ready to turn yourself in," he would say.

On other occasions, the official would simply appear at my office. I'd always welcome him by announcing, straight-faced: "I think the time may be right for me to confess—if I can work out a deal." We would both laugh, even though we both knew my career as a Justice Department prosecutor would be destroyed if I was found to have given the memo to Maitland.

During a telephone conversation with Blumenthal, I mentioned to him that I was coming to Washington on department business. "Oh, by the way," Blumenthal said, "while you're down there, why don't you take a polygraph test?"

Nothing like knowing your agency has faith in you while you're preparing the most important prosecution of congressional corruption in the twentieth century. But having nothing to hide, I agreed readily.

No expense was spared. Paul Minor, the superb FBI polygrapher who had assisted me in the Stabile investigation, was now assigned to polygraph me. Minor, who later polygraphed Anita

Hill on the allegations she made against Clarence Thomas, did a skillful job of questioning me.

I passed the test with flying colors. But as always happens with lie detectors, the results changed nobody's mind. People who thought I was guilty simply blamed the machine: "Well, that proves that the polygraph is all bullshit."

The division of the cases had been made during a meeting in Washington in mid-January 1980. I had run the operation from the beginning, and I wanted to keep control of all the prosecutions. But the U.S. attorney's office in Philadelphia wanted to prosecute their hometown congressmen, Myers and Lederer. The U.S. attorney's office in Washington wanted Jenrette and Kelly. They had, after all, taken their bribe money at the Georgetown town house.

Phil Heymann, the head of the Criminal Division, was in charge of working out a compromise.

"Look," Heymann told me. "We don't want this to be Tom Puccio versus the Congress. We want this to be the United States Justice Department versus the Congress. We really can't have you prosecuting every case."

As a result, the cases involving Congressmen Jenrette and Kelly were given to the United States attorney in the District of Columbia. The United States attorney in Philadelphia received an Abscam spin-off investigation of several Philadelphia city councilmen.

That left me with Senator Williams and four House members. I personally tried all of these cases, beginning with Myers and ending with Williams. The prosecutions were relatively straightforward. The cinema verité videotapes that appeared on the network evening news shows over the next year gave millions of Americans an unprecedented insight into how things really worked in Congress. I don't believe the reaction of ordinary Americans was much different from that of the jurors. None of the juries had any difficulty in quickly arriving at guilty verdicts in each and every one of the cases.

The various prosecutors had, of course, argued about who would go first. We all knew the initial Abscam case would attract a national audience and maximum publicity. The guys from

Washington would have liked to have started the Abscam cases with Jenrette or Kelly, but they were just too slow, timid, and cautious. Philadelphia actually won the race, issuing an indictment in the council case a week before I indicted Ozzie Myers. That case received little notice, however.

I decided to begin with Congressman Myers, whose videotaped civics lesson about money talking and bullshit walking in Washington was just as compelling as his jaunt from the hotel room with $50,000 in cash. The Myers case was the toughest for me because it was the first. I was very worried about the technique we'd used in the case. Would the jury conclude that the government had simply created a fairy tale, full of characters too unreal to be taken seriously? As it turned out, the videotaped venality of the congressmen provided all the reality the jurors needed.

At the time, there was a tremendous amount written about "entrapment," but the entrapment argument actually played a very small role in Abscam. That was because in order to use the argument that they had been "entrapped" in a crime, the congressmen would have had to admit committing the crime. This was not a good approach for an elected politician, and only Congressman Lederer relied on entrapment as a main line of defense.

Myers, on the other hand, claimed that he was only "playacting" and never intended to introduce a bill on the sheik's behalf. In effect, Myers asked the jury to believe that he planned to swindle the sheik—not sell his office. Murphy, through his lawyer, denied knowing there was any money in the briefcase.

Of much more importance to the defense were the "due process" hearings that accompanied the Abscam cases. These hearings received little attention in the press. They were, understandably, regarded as an overly technical sideshow.

But they were no sideshow for me. The "due process" hearings were held by the trial judge to determine if the government's conduct of the Abscam investigation was so outrageous and improper as to have violated the defendants' constitutional rights. Basically, the congressmen claimed that overzealous government agents had unfairly induced them to take bribes. These hearings, in effect, put the prosecutor on trial. And that, of course, was me.

The star witnesses at these hearings were two veteran Justice Department prosecutors, Edward Plaza and Robert Weir. In their desperation to keep New York from prosecuting a New Jersey senator, Del Tufo's aides had complained to Justice Department officials in Washington that I was deliberately withholding information that would tend to show the defendants were innocent. This was a serious charge, of course. Prosecutors have a legal obligation to make such exculpatory material available to the defense. Leaving no stone unturned, Plaza and Weir also sent copies of their complaint to all the judges in the Abscam cases. When the judges, quite properly, informed lawyers for the defendant of this extraordinary development, the defense lawyers subpoenaed Plaza and Weir as witnesses. This was mind-blowing stuff, but there was more in store.

When Plaza showed up to testify, he turned over to defense lawyers a briefcase containing an extensive file of confidential Justice Department memoranda on Abscam. The memos, of course, contained their office's detailed assault on my handling of the case.

If there's one incident in my career that illustrates the destructiveness of Justice Department infighting, this was it. Plaza and Weir, in their eagerness to punish me, were out to destroy Abscam. Plaza had been specifically ordered by Washington not to give any Justice Department materials to the defense unless directed to do so by the judge. But George Pratt, the judge who presided at the Brooklyn trials and two of the due process hearings, had no clear idea of what was happening until Plaza arrived with the documents.

Plaza and Weir presented themselves on the stand as civil libertarians, deeply concerned with the constitutional rights of the defendants. I saw them as bitter bureaucratic enemies, driven by jealousy. By either count, they failed miserably. Judge Pratt completely cleared me and the FBI of any misconduct or impropriety. In a 136-page ruling, he said Plaza had nearly succeeded in obstructing the investigation and that the zealous concern Plaza and Weir had shown for the rights of the defendants was "an apparent attempt to divert Abscam's momentum from Senator Williams."

Cutting to the heart of the matter, the judge said Del Tufo and his aides were "jealous of the obvious importance and success of the investigation." As for the congressmen whose rights Plaza and Weir were championing, Pratt concluded: "Despite their respected and trusted positions, defendants' crass conduct here reveals only greed, dishonesty and corruption. Their major defense is that they were tricked into committing the crime on videotape. The government's need to unmask such conduct more than justifies the investigative techniques in these cases."

Pratt's ruling ended the longest and bloodiest bureaucratic battle of my career. Plaza and Weir later took their road show to Congress, where they received a much more sympathetic hearing before a congressional committee. But Pratt's ruling had effectively discredited them. All of the numerous legal appeals of the Abscam verdicts were rejected.

I wound up Abscam by sending Senator Harrison Williams, D-N.J., to jail. His own sad defense was seriously undercut by his admission on the stand that he paid little attention to Weinberg's "bullshit" remarks.

PUCCIO: When Weinberg told you on June 28, 1979, to talk about your influence to the sheik, did you pay any attention to him?

WILLIAMS: I heard it.

PUCCIO: Did you pay any attention to it or did you do it your way?

WILLIAMS: I heard it. I knew what he was telling me. And I did most of my talking my way.

PUCCIO: How much of it was your way and how much of it was Weinberg's way?

WILLIAMS: I would say predominantly it was my way. Once in a while I did it in their boasting way.

Williams's defense would have been better served by claiming he was only following Weinberg's instructions. But the senior senator from New Jersey couldn't bear to admit he would passively follow the orders of a sleazy character like Mel Weinberg.

Williams, of course, flatly denied the allegation that went to the heart of the case—that he had offered to get government contracts for the titanium mine in which he held a secret interest.

"I never said that I would arrange for government contracts," he testified.

Good old videotapes. Instead of responding with an immediate blizzard of skeptical questions, I simply switched on the monitors in the courtroom to show a portion of the June 28 meeting in which Williams went to work on the "sheik."

"The secretary of state is a neighbor back in New Jersey," the jury heard the senator tell my burnoosed FBI agent. "We live in the same town. Yeah. We're close. Very close."

"Secretary of defense—personal friend," interjected Errichetti helpfully.

"Yeah," agreed Williams.

"Secretary of the navy, Secretary of the army, people that are gonna be utilized . . . ," Errichetti babbled on.

"And the vice president [Mondale], used to work for me on the [Labor] committee," added Williams. ". . . I was his chairman, and we were very, you know, that's the way it goes, very close."

"Well then," said Tony Amoroso, tightening the noose, "in that respect, with you being in that position and contracts and the like would not be a problem."

"No problem, no," said Williams expansively. "In a situation where we can just sit around and describe, they'll see, it will come to pass."

It was a terrible picture for people who like to believe America sends her best and brightest off to Washington. Williams was not an idiot like Kelly or blatantly sleazy like Ozzie Myers. This guy was a major-league U.S. senator, a class act. And there he was, on the screen, dropping names and peddling influence with Angelo Errichetti.

After Williams and the jury watched the senator in action, I was ready to go for the kill.

"I ask you now, Senator Williams, were you telling the sheik that you could get government contracts or assist in getting government contracts when you uttered these words on June 28, 1979?"

WILLIAMS: I didn't have that in mind.

PUCCIO: What did you have in mind?

WILLIAMS: To impress the sheik.

PUCCIO: Impress that sheik with what?

WILLIAMS: The baloney. This was the baloney session.

PUCCIO: When did this become the baloney session?

WILLIAMS: There it is, and I am sure that there are other places in here where . . . with all the suggestions of Mel and Tony . . . meaningless meeting . . . just tell him how important you are, the deal is yours, there is no deal without you, you get the contracts, this is directly following Tony [Amoroso] making—making the suggestion that you would be in that position in contracts of the like would not be a problem. There is no . . .

PUCCIO: Senator Williams?

WILLIAMS: There is no promise of any contracts there, I'll tell you.

PUCCIO: You said you would get government contracts although you didn't mean it, is that a fair statement, sir?

WILLIAMS: That is a complete exaggeration following on what [Amoroso] said.

PUCCIO: Is it fair to say, bearing in mind that you didn't mean it, is it fair to say that you promised to get government contracts or to try to get government contracts?

Am I being fair?

WILLIAMS: No.

PUCCIO: Well, what were you saying you were going to do? What were you describing?

WILLIAMS: That adds up to nothing.

PUCCIO: As a United States senator, you sat there in that room and said things that added up to nothing?

WILLIAMS: I did.

The cross-examination continued, but that, I believe, was the end of Senator Williams.

ABSCAM WAS completely successful, and it brought me a measure of national fame. But the operation had a bittersweet ending. Loud complaints about the investigation echoed through the halls of Congress. It was impossible to charge that Abscam was "political," since the Justice Department was in Democratic hands and six of the seven congressmen were Democrats. But many congressmen continued to believe—or at least maintain—that Abscam was a dark, diabolical plot, even though it had actually unfolded in a completely makeshift—even zany—manner.

The Justice Department made it clear that it, too, was not thrilled with its own success in incarcerating members of Congress. In 1981, the Justice Department announced new guidelines governing undercover operations. The initial changes were quite sensible, but they were only the beginning. New rules and regulations were tacked on as the years unfolded, until now undercover operations are so encrusted with bureaucratic controls that another Abscam is absolutely impossible.

The anti-Abscam message was delivered in other ways as well. John Good and Tony Amoroso performed magnificently in one of the very best FBI investigations of the past fifty years. But neither received any real accolades for a job well done. Amoroso, for example, applied for an FBI liaison job in Rome. (The Bureau has a small number of agents who work overseas.) He received tremendous recommendations from his superiors, but his application for the post was shot down in Washington.

The message to the troops was loud and clear. Good and Amoroso, the Bureau's Abscam heroes, were not being rewarded for their work. Abscam was a frightening aberration—and one that the Bureau was not about to repeat.

I also received an unexpected "rebuke" for Abscam, but mine was delivered by the cold, cruel legal world.

7

VITAS

I LEFT the Justice Department in the spring of 1982. I didn't believe a government case as interesting or challenging as Abscam would ever come along again. Who, after all, was I going to prosecute next? The president?

I'd gone straight from law school to the Justice Department and remained there for thirteen years. If I stayed much longer, I suspected, I'd never leave. It was time to move out into the "real" world. Money played a part in my decision to go, but it wasn't a major factor. I was earning $55,000 a year as chief of the strike force, and with a monthly mortgage payment of $363.48 on my apartment in Brooklyn Heights, I certainly didn't feel crushed by poverty.

I was briefly considered for appointment as the U.S. attorney in Washington, D.C. Some of my friends considered this development absolutely hilarious—the ultimate example of putting the fox into the chicken coop. Needless to say, I was not appointed. I was told, informally, that a black candidate should be named to the post. This sounded reasonable, given D.C.'s large black population, but the lawyer who eventually got the job was white.

I never seriously expected to be named as the chief investigator of crime in the nation's capital. My real goal was a partnership with a top Wall Street law firm. I wanted the prestige and status I then believed were part and parcel of a job with a firm with an old-money, Ivy League aura. Basically, it was the same ambition I had when I left law school.

The outcome was also the same—no takers. Abscam made

great newspaper copy. The videotapes of crooked congressmen were watched intently by millions on the evening news. But running Abscam, I quickly came to discover, was not a great thing to have on your résumé. Some lawyers, clearly, regarded the operation as a small stain on the Constitution. In addition to the old complaint—my lack of an Ivy League education and background—the old white-shoe firms had another reason not to hire me. I was "controversial" because of Abscam.

I had discussions with seven or eight major law firms, but somehow things never worked out. I began to wonder if I'd ever find a spot in private practice. A sympathetic friend, writer Jack Newfield, set up a lunch with me and Mario Cuomo. Jack knows almost everybody in New York and enjoys putting people together, making things happen. At the time, Cuomo was the lieutenant governor. He had a lot of connections, but he was far from the powerful national figure he'd become later on.

The three of us went to an Italian restaurant in Manhattan, where Newfield told Mario about my problem.

"Tom would really like to go into private practice," Jack explained.

"I've got just the thing for you!" Mario exclaimed. "Arnold Biegen!"

"Who?" I asked.

Biegen was the head of Booth, Lipton & Lipton, a Manhattan law firm that didn't even bear his name.

"It's a Park Avenue firm. They're doing very well. Matilda [Cuomo's wife] and I had dinner with Arnold and his wife recently. They'd like me to come there as a partner, but I'm going to run for governor. This sounds like a good situation for you," Mario said.

Cuomo quickly called Biegen and arranged an interview for me. I received an offer from the firm almost immediately. They liked my background and credentials, but I think Biegen was mainly eager to please the lieutenant governor by hiring me.

Biegen, I soon came to find out, was a wheeler-dealer who loved to rub shoulders with politicians. He was ultimately sentenced to three years in prison in 1992 for stealing $158,000 from the campaign fund of New York Mayor David Dinkins and another $900,000 from an eighty-year-old widow whose finances he managed. Back then, however, he was a perfectly respectable member of the New York bar, and I was grateful for his offer— particularly since it was the only one I received.

Like a lot of lawyers making the switch from government service to civilian life, I found the adjustment pretty traumatic. When I left the Eastern District, a friend of mine warned me that if I went into private practice, my phone would never ring. So on my first day of work at Booth, Lipton & Lipton, I was delighted when the secretary announced I had a call.

It was my friend. "I'm calling you so that your phone will ring once today," he said. Later in the day my secretary returned to announce that Ray Brown, a skilled defense lawyer with whom I'd crossed swords in Abscam, had sent me a plant. So much for Day One.

It was depressing—and boring. During my first six months in private practice, I would come into the office, read my mail, make a few phone calls, and then get ready for the big event of the day: lunch. Some days I sat in my office and watched the clock.

I called the lieutenant governor.

"Mario, I'm not practicing law, I'm practicing lunch," I complained.

What a comedown. I was used to directing dozens of lawyers and federal agents in sensitive investigations that involved major criminals and powerful people. My first case in private practice involved a veterinarian who had prescribed large quantities of Percodan (a powerful painkiller) for his secretary. He was facing professional disciplinary charges filed by the state.

I eloquently argued that my client was simply a deeply compassionate man who wanted to ease the suffering of his loyal secretary. My appeal ignored the fact that the vet had prescribed enough Percodan to tranquilize an army. It also avoided another sticky issue: Why was an animal doctor prescribing drugs for a human in the first place?

There was no question in my mind that Puccio the Prosecutor would have eaten up Puccio for the Defense.

I also represented a sweet, grandmotherly lady who had

embezzled money from the company where she worked. She was in trouble with the IRS. When she couldn't come up with the money to pay me, she gave me a sweater she had knitted.

As a prosecutor, I had an endless supply of lawbreakers to choose among, and I spent a lot of time selecting the best quality cases. Defense lawyers, I learned quickly, couldn't afford to be too picky. It's understood that a lawyer coming into a firm from government service will need some time to establish himself. Nevertheless, I knew that I wouldn't survive very long if I didn't bring in money. I had fancied myself becoming a specialist in white-collar crime, but when you get into private practice, you realize that you do what pays.

I also began to realize that when I did come up with cases, they were likely to be boring. I was discovering that people and corporations generally have pretty mundane legal problems. All you can do is hope you'll eventually snare one of those rare, wonderful cases that are both interesting and profitable.

After six forgettable months in private practice, I got my first big case, thanks to another lawyer at the firm who liked tennis and backgammon. (The two went together that year—backgammon was a popular pastime on the professional tennis circuit.) The lawyer asked me if I would be interested in representing Vitas Gerulaitis.

Gerulaitis was a top-ranked professional tennis player who made the Studio 54 scene with the likes of model Cheryl Tiegs. He was earning a great deal of money on the tennis circuit, not to mention his lucrative product endorsements. Suddenly, all that was in jeopardy.

Tony Goble, who was one of Gerulaitis's friends, had been arrested by federal drug agents. Goble was a low-level cocaine dealer who claimed to be a professional backgammon player. He was one of many hangers-on who followed the professional tennis circuit and basked in the glow of the stars. Goble bragged about his friendship with Vitas and claimed that Gerulaitis was financing a cocaine purchase Goble was making. The sellers, unfortunately, were undercover agents who tape-recorded his every cough and comma.

Goble made a deal to cooperate with the feds following his

arrest in exchange for leniency in his sentencing. He pled guilty to conspiring to buy cocaine from the undercover agents and was secretly sentenced to a year in jail by Judge Kevin Duffy. Soon thereafter, Vitas became the target of a federal grand jury investigation. The star witness—indeed the only witness—was Tony Goble.

At the time I was approached about entering the case, Vitas was being represented by another lawyer. This lawyer had also represented Nicky Barnes, one of the most notorious drug dealers in New York history. A good deal of Vitas's income was derived from product endorsements, and somebody in the management company representing Gerulaitis apparently realized that Vitas's image would not be enhanced if word got out that he was sharing an attorney with Nicky Barnes.

My first meeting with Vitas took place at Windows on the World, the restaurant atop the World Trade Center in Manhattan. Mario Cuomo had an office in the World Trade Center, and I was helping out in his gubernatorial campaign at the time. I killed two birds with one stone by meeting with Mario and then shooting upstairs for my lunch with Vitas.

Gerulaitis showed up in tennis sweats, but the waiters couldn't have been happier to see him if he'd been wearing a tuxedo. The world has different rules for famous athletes. We instantly got along with each other. I liked his manner and personality, and he liked me. Vitas was delightful to deal with. He was even-tempered and had a good sense of humor. He was somebody who always came into the office when I needed him. And he was honest. He was always totally straight with me.

I thought the government's case against Gerulaitis made no sense. Even if Goble's story was accepted as fact, Vitas would not have been purchasing enough cocaine to be a drug trafficker. At worst, he had shown himself to be a private user. But the government was accusing Vitas of distributing cocaine, a much more serious matter than simple possession. They were arguing he'd bought the drugs and given some to his friends. Given all the major-league drug dealers running around unscathed, it was an incredibly cheap case. But the country had shifted to the right in the early 1980s. Ronald Reagan's attorney general, William French Smith, was saying that the Justice Department would prosecute people for using marijuana.

Vitas had an additional problem. His previous lawyer had attempted to stave off an indictment by taking Gerulaitis to the U.S. attorney's office in Manhattan and having him give prosecutors an off-the-record statement. Vitas's basic pitch was to suggest that he might have tried cocaine and to deny that he had ever sold the drug.

This approach turned out to be an incredibly bad move. The prosecutors were unmoved by Vitas's personal pitch. And the fact that he'd made it narrowed my maneuvering room. It would be impossible, for instance, for Vitas to take the stand in his own defense. While the government could not use the off-the-record statement to build a case against him, it could be used on cross-examination to impeach his testimony. And Vitas had no record of exactly what he told the prosecutors, so I could not be entirely sure of what the government might spring on him. All in all it was a dangerous situation for Gerulaitis—a very dangerous situation.

I initially took a standard approach to Vitas's defense by trying to persuade the prosecutor, Michael Feldberg, to drop the case. At most, I argued, Vitas was guilty of drug use. And Goble could be lying about everything to save his own skin. While it was true Goble had mentioned Vitas to the undercover agents on tape, that really proved nothing. Tennis tour hangers-on like Goble loved to drop the names of the top players.

Feldberg wasn't swayed. I moved steadily up the ladder in a process that was standard operating procedure for a lawyer trying to save his client from indictment. I first appealed to Feldberg's boss, Rhea Neugarten, the chief of Narcotics in the U.S. attorney's office. Then I made my pitch to John Martin, the U.S. attorney in Manhattan. When these efforts failed, I flew to Washington and tried to persuade Lowell Jensen, chief of the Criminal Division in the Justice Department, to back off the indictment.

No dice. The government refused to back off its contention

that Gerulaitis was "financing" a major drug purchase. This was, after all, a war on drugs. Indicting a celebrity like Vitas would be a major victory on the all-important public relations front.

In late January, the Justice Department informed me that all my appeals had been rejected, and that Vitas would be indicted by a grand jury on Thursday, February 3, 1983. I received the bad news while attending a federal bar conference in the Caribbean. I flew back to New York to tell my client.

"Vitas, here's the bottom line," I said. "The prosecutors in Manhattan are insisting that you be indicted, and Washington has backed them up. We have to prepare."

I was reasonably confident Gerulaitis would be acquitted if his case came to trial. But like the government, he had to regard the case from a public relations perspective. Even an acquittal might not protect his lucrative endorsement deals. You can't put an athlete's face on a cereal box if there's a suspicion he really gets his energy from something less wholesome than Wheaties.

"When you're indicted, these endorsements could go down the drain," I said. "We have to do something to get out in front on this case."

Vitas readily agreed. I called in Howard Rubenstein, a legendary New York public relations man and an old acquaintance. Howard had a "let's get it done" kind of attitude that I liked. He was always up for an offbeat challenge. We sat down to come up with a plan to mitigate the disaster that was about to befall Gerulaitis.

"The government's going to kill you on the day it returns the indictment," Howard said. "You've got to concede that day to the government." He pointed out that no matter how forceful our statements, the newspaper headlines would be the same: "Gerulaitis Charged with Drug Dealing."

"That's the way the story is going to read. Not 'Gerulaitis, Claiming Innocence, Charged with Drug Dealing,'" Howard concluded.

This gave me an idea.

"Okay," I said. "We've got to give that day to the government. But if a knockout punch is delivered the first day, we're not gonna be able to get up after that. What about the day *before* the indictment? Why don't we make something happen on that day?"

"Is there any way the government might be bluffing?" Howard asked.

"No way," I said.

"If you do something the day before, and the government isn't planning to indict, you'll force them to take action," Howard warned.

But I knew the government wasn't bluffing and that it would go ahead with Vitas's indictment as planned. The more we talked, the better I liked the idea of a preemptive publicity strike.

Howard didn't say yes and he didn't say no. He just told me how to handle it. "You should deal directly with the major publications yourself," he suggested. "They'd rather deal with the principal than with a flack."

It was good advice, which Howard took himself. He always liked to stay in the background.

I explained the situation to Vitas, and he approved the strategy. I planned to summon eight or nine reporters to my office on the day before the indictment to lambaste Tony Goble and proclaim Vitas's innocence. If I did the job well, maybe we could turn the "expected indictment" of Vitas Gerulaitis into the "expected tainted indictment" of the tennis star.

The kind of preemptive publicity assault I was planning was unprecedented as far as I knew, but over the years I'd been involved in many unorthodox situations.

I didn't ask any other attorneys whether they thought my plan was unseemly. But I did read the rules governing proper behavior for lawyers. The rules said you can't issue public statements attacking the credibility of witnesses after legal proceedings have begun. But proceedings against Vitas hadn't started.

So on Wednesday, February 2, I invited reporters to come to my office one by one beginning at eight-thirty. Vitas, dressed in a sweatsuit, sat next to me. I delivered my pitch about Goble being a liar and Vitas being innocent. Vitas sat there while I did the talking. I'd given him one line to say, which he repeated to each of the reporters.

"I'm totally innocent of all these charges," Gerulaitis said.
"I'm definitely going to plead not guilty if they go ahead and
indict me."

The reporters who showed up were delighted with the
"scoop" I was giving them. They didn't seem to give a damn
about questioning Vitas. They agreed to my ground rules: I
would do all the talking. No questions for Vitas. He just nodded
and repeated his one line.

We did eight interviews. I thought the day to be a grand success—though I had no idea just how grand it would turn out to
be. When the newspapers hit the stands the next morning, New
York got a chance to read my description of what a sleaze Tony
Goble was. What I hadn't anticipated was that some of those
interested readers would be grand jurors, en route to the federal
courthouse where the government was going to ask them to deliver an indictment against hometown hero Vitas Gerulaitis of
Long Island.

When Goble appeared before them as a witness that very day,
they gave him a hell of a time. They became a runaway grand jury
and refused to indict Gerulaitis.

I never dreamed of anything like this. I had only hoped to get
a jump on the story and maybe keep Vitas's endorsement contracts alive. The fact that the grand jury declined to indict Vitas
genuinely shocked me. I knew from years of experience that the
grand jury was a rubber stamp for prosecutors. (After all, I was a
firm believer in the proposition that a prosecutor could get
grand jurors to indict a ham sandwich.) But the nearly impossible had happened.

The first inkling of this disaster for the prosecution came late
Thursday afternoon. The government had scheduled a press
conference for 4 P.M. to announce the indictment. But it was
canceled without explanation.

At that point, I phoned Howard Rubenstein. "Call a massive
press conference," he said. "Get everybody up to your office!"

Soon, there was a media traffic jam in my waiting room.

"We've just been notified the government has canceled its
press conference," I told the assembled reporters. "We haven't

been told why, but it appears they're reconsidering the case against my client, and I think that's good. They should reconsider for the following reasons."

Then I went through the whole rigmarole about Tony Goble. "This case is based on the flimsiest of evidence," I said. "Vitas is totally innocent."

Dan Rather called later the same day.

"I'd like to talk to Vitas," he said.

"You can't do that," I replied.

"Can we at least photograph him?" he asked.

"Sure," I said.

Anything to oblige Dan and his millions of viewers. Vitas and I walked up and down the block a couple of times for the benefit of the CBS camera crew.

Rather's piece appeared a day or two later. He showed Vitas playing Jimmy Connors and me going after Tony Goble and the United States government.

There was also a shot of red-faced U.S. attorney John Martin.

The piece ended with Vitas hitting a shot Connors couldn't get and Dan Rather saying: "The ball's in the government's court."

Well, if that didn't nail those endorsement contracts down, nothing would. But Vitas was not yet off the hook. I kept up the pressure on Martin and the U.S. attorney's office by requesting the Justice Department in Washington to review his effort to obtain an indictment against Gerulaitis.

I went before Kevin Duffy, the judge who had secretly sentenced Goble, and asked him to unseal the transcript of the sentencing hearing. The judge readily agreed, saying he had ordered it sealed in the first place to protect Vitas because he believed federal prosecutors wanted to use Goble's sentencing for publicity purposes.

Judge Duffy also referred to a letter he had received from Rhea Neugarten, the chief of Narcotics, outlining the extent of Goble's cooperation with the government. Duffy had also ordered the letter to remain sealed.

"I consider the letter signed by Ms. Neugarten to be an attempt to obtain publicity by mentioning in great detail the supposed information gathered against one Vitas Gerulaitis—a person of some public note," Duffy said.

The government was getting killed—in and out of the courtroom. The Justice Department review was conducted by then-Associate Attorney General Rudy Giuliani. Rudy, of course, went on to succeed Martin as the U.S. attorney in Manhattan. I believe he already had his sights set on Martin's job when he undertook the review. He did nothing to quash an indictment of Gerulaitis, but I think he increased the pressure on Martin by making it very clear that the U.S. attorney had better well know what he was doing in the Gerulaitis case. I also think he enjoyed Martin's embarrassment.

In any case, after several weeks of maneuvering, I received a phone call from Martin.

"Look," he said. "I'm sending over a letter. You keep your mouth shut, and we're not going to bring this case."

And that was the deal we made. On March 22, 1983, Martin formally announced that a grand jury had declined to indict Gerulaitis and that the investigation against him was "terminated."

I wish I could say this story had a happy ending, but life doesn't imitate the law. Vitas died in a tragic accident in September 1994 at age forty. He was killed in his sleep by carbon monoxide gas that escaped from the heating system in the bungalow of a friend on Long Island. Vitas was a bright, down-to-earth, decent, and extremely good-hearted guy. The lifetime of tennis lessons he had promised me would never take place.

I WAS a winner in the Gerulaitis case, but once again I was "controversial." There was all kinds of fallout in the legal community, ranging from lawyers who said I had handled the case brilliantly to those who said I acted unprofessionally by going public the way I did. In fact, neither assessment was on the mark. I had no way of knowing my actions would cause a grand jury to refuse to indict Gerulaitis.

Certainly, it was a once-in-a-lifetime success. No other lawyer has ever been able to duplicate it. That's partly because the rules governing the conduct of lawyers in such matters were changed following the Gerulaitis case. Now, they say that if a proceeding is *contemplated,* you are barred from making public comments on the evidence.

Apart from the rule change, getting a grand jury to refuse to indict rarely happens. You just can't count on that kind of miracle dropping into your lap. And, of course, prosecutors don't usually tell defense attorneys when they plan to indict somebody.

Over the years, I've given many talks on this case. I always end every discussion by making one point: "The problem is that the government is going to get its press and the defense has to do something to counteract the publicity. Do we need a rule? Fine, let's have a rule: The government gets no press and the defense get no press. No publicity on either side."

Nobody from the government has ever taken up my offer.

THE GERULAITIS CASE gave me instant credibility, even though the outcome was largely luck. I had become, in pretty short order, Tom Puccio defense lawyer. Soon after the Gerulaitis case, I struck out on my own by forming a new law firm with two other lawyers. The three of us decided to go our separate ways after two years. I joined another Manhattan law firm, Stroock & Stroock & Lavan. And about the time I became a partner at Stroock, I got a new client—a Danish aristocrat named Claus von Bulow.

8

Claus

■

THE PHONE CALL came in the fall of 1984.

"This is Claus von Bulow," the caller announced in a deep voice with an old-world accent.

Of course, I knew who von Bulow was—that he had been convicted of attempting to murder his wealthy wife, Martha "Sunny" von Bulow, with insulin injections. I also remembered thinking while watching a TV report about the reversal of von Bulow's conviction by the Rhode Island Supreme Court that this would be a nice case to handle.

Von Bulow came straight to the point.

"I've done a complete and thorough search for counsel," he said. "I've narrowed it down to two people, you and Ed Williams, and I would like to speak with you as soon as possible."

I was flattered to be mentioned in the same breath as Edward Bennett Williams, once the nation's top trial attorney. He had always been one of my idols. I was also somewhat puzzled. I didn't know I'd been in the running to become von Bulow's lawyer, much less one of the finalists to handle a case I hadn't agreed to take.

Naturally, I was intrigued by the possibility of handling the von Bulow defense. I quickly agreed to meet von Bulow the next day at 960 Fifth Avenue, the address of a fabulous fourteen-room apartment overlooking Central Park that Sunny and Claus had shared during their fourteen years of marriage.

I walked through a darkened lobby and into a small, wood-paneled elevator for the trip to Claus's floor. There was a jolt of surprise that shouted "wealth" when the elevator opened to the marble vestibule in Claus's apartment instead of a typical New York hallway lined with double- and triple-locked doors. Claus, dressed casually in corduroy slacks and an ascot, looked much more pleasant than the sullen-looking defendant I remembered seeing on TV. He greeted me warmly and ushered me into a place filled with marble, oak, priceless antiques, and enormous fireplaces. We walked by a huge kitchen that looked like a restaurant and a circular dining room with a marble floor and glass shelves and mirrors that were given a glittering effect with indirect lighting. Our destination was a large study dominated by a fireplace, where Andrea Reynolds was waiting for us.

Andrea was Claus's girlfriend, an attractive, middle-aged woman who appeared to have had a fair amount of plastic surgery. Before we were more than ten minutes into the conversation, it was clear that Andrea had every intention of playing a central role in everything that happened.

The presentation lasted about five hours, during which Claus and Andrea did most of the talking. They bombarded me with their ideas—what had gone wrong at the first trial, what sort of strategy they thought would work better next time around. Like many people who've been involved in a case for days, months, and years, they were consumed by the whole affair. The case was their life. Of course, it was agonizing to them, but in a way you got the feeling that if it disappeared from their lives, they'd miss it.

Von Bulow had been convicted of twice attempting to murder his wife with insulin injections by a Rhode Island jury in 1982. Despite the bizarre nature of the charge, the state had presented a clear and convincing case for his guilt based on strong medical testimony and two powerful motives: a $14 million inheritance and the love of a beautiful woman, soap opera actress Alexandra Isles.

At the time I met him, Von Bulow was practically a career defendant—found guilty, freed on appeal, and now facing a second trial. He appeared to have an encyclopedic mastery of everything about the case, particularly the medical evidence. I was a little awed, actually, by the kind of proficiency he seemed to have. I found out later that, like most clients, he sounded a lot more knowledgeable than he was. But at the time, he was pretty impressive.

He was, in many ways, an extraordinary character—six foot three with an old-world demeanor that approached, but did not cross, the line into self-parody. Claus had a magnificent, expressive jaw and a stiff, aristocratic bearing that reminded me of Hollywood's vision of a U-boat commander. Unfortunately, as I would soon discover, his formidable bearing was not always matched by a steely resolve. He could seem indecisive—even with his life on the line.

"I don't really know what happened to Sunny," Claus said as Andrea passed around coffee and croissants. "I can certainly assure you I had nothing to do with her death." (Sunny, at the time, was in Columbia-Presbyterian Medical Center, in an irreversible coma. But everyone tended to refer to her as if she was no longer living.)

Like an unnerving number of the people I've run across in my career, Claus was Soon to Be a Major Motion Picture. The British actor Jeremy Irons won an Academy Award portraying him in *Reversal of Fortune,* and I'm sometimes asked if my client was really like the chilly snob Irons created. The Claus von Bulow I met in 1984 was intelligent articulate, and had an engaging but self-deprecating sense of humor. He spoke French, German, Danish, and English and could hold forth at great length on the British aristocracy, fine French wines, opera, literature, and almost any other subject thought to be socially desirable. He was implacably pleasant and cordial. Indeed, being pleasant seemed to be one of his main missions in life and may explain why he seemed at such a disadvantage with strong-willed women like Andrea Reynolds. It was easy for me to imagine Claus effortlessly cruising from table to table as the headwaiter at New York's finest French restaurant.

His frugality was something to behold. He would give cab drivers a quarter tip. Old suits were endlessly taken to the tailor for repairs and mending. Claus sometimes rewarded friends and associates with "gifts" that turned out to be unwanted items that were lying around his house. I became a Christmastime recipient of just such a gift: a pair of used books Claus had obviously finished reading. One of them was *White Mischief,* the true-life tale of murder and marital infidelity among upper-class whites in colonial Africa.

He was born Claus Borberg in Denmark on August 11, 1926, the son of Svend Borberg, a playwright, and Ionna Bulow, who came from a wealthy and distinguished family. Both he and Sunny grew up in single-parent households with domineering mothers—Claus's parents divorced when he was only four years old, and he was raised in Copenhagen by his mother, who changed his name to Bulow. (Asking Claus how he acquired the lowercase "von" is letting yourself in for more than you bargained for. He's likely to produce a copy of the German registry of the nobility and a letter from a princess named Bismarck to prove that his use of "von" is appropriate.)

Young Claus was educated at exclusive boarding schools in Switzerland and Denmark. His mother, who was in France when Denmark was invaded and occupied by the Nazis, used her connections to get her son out of the country in 1942. The two of them settled in London, where Claus graduated from Cambridge in 1946 and became a lawyer in 1950. He led the life of a European socialite and worked for a time as the executive assistant to oil baron J. Paul Getty.

He was, by all accounts, an astonishingly handsome young man with polished social graces. He also had a reputation for kinkiness. According to Andrea, friends of Claus had—as a joke—started a story that he was necrophiliac because of his dazzling good looks. This and other rumors about Claus's exotic behavior were, of course, hardly helpful to the defense. Public interest in the von Bulow affair was so intense that people who had never met Claus or Sunny were authoritatively announcing that Claus routinely put his women into deathlike comas before making love.

During the time I knew Claus, his existence was dominated by Andrea, a human dynamo with an Eastern European accent and a way of ending her sentences in a question. By her own account, Andrea was "well-born" in Hungary and raised in Switzerland, where she went to exclusive boarding schools and studied under the great psychologist Piaget at "the university in Geneva."

Nothing in Andrea's life seemed to be ordinary or pedestrian. She claimed to have met Sunny in St. Moritz in 1960, when Sunny and her then-husband Prince Alfred von Auersperg were having a "huge fight" in the Palace Bar because the prince was seeing another woman. (I was later told the woman was actress Gina Lollobrigida.) Andrea, who says she was seated at the next table, witnessed the prince hit Sunny over the head with a wine bottle.

"I helped Sunny remove the glass from her head," Andrea recalled matter-of-factly. She claimed the glass-removal process resumed the following day "at the hairdresser's." Sunny, she said, was not a friend but a "bit more than a casual acquaintance."

During the first trial, Andrea and her then-husband, television producer Sheldon Reynolds, wrote Claus a sympathetic letter. Claus phoned her during jury deliberations and later invited her to tea at 960 Fifth Avenue on St. Patrick's Day, 1982. She soon moved into his apartment and into his life. (One of the more bizarre aspects of the Reynolds-von Bulow household was that it originally also included Sheldon Reynolds, who cheerfully joined with Andrea and Claus in planning his appeal. For a time Andrea actually had *two* of her ex-husbands ensconced in Sunny's home.)

Andrea found Claus to be emotionally shell-shocked, apathetic about his case, and fully prepared to go to jail. He talked about leading a useful life in prison by giving his fellow inmates legal advice and teaching them French and German.

Andrea had a somewhat more realistic view of prison life.

"You will be held down by four guys and the fifth one is going to bugger you," she told Claus.

Andrea motivated Claus by telling him he must fight the charges for the sake of his daughter, Cosima. Still, she complained, Claus never got wholeheartedly into his own defense. He always had to be prodded.

"I reminded Claus of his mother—she was choleric," Andrea said. "Every time I raised my voice, Claus immediately gave in." According to Andrea, Claus always listened to the last person he spoke with. She always made it her business to be that person.

All in all, they were quite a couple. Their nicknames for each other may shed some small light on the nature of their relationship. Andrea liked to call von Bulow "Claus-a-kins," while von Bulow playfully referred to Andrea as "my Hungarian armored truck." Listening to them talk that first afternoon on Fifth Avenue, I felt reasonably confident that Claus would be a client I could work with. Andrea, however, looked a little more problematic.

Claus made only one reference to Alan Dershowitz, the Harvard Law School professor responsible for the appeal that resulted in Claus's getting a new trial. Von Bulow said that Dershowitz was eager to be his defense lawyer, but that he did not believe Alan had the trial experience necessary to do the job. "I think we're going to say Alan's schedule at Harvard is too demanding for him to take the time to handle the case, even though I want him as my lawyer," Claus explained. That was fine with me. I did not know then that Dershowitz would run a distant second to Andrea Reynolds in the Headache-of-the-Month sweepstakes.

I sat on the couch while Claus chain-smoked and spun out his story in a conversation that lasted from noon to 5 P.M. He was remarkably detached; he talked very little about himself, and what he did say was generally couched in the third person. It was the account of the ultimate insider—a man who took into careful consideration the way his words and actions might "play" with the press and public. I was soon at sea, since Claus's conversation assumed that the listener also had a detailed mastery of what had been written about him in the gossip columns.

Andrea, who was embarrassingly obsequious throughout the meeting, was particularly aggressive in pushing the idea that Claus had been framed by his stepchildren, Alexander and Ala, and that the best line of defense in the second trial would be to attack Sunny's kids. Their joint objective, however, appeared to be to send me out of the apartment thinking: "Here's a guy who definitely didn't do it."

I left without the foggiest idea of whether he did it or not. But I must say I was taken by the way Claus talked about the case— the ease and conviction with which he denied any guilt. Over the upcoming months, my opinion about von Bulow's guilt never changed, or grew any more informed. I don't know any more today about what happened between Claus and Sunny than I did on that day in the fall of 1984.

SUNNY VON BULOW was in many ways the most elusive character in the case. She was born in 1931, the only child of George Crawford, the elderly millionaire owner of a utilities company, and his wife, Annie Laurie. Crawford died when Sunny was only four years old. Annie Laurie inherited his fortune and endeavored to make Sunny a daughter of the American aristocracy. She moved east from Pittsburgh, purchasing homes on Fifth Avenue and in Greenwich, Connecticut.

According to several of Sunny's old friends, she was an intensely shy young girl—extremely tall and often the wallflower at school dances. She grew into a beautiful woman but never lost her inferiority complex. Her sense of self-esteem was almost nonexistent. She did not, for example, believe that she was intelligent enough to go to college.

Instead, Sunny came out as a debutante in 1951. She lived the proverbial life of the idle rich in America and Europe, until she met her first husband, Prince Alfred von Auersperg, at an Austrian mountain resort in the mid-1950s. They married and had two children: a son, Alexander, and a daughter, Annie Laurie, who was nicknamed Ala to avoid confusion with her grandmother. Prince Alfie was, by all accounts, a philanderer who spent long periods of time away from home as a safari guide in Kenya. They were divorced in 1965.

Claus and Sunny, who met in England, married in 1966. A prenuptial agreement eliminated any claim that Claus might have on Sunny's fortune in the event of a divorce. Obviously, they were not exactly walking on clouds when they decided to tie the knot, and everything that followed seemed to flow from that defensive, legalistic prelude. The marriage was basically unhappy, and Claus claimed their sexual relationship ended following the birth of their only child, Cosima, in April 1967.

The von Bulows followed a long tradition of the nouveau

riche by purchasing a home in Newport, Rhode Island, the summer colony of "old money" society. After a search, the couple settled on Clarendon Court, a seaside mansion set on ten acres along millionaires' row. Sunny's ever-present mother, Annie Laurie, purchased a house virtually next door. Claus and Sunny shuttled back and forth between Clarendon Court and Fifth Avenue during their years of marriage. Despite her own insecurities, Sunny appeared to have the stronger will and dominated both the household and Claus. Still, she managed to carry on only a minimal sort of existence. A typical day in New York for Sunny, during the crucial 1979 to 1980 period, would begin at 9 A.M. with breakfast in bed. She would then talk on the phone for an hour with her mother before getting dressed and sitting in the library. Shortly before noon, the family chauffeur would drive Sunny to her daily exercise class. After exercising, Sunny would go shopping or to the beauty parlor. The chauffeur would then take her home around three or three-thirty. She would eat a grilled cheese sandwich, take a nap, and do some reading. This would be followed by an early dinner with the family at five or five-thirty. Sunny, who was perpetually dieting, would often refuse to eat.

At Clarendon Court, the time of breakfast in bed was more variable and could come as late as eleven-thirty. Sunny's devoted maid, Maria Schrallhammer, always delivered the breakfast tray. From time to time, Sunny would take all of her meals in her room and might not be seen around the house for two or three days.

Despite a continuing preoccupation with her health and appearance, Sunny smoked heavily, gobbled aspirin and laxatives, and took Valium and barbiturates. She also tended to eat in binges and was hopelessly addicted to sweets. Her marriage was scarcely more fulfilling than her daily routine. Claus was, by his own admission, seeing other women. The couple began an ongoing discussion of divorce at least six months before Sunny's first coma.

Not surprisingly, a Newport Hospital psychiatrist who spoke briefly with Sunny following her first coma reported that she was frequently bored, "almost never happy," and was sometimes unwilling to get up in the morning. "I have often wished myself dead," she told the psychiatrist.

During the first trial, Sunny's maid, Maria Schrallhammer, had testified in devastating detail about that first coma. She told the jury she was on her way to the bedroom shared by Sunny and Claus at Clarendon Court on the morning of December 27, 1979, when she encountered Claus, who told her that Sunny was ill, and that she should not attempt to wake her. A short time later, Maria heard Sunny moaning as she passed the bedroom.

According to the maid, she knocked and entered the room to an extraordinary sight: Claus was lying in bed calmly reading a book while his wife lay next to him in an unconscious state, her body ice-cold.

Over the next five hours, Maria claimed, she made a series of urgent pleas to fetch a doctor. Her requests were coolly rebuffed by Claus, who insisted that Sunny was only "sleeping."

In desperation, Maria testified, she finally presented Claus with an ultimatum: "Either you have to call the doctor now, or I have to do it."

Claus phoned Dr. Janis Gailitis, but the doctor could not be reached right way. When he called Claus back about an hour later, Maria testified she overheard von Bulow tell the physician that Sunny had been out of bed and had taken a drink of soda.

About 6 P.M., more than eight hours after Maria had discovered Sunny in an unconscious state, Claus again phoned Gailitis and urgently begged him to come to the house immediately. By now, Sunny's condition was grave. She was gasping for breath and making a sound Maria described as a rattle.

Gailitis arrived barely in time to save Sunny's life by administering mouth-to-mouth resuscitation. She was rushed to a nearby hospital, and soon recovered. But the maid, Sunny's son and daughter, and her mother, Annie Laurie, all became suspicious of Claus.

Some weeks after the first coma, Maria Schrallhammer testified that she made a disturbing discovery while cleaning at the couple's Fifth Avenue apartment. In a clothes closet, she spotted a little black bag inside a suitcase used by Claus. She opened the bag and found it contained vials of pastes and powders. There was also a prescription bottle in the name of a prostitute Claus patronized—another little public relations setback for the defense. The maid called Sunny's daughter, Ala, who decided to take samples of the drugs to Dr. Richard Stock, the family physician. An analysis of the drugs showed them to be Valium and a barbiturate. Sunny had used both of these drugs, but never crushed into powder or made into a paste. The little black bag remained a mystery. The maid kept a watchful eye out for the bag and discovered it again, this time in Claus's room in the New York apartment, at the end of November 1980, about a month before Sunny slipped into a second coma.

The maid again examined the contents. This time, she testified, she found a bottle marked INSULIN as well as needles and syringes. Alexander and Ala were quickly informed of the latest discovery.

"Insulin, what for insulin?" Maria asked. It was further damaging testimony that would help sink Claus.

Early in December, Sunny took an overdose of aspirin. She collapsed on the floor of her bedroom in New York and cut her head. After she was released from the hospital, the family went to Clarendon Court for the holidays. It was there that Sunny's body was discovered on the marble floor of her bathroom. She was rushed to the hospital, and never returned. To this day she lies at Columbia-Presbyterian Medical Center, unconscious, oblivious to the passage of time.

A high level of insulin was found in Sunny's blood following the second coma, according to a lab test that would haunt Claus for years to come. Except for Cosima, everyone in the family suspected that Claus was behind the tragedy. They decided to hire Richard Kuh, a former Manhattan district attorney, to investigate. Needless to say, one of Kuh's first actions was the recovery of the black bag, which was found in a closet at Clarendon Court. In addition to drugs, it contained several hypodermic needles, including one that appeared to have been used.

The contents were again given to Dr. Stock, the family physician. A test conducted by the same lab that analyzed Sunny's blood showed there was insulin on the used needle. These findings were turned over to Rhode Island authorities, and Claus was soon charged with twice attempting to murder Sunny.

The trial was, to put it mildly, a media sensation. Platoons of reporters from news organizations all over the world descended on the courthouse in Newport to cover the proceedings. Since television is permitted in Rhode Island courts, literally millions of people worldwide saw some portion of the von Bulow trial.

To buttress the claims that Claus had a financial incentive for doing away with his wife, Morris Gurley, the lawyer who handled Sunny's finances, testified that Claus stood to inherit $14 million if Sunny died, including Clarendon Court and the Fifth Avenue apartment. And then there was the media's favorite motive—Claus's love for Alexandra Isles, a beautiful doe-eyed soap opera actress. Claus and Alexandra met in New York in 1978 and were soon having an affair. Claus proposed marriage, and Alexandra quite naturally pressed von Bulow to follow through and divorce Sunny. But despite his protestations of love, Claus temporized. (Morris Gurley had testified that in the event of a divorce, Claus would only receive a yearly income of $120,000 from a trust fund.)

The pattern seemed to repeat itself endlessly. Claus proposed, then backed off. Alexandra would angrily walk away from the relationship, only to be pursued by a lovesick Claus once again offering marriage. Alexandra seemed unable to end the cycle. On December 1, 1980, Isles angrily delivered a shopping bag stuffed with love letters and other mementos of her relationship with Claus at the Fifth Avenue apartment. About three weeks later, she dropped off another shopping bag filled with Christmas gifts for Claus. (The real significance of these deliveries did not become clear until Claus's second trial.)

Claus resumed his relationship with Alexandra after Sunny's coma, but the actress decided to stop seeing him following his indictment in July 1981.

Isles was a star witness at Claus's first trial. Her testimony about the affair and her ultimatums was damaging enough. What destroyed the defense, however, was the halting, reluctant way in which she delivered it. Alexandra sure did sound like a woman in love. She also sounded like a woman who believed her lover was guilty as sin. Claus made things even worse by announcing a "gentleman's" decision to forgo cross-examination of the woman he loved.

The public, naturally, found the whole matter riveting. Much less attention was given to the medical testimony, even though it was the most crucial part of the prosecution's case. Proving that Claus had caused Sunny's coma was much tougher than proving he might have wanted to: attempted murder by insulin is hardly an everyday event.

The prosecution's ace in the hole was Dr. George Cahill of the Harvard Medical School. Cahill was one of the world's foremost endocrinologists. (Endocrinologists are specialists in blood sugar and related disorders.) He had a tremendous bearing and presence that made him a highly effective witness. Cahill told the jury—very convincingly—that both of Sunny's comas had been caused by "exogenous insulin"—insulin from outside the body.

The defense was left with the task of coming up with a good explanation for how insulin got into Sunny's body if Claus didn't put it there. His lawyer at the first trial, Herald Price Fahringer, presented what might be called a diet defense. It relied, disastrously, on the testimony of a New York woman named Joy O'Neill.

O'Neill was an exercise instructor at Manya Kahn, an exclusive Manhattan health club where Sunny worked out. (Like almost everything Sunny did, the workouts sounded bleak. After they were over, O'Neill said, Sunny would hide in a back room, smoking cigarettes and staring into the mirror.) O'Neill claimed that she had given Sunny private lessons at the health club four or five times a week over a four-year period, and that she and Mrs. von Bulow slowly became close friends, who shared the most intimate details of their lives. On one occasion, Joy said, she complained to Sunny that she was having difficulty keeping her weight down, and Sunny suggested a solution: an injection of insulin or vitamin B. Insulin, Sunny said, would eat up the sugar in her system.

O'Neill was obviously not the perfect defense witness. Her story about a self-administered insulin injection could clear Claus, but the jury would have to buy the idea that Sunny, who did not discuss her private life with her oldest friends, was sharing her most intimate secrets with an exercise instructor. Nevertheless, O'Neill was put on the stand, where her testimony was demolished by the prosecution. Records from Manya Kahn introduced as evidence established that O'Neill had only been Sunny's instructor on a few occasions over the years, and not at all during the period when Sunny supposedly made revealing comments about insulin use.

The defense also introduced some medical evidence, but it did not come close to counteracting Cahill's testimony. The jury found Claus guilty on both counts of attempted murder. He was subsequently sentenced to thirty years in jail.

Broke and convicted of a monstrous and cowardly crime, Claus was at his lowest ebb when J. Paul Getty, Jr., came to the rescue. Getty, the son of von Bulow's previous employer, provided Claus with the $1 million he needed to make bail. Getty also financed Claus's successful appeal.

Winning the appeal was a great victory, but Claus's conviction had been reversed on narrow technical grounds. The Rhode Island Supreme Court ruled that the defense should have been given notes made by Richard Kuh, the attorney hired by Sunny's children. The court also said that the Rhode Island state police should have obtained a search warrant before analyzing certain drugs taken from Clarendon Court.

The ruling left the very compelling prosecution case largely intact. Somehow, the same evidence that convicted Claus at the first trial would have to be overcome. It was a huge challenge. Nevertheless, the case presented a great opportunity for any defense lawyer, and I was eager to become involved.

The only other lawyer Claus seriously considered was Edward Bennett Williams. Although Williams was one of the best lawyers of his generation, he was the wrong lawyer for this case.

Two days after our first talk, Claus called to set up a meeting at my office. He wanted me as his lawyer.

"There are a couple of young people who worked with Alan Dershowitz on the appeal who I would like to keep on the case," Claus told me. He was referring to Joann Crispi and Andy Citron, two former Harvard Law School Students who had been hired by Alan Dershowitz to help on the von Bulow appeal. I agreed without enthusiasm. I worked alone, for the most part, as a defense lawyer. And as a federal prosecutor, I had managed the lawyers on my staff like a field marshal. They were simply troops who carried out my orders.

Andy and Joann were a couple no less interesting in their own way than Claus and Andrea. In addition to being bright young lawyers, they were accomplished musicians who played in a punk rock band called "Five Graves to Cairo." They often dressed in black, a perfect look for the small clubs in the East Village where the band played.

I began our relationship by giving them specific assignments, like researching a point of law. I also kept them at arm's length. But a couple of weeks after I entered the case, they urged me to give them a greater role. I decided they were right. "From this day forward," I announced, "anything I do, you guys are going to do it with me." Thereafter, Andy and Joann became my shadows. If I conducted an interview or went on a trip, they were there.

Alan Dershowitz had hired Joann to work on the case in the summer of 1982, not long after von Bulow had been convicted of attempting to kill Sunny. At the time, Joann was an associate for one of New York's most prestigious law firms, but she jumped at the chance to work on the von Bulow case for only $400 per week.

Joann was just one of a dozen or so people assembled by Dershowitz to work on the appeal, but she came to play a pivotal role. Since she was living in New York anyway, Dershowitz assigned her to hold Claus's hand. Von Bulow and Andrea Reynolds were living at 960 Fifth Avenue, and Andrea decided the apartment would be used as the headquarters for the appeal.

"From now on, you work here," Andrea commanded.

Joann commandeered Alexander's old bedroom as an office and became immersed in what she came to think of as the Bathrobe Case. The young lawyers felt completely surrounded by people in nightclothes. Meetings would literally take place in bed, with Andrea and Claus snugly under the covers while Joann and Andy sat perched on the edge of the mattress. At the time, Claus and Andrea were sharing 960 with Andrea's two ex-husbands, TV producer Sheldon Reynolds, and Pierre Foutier, who Andrea described as a "minitycoon." Reynolds and Foutier, also dressed in their bathrobes, peppered Joann and Andy with advice and suggestions about the case.

Joann and Andy shared a small apartment in the Chelsea section of Manhattan. By day, they were von Bulow investigators. By night, they played with their band at small clubs. (They dropped the band as the second trial approached, reasoning that Claus's already racy reputation could not be helped by news that two of his lawyers were punk rock musicians.)

Dershowitz, who had controlled the appeal effort from his office in Cambridge, Massachusetts, assigned himself the juicier aspects of the case. This included David Marriott, a young Massachusetts man who claimed to have delivered drugs to Sunny's son, and Truman Capote, who claimed to have known Sunny for thirty years and to have done drugs with her on a number of occasions. There was also a gaggle of high society types who might have stepped right out of the Marx Brothers' *A Night at the Opera*. These people usually claimed that Sunny was a hardcore alcoholic.

While reviewing correspondence from the first trial, Joann came across the name of an endocrinologist named Dr. Harold Lebovitz, a professor of medicine at New York's Downstate Medical Center. She tracked down Lebovitz, who was newly divorced and happy to find friends in Joann and Andy. "Harry," as he was fondly called, agreed to help the defense but refused to take money, not wanting to be known as a paid witness. They delivered the medical records to Harry's Brooklyn apartment, where Lebovitz pointed out a number of weaknesses in the state's medical case. He also agreed to put Joann and Andy in touch with some of the big names in endocrinology.

It was an important breakthrough. Joann and Andy rushed from Lebovitz's apartment to Fifth Avenue, picking up a six-pack of beer along the way to celebrate the good news with Claus and Andrea.

"When this is over, my children, I shall have to commit a crime so we can all be together again," Andrea joyfully exclaimed. (Andrea liked to call Joann and Andy "my children.")

By the time I entered the case, Joann and Andy had probably spoken with most of the endocrinologists in North America. Some were helpful and some were hostile, but even some of those who were hostile offered some valuable insights for the defense.

Of course, when I came onboard I wanted to examine all the possible lines of evidence. (One potential strategy was the one that had interested Dershowitz during the appeal—the testimony of David Marriott, Truman Capote, and the high society chorus. I called this the Page Six defense after the gossip column of the tabloid *New York Post.*)

I never considered a Page Six defense, per se, but it might have been possible to mount a defense that operated on two tracks with testimony from some high society types about Sunny's unhealthy lifestyle and medical experts who might challenge Cahill's conclusions.

Despite the disastrous results that had been obtained from putting Joy O'Neill on the stand at the first trial, Claus remained preoccupied with the discovery of "magic" witnesses who would confirm his view of the case. There were three potential candidates for Magic Witness title: David Marriott, a young man from Wakefield, Massachusetts, with no apparent occupation; the Reverend Philip Magaldi, a parish priest from Providence; and the late Truman Capote, the celebrated writer.

Marriott called Claus a few days after his conviction to report he had information about Alexander von Auersperg's alleged drug use. In a nutshell, Marriott, twenty-six, claimed to have delivered drugs to Alexander at Clarendon Court.

This was music to Claus's ears. He and Andrea were convinced that Alexander and Ala had framed him, at the urging of Sunny's maid, Maria. The best way to defend Claus, they felt, was to undermine the credibility of Sunny's two older children. Andrea was even more enthusiastic about this line of attack than Claus, but I felt the idea was a nonstarter. Alexander and Ala seemed like decent people; they were well spoken and certainly sympathetic figures to a jury. At the time they had not one but two parents in tragic, irreversible comas—their natural father, Prince Alfie, had been injured in an automobile accident and never regained consciousness.

Marriott was one of those witnesses with a story that covers every possible angle of the defense case. He claimed over a two-year period in 1977 and 1978, he delivered packages to Alex on behalf of a friend named Gilbert Jackson, who was a drug-dealer. Marriott claimed that he was never told—and never asked—what was in the packages. But during one delivery, when he was waiting in his car for Alexander to return home, Marriott decided to take a peek. Inside the package, he said, was a veritable pharmacy: syringes, hypodermic needles, a plastic bag with white powder, Demerol, and various pills and potions.

Marriott's story got even better after this. He returned to the house and again knocked on the door. This time, an older, blond-haired woman answered the door and calmly accepted the package, announcing that Alexander was expecting a delivery.

This would have been more than enough for most defendants, but the helpful Marriott had more: He described the delivery of another package overflowing with drugs. This time, Marriott asked Alexander about the vast quantity of pharmaceuticals.

"Oh, I give some to my mom to keep her off my back," Alexander supposedly revealed.

This was better than hitting a Lotto jackpot. Not only did Marriott's story provide an explanation of Sunny's death, it also showed Alexander to be a drug addict who presumably contributed to his mother's coma by feeding her drugs.

The only witness who might have corroborated Marriott's tale was drug-dealing Gilbert Jackson. Alas, he had been murdered. But the resourceful Marriott made Jackson's death into something of a virtue by saying that within days of the murder, a worried Alexander phoned Marriott—and even Marriott's mother—with anxious questions about Jackson's demise.

Still, there was no one to back up Marriott's story, or so it seemed, until Marriott himself produced a priest named Philip Magaldi, who claimed to be Marriott's counselor. Father Magaldi announced that Marriott had confided to him about his drug deliveries to Alexander at Clarendon Court. The story the priest repeated was the exact same story Marriott had given to Dershowitz.

This was great stuff. About the only thing missing was an eyewitness account of Sunny's drug abuse. That problem was solved straightaway by the late Truman Capote. The author of *Breakfast at Tiffany's* and *In Cold Blood* also waited until shortly after Claus's conviction to reveal, in an interview with *People* magazine, that he and Sunny had been friends for thirty years.

In subsequent interviews with Alan Dershowitz, the writer recounted another amazing story.

Capote said that he first met Sunny about 1952 at the Long Island estate of C. Z. Guest, a famous New York socialite and longtime friend of Capote's. The writer and the young heiress quickly agreed to meet for lunch at the Colony Club in New York a few days later. With lightning speed, it appeared to me, their first luncheon meeting turned to talk of injections and drugs. Capote confided that he was receiving injections of vitamin B_{12} from a Manhattan physician named Max Jacobson to raise his energy level. Frequent visits to Dr. Jacobson's office for injections had played havoc with Capote's writing schedule. As it turned out, Capote had come to the right socialite.

Why, Sunny wanted to know, wasn't Capote injecting himself?

"It's the simplest thing in the world," Sunny explained. "Once you do it, there's nothing to it at all."

Naturally, the twenty-one-year-old Sunny offered to show Capote the ropes, using her personal supply of "disposable hypodermic needles." The writer proved to be a bad pupil, but their lifetime friendship was evidently cemented. Capote said the two continued to meet for lunch over the years and would occasionally do drugs together. Sunny would always pull out the same black bag stuffed with drugs and needles. She injected herself and Capote with a mixture of amphetamines and vitamins.

It's worthwhile noting that at the time Capote was spinning out this story for Dershowitz, the writer was a hardcore alcoholic and drug addict shuttling in and out of hospitals.

Unfortunately, Capote's story did not withstand even cursory scrutiny. Apart from the writer's dubious credibility as a witness, there were serious problems with the story he told. Many of the details in his account—like the little black bag—would be known to anyone who read about the case. Facts recounted by Capote that were not in the public record proved impossible to confirm. The "disposable hypodermic needles" that Sunny pulled from her little black bag following her first lunch with Capote in 1952 were not invented until years later. Most importantly, there was nothing in Sunny's medical history to support Capote's claim that she had been a hardcore drug addict for decades.

Capote died at the home of Johnny Carson's ex-wife, Joanna, in August 1984. On the night before his death, Carson said, Capote talked about the withering cross-examination he might be subjected to for testifying at the second von Bulow trial. Unfortunately, I wasn't around to put Capote's mind at ease. There was no way I would have put him on the stand in a million years.

Capote, at least, had not been a major drain on the time and energy of the defense. David Marriott was another matter. During the appeal, this strikingly handsome and deeply stupid young man demanded—and received—constant attention. Claus, Andrea Reynolds, and Dershowitz turned Marriott into a veritable cottage industry.

Soon after Marriott gave the defense an affidavit swearing to the truth of his story, he began to report that he was the target of murder attempts by unknown assassins as well as anonymous telephone calls from people who threatened to kill him if he testified in court. The assassins and the anonymous callers all seemed to speak in the same grade B movie dialogue.

"If you plan to live a healthy life," one thug said, "you'd better forget about this case."

On one occasion, Marriott told Dershowitz that he was driving a "borrowed" Cadillac near his Massachusetts home when two men in a Lincoln Continental tried to force him off the road. Marriott said he lost control of the car when a masked man popped up through the sunroof of the Lincoln Continental and hurled a boulder through the driver's window of his car.

But the police who found Marriott lying next to the Cadillac were puzzled by the fact that he was not cut by flying glass. Nor were there any skid marks on the portion of the road where the Lincoln Continental attempted to force Marriott's car from the road. Marriott told the police he had borrowed the car from none other than Father Magaldi, who was staying at a Boston hotel. The priest not only confirmed Marriott's claim but said he had received an anonymous phone call at the hotel from someone who threatened to kill his young friend. (Magaldi also told the police that Marriott was the only person who knew he was staying at the hotel.)

I found Marriott's story to be utterly unbelievable: Shouldn't masked assassins be carrying guns instead of boulders? Of course, this all occurred before I entered the case, so I heard the details secondhand. Maybe you had to be there.

Marriott, at any rate, used the alleged attempts on his life to step up his demands on Dershowitz and Claus.

"Count me out," Marriott told Dershowitz. "I'm not testifying under any circumstances. Claus is going to end up a free man. And I'm gonna end up dead. No way."

Dershowitz mollified the jobless Marriott by placing him on the defense payroll as an "investigator." Marriott also ran up a steep bill for "expenses" that included taking a chauffeured limousine back and forth to his meetings with Claus and Andrea in New York and trips to Puerto Rico and Florida. (Andrea suspected the young man had also helped himself to a $4,000 ring from her apartment, where Marriott stayed on one trip to New York.)

The intrigue seemed endless. Marriott, as Andrea told the story, had secretly tape-recorded a damaging conversation with her ex-husband Sheldon Reynolds. (Sheldon, she complained, was motivated by spite since she had dropped him for Claus.) Andrea arranged to meet Marriott in a hotel room in Boston to discuss the matter. During the meeting, Andrea somehow managed to grab the tape and stuff it into her bra, thereby thwarting Marriott's evil designs, whatever they may have been.

Despite all this, Marriott remained on the defense payroll until I entered the case. I refused to meet with him, and after reviewing the history of his involvement with the defense, I quickly concluded that he was a walking disaster.

Marriott reacted by switching sides and cooperating with the prosecution! He now claimed that *Claus* was the recipient of the drugs he delivered to Clarendon Court and that his secret tape recordings would implicate Claus in various unspecified crimes.

The publicity was bad, but I was delighted that Marriott was now the headache of Rhode Island prosecutors. He had no impact whatsoever on the outcome of the case.

In addition to Marriott, Magaldi, and Capote, Dershowitz had recruited a small army of society types who were prepared to testify that Sunny was an alcoholic or a drug addict. Most of them were friends and supporters of Claus. But I regarded their claims as highly suspect. Rich socialites make the worst kind of witnesses. A jury of ordinary citizens might have voted to convict Claus based on the fact that these people were his friends.

In a matter of a few months, it became clear to me that if Claus was to win, he would win on a medical defense. The case with fantastic wealth, sexual infidelity, drugs, rivers of blue blood, suspicious servants, and intrigue would have to become a case of blood sugar levels, endocrinologists, and arcane medical terminology.

I don't believe cases are won by disputing every fact introduced by the prosecution. Some lawyers believe you should wreak havoc on the state's case by trying to throw everything presented by the prosecution into doubt. But when I analyze a case, I try to isolate the key facts that provide the foundation for the state's case. Change one or two of these facts, and the state's case becomes weak or collapses.

In the case against Claus von Bulow, the number one fact was insulin. Insulin was found on a needle in the black bag that was tied to Claus; Sunny's maid testified that a bottle marked INSULIN had been found in the bag; and, of course, prosecution experts had testified that "exogenous insulin" was the cause of Sunny's death.

The state's success in establishing that she was injected meant there were only two people who could be responsible: Sunny or Claus. The defense at the first trial suggested that Sunny had injected herself with insulin to lose weight, a premise I found somewhat absurd.

The best thing we could do was to refuse to concede the insulin issue. If there was no insulin injection, there was no crime and no need to worry about Sunny's fortune, the beautiful Alexandra Isles, suspicious servants, high society, or any of the other gossipy elements that gave the case so much public appeal.

Things would not be quite that simple, of course. If there was no insulin injection, how did Sunny end up in a coma? I wanted to provide the jury with a convincing explanation for this event—one that didn't involve shooting up with the likes of Truman Capote.

Sunny had clearly used various kinds of drugs over the years. She also took a drink now and then—although there was no evidence she was ever an alcoholic. I believed a combination of drugs and alcohol provided a much more plausible way of explaining her death than insulin injections.

I had Joann Crispi prepare a medical biography of Sunny. One thing that caught my attention right away was an event that had received very little attention at the first trial. On the evening of December 1, 1980, three weeks before Sunny's final coma, she had been rushed to Lenox Hill Hospital in New York for treatment of an overdose of aspirin. Claus had quickly called 911 when Sunny's distress became evident and summoned maid Maria Schrallhammer to help him with Sunny. (The maid slept in a separate apartment near 960.)

It was clear to me the aspirin overdose was a desperate suicide attempt by Sunny. On December 1, Alexandra Isles had decided to force the issue with Claus by sending a shopping bag filled with "mementos" of their relationship—including love letters— to the Fifth Avenue apartment. Claus was not at home that day to receive the shopping bag, but Sunny was.

That night, Claus discovered his wife collapsed on the bedroom floor. He immediately summoned help. In fact, he did everything he could to save Sunny when it would have been very easy to ignore her plight. Why, I wondered, would a man bent on getting rid of his wife go to this trouble to save her just three weeks before her final coma? It was a question I was confident the jurors would ask as well.

At the first trial, the prosecution had passed over this episode by suggesting that Sunny was not in serious danger—only engaged in a little overmedicating. I looked at the situation differently. I wanted to find a leading medical expert—a "Mr. Aspirin" if you will—who could testify with authority about the quantity of aspirin Sunny had consumed. If it was a dangerously large amount of aspirin, as we believed, the prosecution would be hard-pressed to claim it was not a suicide attempt. (I ultimately came up with two "Mr. Aspirins"—medical experts who would testify Sunny swallowed sixty-five aspirin tablets on the night of December 1.)

I naturally looked closely at each of the comas. No evidence of alcohol or drugs had been found in Sunny's system following the first coma. But on the night before the second, we knew that Sunny had been drinking eggnog spiked with bourbon. What role might alcohol have played, and what other factors, besides insulin, might explain what happened to her?

Sunny's medical history showed another interesting incident: In April 1980, she woke up in her New York apartment feeling weak. Her speech was slurred and her actions uncoordinated. She underwent a comprehensive medical workup and was diagnosed as having abnormally low blood sugar as a result of a condition called reactive hypoglycemia. Reactive hypoglycemia is brought on by the consumption of carbohydrates. The treatment is simple: Avoid sweets, alcohol, and other foods high in carbohydrates. But Sunny, the well-known chocoholic, did not seem to make any changes in her lifestyle.

On the night of Sunny's second coma, she was assisted into bed by her son, Alexander, after she complained of feeling weak. Even though it was extremely cold outside, Sunny asked him to open the bedroom windows. It was not an unusual request. Sunny liked to sleep under an electric blanket in a cold room. The next morning, Claus discovered Sunny's body on the floor of the marble bathroom that adjoined the master bedroom. She was ice-cold and unconscious. She was rushed to Newport Hospital, where her body temperature was recorded at 81.6 degrees—astonishingly low. This time Sunny did not recover from her coma. Blood tests showed traces of alcohol, aspirin, and barbiturates in her system. Could the drugs, alcohol, low body temperature, or other factors account for her condition?

I prepared a list of questions for medical experts who specialized in the areas we were interested in: insulin, aspirin, alcohol, and drugs. I wasn't interested in using the same old tired faces. There are a group of experts in various fields who make their way from courtroom to courtroom as professional witnesses. Some of them are very persuasive, but they just don't have the prestige or authority of top academic experts.

I wanted to start at the top with the most widely respected authorities in a given field. You don't normally see these guys on the witness stand—they're usually deeply involved in research and have no interest in taking the time to testify in a court case. Why should they place their impeccable reputations on the line in an arena where skilled prosecutors might try to tear them apart with hostile questions? Why should they go out of their way to help a lawyer—a member of a breed most physicians regard as one step up the evolutionary scale from Cro-Magnon?

Of course, we had a couple of advantages in the von Bulow case. The trial was, to say the least, high profile. And it raised interesting medical and scientific questions. That was very important. The people we were pursuing did not care about witness fees. Not one of them ever brought up the subject of money. Of course, we encouraged them to submit bills when their work was completed. The bills we received were very modest.

We had already spoken to many of America's top endocrinologists, who are specialists in blood sugar. One who impressed us was Dr. Arthur Rubenstein, chairman of the Department of Medicine at the University of Chicago. He had examined some of the material in the case and concluded that the test used to identify insulin on the needle in Claus's bag was flawed.

If I'd still been a federal prosecutor, I would have shipped out a subpoena and waited for Dr. Rubenstein to come to me. Unfortunately, things don't work that way when you're working for the defense. I embarked on a sales campaign. First, I called Dr.

Rubenstein and urged him to testify, emphasizing the human stakes: Claus's life was on the line. I also suggested the case might well have an impact on his specialty, since the medical testimony in the case was bound to be widely discussed.

I followed the phone call with a trip to Chicago. Dr. Rubenstein and I met for an hour, and he agreed to testify. He also allowed us to use his name with other specialists. This did not mean the doctor was at our beck and call. Though we talked on the phone a few times, I did not see him again until the night before he testified in Providence.

I went on a coast-to-coast recruiting trip in our search for suitable experts. In the months leading up to the trial, we spoke with dozens of authorities. We received surprisingly few rejections. We eventually wound up with medical experts from New York, Chicago, Ohio, Texas, Connecticut, Oklahoma, and even England. These witnesses could weave together a powerful argument that Sunny's comas were almost certainly self-induced. They'd allow us to cast serious doubt on the prosecution's contention that insulin caused Sunny's death and point to other factors that were much more likely to have caused the comas. And we would do so with nary a word from a celebrity, society debutante, or loyal servant.

We were ready. Now all I had to do was try the case.

9

THE SECOND TRIAL

JOHN SHEEHAN was Claus's lawyer in Rhode Island. If you've seen Paul Newman as the hard-drinking Boston lawyer in the movie *The Verdict,* you've seen John Sheehan. He was an old-timer with a Sam Spade kind of office.

John was not only one of the most delightful people I've ever met, but a shrewd lawyer who seemed to know everyone in the Rhode Island judicial system. He had been with Claus from the beginning of his troubles and had recommended Herald Price Fahringer, Claus's lawyer at the first trial. Claus and Sheehan were definitely an odd couple: Claus the tall, ramrod straight aristocrat and John, an earthy, rumpled-looking country lawyer type.

John was unhappy when Claus chose me as his attorney. He had played second fiddle to Fahringer at the first trial, and now he would have to play the same role with me. I was indifferent, early on, to his wounded feelings. But Claus was careful to placate Sheehan.

"We need him in Rhode Island," Claus explained. And he was right. Rhode Island is a very clubby state. Without the help of a savvy local lawyer, you could get your legal head handed to you.

I discovered that pretty fast. Rhode Island has the most stringent rules in the nation when it comes to getting permission for an "outside" lawyer to handle a local case. In most states, you can try a case with the sponsorship of a local lawyer. But in Rhode Island, you have to file a sworn affidavit with the court attesting to the fact that there is no lawyer in the state who can handle the case in question as well as you can. You're treated pretty much like an illegal alien trying to sneak past immigration officials. This outrageous rule was mainly intended to prevent the Boston bar from taking business away from local lawyers, and it succeeded admirably.

My first duty in the case was to get myself admitted in Rhode Island as Claus's lawyer. To that end, Claus hired a Chevrolet to take us from New York to Newport, where the first trial took place. I was scheduled to appear before Judge Albert DeRobbio, a burly-looking former prosecutor. He and John Sheehan were old drinking buddies, and Sheehan was supposed to guide me through the admittance process. But when Claus and I arrived at the courthouse in Newport, we discovered that John had called in "sick" with a cold. He simply couldn't venture out, we were told.

Claus phoned Sheehan and begged him to dispatch another lawyer. Peter DiBiase, a young Rhode Island lawyer who was also part of the first-trial defense team, came to the courthouse. But DiBiase, of course, didn't have any connections with the judge.

DeRobbio was sitting behind the desk in his chambers in shirtsleeves. He was a short man in his fifties with jet black hair, a dark complexion, and thick, muscular arms. I thought he looked like a little boxer. After an hour of his questioning, I felt like I'd gone a few rounds with Rocky Marciano.

DeRobbio peppered me with skeptical questions about who I was and what cases I had tried. "We run a tight ship here in Rhode Island," he said. "I want somebody I can count on to be here. Can you be here? This is not going to be a picnic." The judge went on and on in this vein. About every ten minutes, DiBiase would gently try to raise the issue of my admission to the case. But DeRobbio was noncommittal.

"Let me think about that," he said.

Claus was crestfallen. When we got back into the car, he looked at me and said, "I suspect a trick by Sheehan."

There was no question in my mind but that Sheehan had arranged the whole thing. But I wanted his help, not an ongoing battle.

"Let me handle it," I told Claus. "I've never had a problem with other lawyers. I think John and I will wind up seeing eye to eye on things."

When we got back to New York, I phoned Sheehan.

"John," I said, "I'd like to come to Rhode Island and talk to you."

Over lunch in Providence, John and I made peace. He clearly resented the fact that Claus had passed him over for another New York lawyer, but I think he was also resigned to the fact that he wouldn't be handling the second trial. We hit it off. I very quickly took a liking to John, and I believe he felt the same way about me. Needless to say, my problems with DeRobbio evaporated.

My next trip to Newport nearly led to disaster. As I got more deeply into the facts of the case, I wanted to review all the documents that were introduced as evidence at the first trial. Unfortunately, there were no copies. So I decided to drive to the courthouse where Claus had been tried and personally photograph everything of importance. I had done some amateur photography, and I dug out a Nikon camera that had been sitting in my closet. My next stop was a photo store, where I purchased a powerful light to illuminate the documents I'd be photographing.

I packed everything into a car and headed for Newport. By then I was too wise in the ways of Rhode Island even to approach a courthouse without some local help. Peter DiBiase agreed to accompany me, and he was a great guide. He introduced me to the clerk of the court, who was very friendly. We were soon ushered into the hot, dusty basement where the records of the first trial were stored in cardboard boxes. If it hadn't been for Peter, I might have needed a court order or an act of God to get in there.

I set up my equipment on a table. The light was certainly doing a good job—the place seemed as bright as the center of the sun. As I carefully focused my camera on a document I wanted to photograph, something made me look up at DiBiase. There was a look of pure terror on Peter's face.

"The place is on fire!" he cried.

Sure enough, my photographic light had touched off a smoky fire amid the boxes containing the records of the trial. For a minute, we frantically stomped away on the boxes until the fire was out. No serious damage was done, but the smell of smoke filled the basement. Visions of headlines danced through my head.

"Smart-Ass New York Lawyer Burns Down Newport Courthouse!"

That was the end of the career of Tom Puccio, courthouse photographer. Peter and I walked to a nearby restaurant, where we each sipped an Irish coffee. It was a few days before Christmas 1984, and a small Christmas tree was twinkling merrily at us from behind the bar.

I thought about picking up the phone and informing Claus: "Von Bulow, you lucky bastard, I have just saved your ass. I'm going to be the one who's breaking rocks in the Rhode Island state prison—for burning all the evidence in the case against you."

But I managed to restrain myself. In fact, I never told Claus a thing about setting a fire in the courthouse. Still, I couldn't help but wonder what Rhode Island would serve up next. I didn't have long to wait.

Richard Kuh, the lawyer hired by Claus's stepchildren to investigate Sunny's death, had been ordered to turn over his notes to the defense. Those notes had been a central issue in the appeals case but seemed unlikely to be as crucial in the retrial. Still, since Kuh had interviewed Sunny's maid, Maria Schrallhammer, and other witnesses before the police entered the case, his notes might well make interesting reading. A hearing on exactly what would be turned over to the defense was going to be held before Judge DeRobbio.

Alan Dershowitz called me up and said he'd like to be involved in the hearing on the Kuh notes.

"I'd like to ask some questions," he said.

Von Bulow was dubious about Alan's request, but I had no problem with bringing him in on the hearing.

"He won the appeal for you," I told Claus.

I'd known Alan Dershowitz for some time, and I thought I had a good relationship with him. Before I'd become immersed in the von Bulow case, Alan had done a brilliant job in winning Claus's appeal. It seemed to me that he deserved more than a little deference. What I didn't know then, of course, was that Dershowitz was writing a book about the von Bulow case, starring Alan Dershowitz as Claus's crusading lawyer. Because of the book—which became *Reversal of Fortune*—Dershowitz had to carve out some kind of role for himself in the second trial.

The hearing took place on January 4, 1985. I arrived in Providence the night before the hearing to discover half the Harvard Law School faculty in Alan's hotel room. Both of his sons were there as well. Slowly—too slowly—it began to dawn on me that they had all come to see Alan put on a show.

They sure did get what they came for. The televised hearing turned into a circus not long after I announced to the court that Professor Dershowitz was going to handle the questioning. My announcement immediately pissed off the prosecuting attorneys who—like almost the entire Rhode Island legal community—appeared to hate Dershowitz's guts.

Dershowitz got Kuh on the stand and lashed out at him with a series of questions that had nothing to do with the issue of the hearing. DeRobbio finally called a halt to the proceeding, but the two combatants simply resumed their fight on the courthouse steps. It was like a barroom brawl that had spilled onto the street. One group of reporters with notepads and microphones gathered around Dershowitz. Another circled Kuh. Both men were screeching, calling each other names, attacking each other's liberal credentials.

"You voted for me when I ran for DA!" Kuh screamed at one point. Alan yelled back something equally ridiculous.

It was the Fourth of July and Christmas all rolled into one for the Rhode Island media, which had a field day with the story. It also agitated the prosecution and the judge. From Alan's viewpoint, it did the job, which was to create the impression Dershowitz still had an important role in the case.

John Sheehan thought I had been taken to the cleaners. "Don't allow this guy near the case ever again," he advised.

I had made a mistake. But I had no way of knowing that Dershowitz's prime-time performance had set Rhode Island's weird wheels of justice in motion. This time, they wound up rolling in my favor.

About a week after the hearing, I was at my office in New York when I received an urgent phone call from Sheehan.

"You gotta get to Rhode Island immediately," he said. "The chief judge wants to meet you. He has something very important he wants to discuss with us and he won't talk about it on the phone."

I literally dropped everything and headed straight for the airport. Sheehan was there to meet my plane. We immediately drove to the courthouse in Providence for a meeting with Anthony A. Giannini, the presiding justice of the Rhode Island Superior Court.

The presiding justice was a little old man who sat behind a desk in a huge, darkened chamber. None of the prosecutors were present. That was very unusual—a representative of the prosecution should have been present for any discussion involving the case. This oversight, as it turned out, was small potatoes compared to what was to come.

Giannini wasted no time in expressing his unhappiness with the hijinks at the Kuh hearing.

"The state of Rhode Island is being made to look like a laughingstock," he complained. "DeRobbio wasn't able to control things, and we aren't going to permit that to happen again. This case is going to be tried in Providence."

"Your Honor," I interrupted. "My client has a preference for Newport." (This was something Claus had mentioned to me many times.)

A look of weary impatience crossed Giannini's face. It was the kind of expression a frustrated teacher might shoot at a slow pupil. "Let me put it this way," he said. "This case is going to be tried in Providence whether you like it or not. We can either do it the easy way or the hard way. The easy way is for you to agree to have the case moved. If that happens, I'll let you pick any judge in the courthouse to try the case. If you kick up a fuss, it will come to Providence anyway and *I'll* pick the judge."

Nothing quite like this had ever happened to me before. I'd been around the courts for many, many years and I never heard of a defense lawyer being allowed to pick his own judge for an important criminal case.

I looked at Sheehan for help.

"Your Honor," he said smoothly. "May we have a few minutes to discuss the matter."

Outside Justice Giannini's chambers, Sheehan gave me a fatherly talk on the Rhode Island legal system. "Let me tell you the facts of life," he said. "This guy means what he says. He wants this case taken away from DeRobbio. The trial is coming to Providence, and there isn't a goddamned thing you can do about it."

"You'd better call Claus," he added.

I phoned von Bulow in New York. "This is outrageous," Claus sputtered. "As a matter of principle, I want to be tried in Newport. We shall go to the newspapers. We shall appeal to the Supreme Court—"

"Claus," I interrupted, "have you forgotten you were sentenced to thirty years in jail in Newport? You can't win this case without a fair trial, and getting a fair trial means getting a judge who won't screw you. This isn't a bad deal at all."

Claus capitulated. I hung up the phone and turned to Sheehan. "OK," I said. "Claus is onboard. But I've got to rely on you to choose the right judge. Who do we want?"

John thought for a moment. "There are two people, equally good," he said. "One is a guy named Joe Rogers. He went to Brown. He used to be a football player. Good guy. He'd be a perfect judge. Another is Corrine Grande. She's smart. She's good. And I know her really well."

John said both judges would be even-handed.

"There's no way you'll get a judge who will favor the defense in Rhode Island," Sheehan said. "They eat, drink, and pal around with the prosecutors. The questions is, are you going to get the shit kicked out of you by a judge who favors the prosecution, or are you going to get a fair shake? These two judges will give you a fair shake."

"You choose," he added.

The idea of a woman in the case appealed to me. There was nothing scientific about it, but I'd noticed that women in the forty-to-sixty-year-old range always seemed sympathetic to Claus. Grande was fifty-five. She was also something of a pioneer in the Rhode Island criminal justice system—the first woman lawyer to serve in the state attorney general's office, the first woman to be named a district court judge in Rhode Island. And as John suggested, she had a reputation for fairness.

"Let's go with Corrine Grande," I said.

So we went back into Giannini's chambers and told him we'd go to Providence. The deal was struck then and there.

I had a strong suspicion that Sheehan had discussed the matter with Giannini before I was summoned to Rhode Island. It's just a guess, but I think they went over Sheehan's choices and how I was likely to react to the proposal.

On the plane from Providence to New York that night, I couldn't stop wondering about what I had gotten myself into. The events in Giannini's chambers made me realize just how much of an outsider I was in Rhode Island. Without John, I might have been dead before I started. Sheehan was my eyes and ears. He was the guide, and this was Africa. Darkest Africa.

Giannini's official announcement of the change in venue and appointment of a new judge cited a large backlog of civil and criminal cases at the Newport court. The presiding justice said he did not want the small courthouse tied up for the six weeks the trial might take. Giannini really laid it on by saying he was making the change over von Bulow's objections. He said Claus's lawyers (John and I) had failed to supply him with a convincing reason why the trial should remain in Newport.

I have no idea how the prosecutors reacted to all this. I'm sure they had their own ideas about a suitable judge for the case. I think it's likely Giannini told them they had no choice.

I talked to Sheehan on the phone the next day. He'd talked to Judge Grande, who was very excited about handling the biggest case of her career.

"She said she was gonna go downtown and buy herself a whole bunch of new blouses," Sheehan reported.

(That's all the opportunity a judge gets to exhibit a sense of fashion. While Grande would be wearing the traditional judicial dress for the trial, the top of her blouse would peek out over the black robes.) With the locale and the judge in the case set, I resumed preparation. I carefully reviewed the transcripts from the first trial. This was much more than a matter of familiarizing myself with the facts. There were lines of questioning pursued by Stephen Famiglietti, the prosecutor at the first trial, that I believed were inadmissible. But for one reason or another, Herald Price Fahringer had failed to object, and Famiglietti's questions went unchallenged. If, as I anticipated, prosecutors Mark DeSisto and Henry Gemma stuck closely to Famiglietti's script, we would be ready with an objection almost before they asked their questions. (We eventually had the prosecution so well clocked that I once made an objection before the prosecutor even got the question out.)

In addition to reviewing the transcripts, I had also watched the videotapes of the first trial. The atmospherics were not good. Claus was stiff, solemn, and somber. He wore dark suits. It might have been the trial of a U-boat commander accused of torpedoing a ship filled with civilians. Herald Price Fahringer was every bit as stiff and aristocratic as Claus, if slightly better dressed. The judge gave Fahringer a tremendously hard time, probably because he secretly regarded Fahringer as a dandy from the big city.

Andrea Reynolds had already encouraged Claus to change his wardrobe for the second trial. For once, I could enthusiastically support an Andrea campaign: I also urged Claus to dress differently, and he did. Tweed jackets and soft colors were the order of the day. Instead of an undertaker, Claus looked as if he might have been a professor at nearby Brown University. Claus also agreed to change his behavior. He had spent most of the first trial with his lawyers, largely isolated from the press and public. The "new" Claus would be more cheerful and accessible to the media.

One pressing matter I'd been unable to resolve before the trial began was the ongoing question of Andrea's role. Claus had made it clear—mostly by his inaction—that it was up to me to handle the energetic Ms. Reynolds. Once, while we were in New York, Claus and I had lunch alone and he confided in me that he felt it would be a great idea if I could somehow get Andrea into the background. But he also seemed worried about what kind of turmoil she might cause if she defected.

I didn't share that concern. But there was plenty about Andrea that *did* keep me up nights. For one thing, I'd learned that Andrea was wearing Sunny's clothes. She'd had them altered to fit her more substantial frame, but they were Sunny's all right. Claus's wife lay in Columbia-Presbyterian, comatose, and his girlfriend was rummaging through Sunny's closets, picking out a new wardrobe. I couldn't imagine how the jurors would react if they got a whiff of that detail.

Not long after Claus and I had our talk, I had lunch with him and Andrea at the Four Seasons, one of Claus's favorite restaurants. I have to admit my thoughts were wandering—Andrea's conversation tends to be a bit repetitive—when I suddenly realized she was talking about being at Claus's side during the trial.

Well, that certainly got my attention.

"What do you mean, 'By his side'?" I demanded.

She said, "Well, of course I'm going to be there next to him during the trial."

"You've got to be kidding. You're joking, right?" I said hopefully.

"No," said Andrea. "I've got to be there. I'm part of the defense team."

I turned to Claus. "Hey, this is a wonderful idea. Why pay me? Why don't you just surrender now, go check into Rhode Island state prison right away? You're going to go on trial for attempting to murder your wife, and have your girlfriend sitting right next to you!"

Claus just sat there, looking sort of nonplused.

"I see your point," said Andrea, taking another tack. "But we have to live with the fact I do exist."

I was so angry I made a major strategic mistake. "I don't think that's true, Andrea," I said. "Ninety-nine percent of the people in Rhode Island don't even know you exist."

Of course, this was a terrible affront to Andrea, who saw herself as the internationally known consort of Claus von Bulow. And I paid for it. When I arrived in Providence on the eve of the trial, I discovered the *Providence Journal*'s Sunday magazine featured a big story on—you guessed it—Claus's new love. There she was, in living color, on the cover. Inside, there were photos of Claus and Andrea frolicking in Central Park. The *Journal* was read by just about everybody in the state.

Andrea appeared at my hotel room the next morning ready to go to trial. She had, of course, engineered the newspaper story but treated it like an act of God.

"Oh, the *Providence Journal* has put this all over the state," she told me. "I must come to the courtroom now. Everybody knows who I am." Andrea then informed me it was her plan to appear in the courtroom with "Professor Dershowitz."

I deeply regretted having told her she was not a household name in Rhode Island.

"Alan hasn't called me, and I don't expect him to show up," I said. "I don't want you there, either." I managed to get Andrea to stay away from the courtroom during jury selection, but it was only a temporary victory. She still planned to make a grand entrance when testimony in the case got under way. Claus still refused to say anything to her about the matter. It was left to me to confront her.

A solution to the problem emerged during one of my discussions with the prosecutors, Mark DeSisto and Henry Gemma. It turned out that they had their own cross to bear in the form of Richard Kuh, the lawyer hired by Sunny's children to investigate her death. Kuh had become an anti-Claus zealot in the years that followed his original involvement in the case. He was also, according to DeSisto and Gemma, bossy, supercilious, condescending, and intractable. The prosecution, understandably, did not want him in the courtroom.

Since this was, after all, Rhode Island, I suggested a deal. I would put Kuh on my witness list if they would put Andrea on theirs. Having your name placed on the list by the prosecution or the defense did not necessarily mean you would actually be called to testify. Potential witnesses are, however, barred from the courtroom.

The deal was sealed with a handshake. I thought I had neatly removed a major headache, but the very next day I was double crossed. Gemma approached me during a break in jury selection and delivered some bad news.

"I've got to tell you, in all candor, that we thought this over last night and we can't do it," he said. "It's just too good for us. If this woman comes into court, it's gotta help us. So we don't want the deal."

"But we shook on it!" I replied. This seemed as good an argument as any in Rhode Island.

"Sorry," Gemma said, "but the boss [State Attorney General Arlene Violet] says no."

I didn't really believe that they had even discussed it with Violet, but it didn't matter. I was worried. I decided to go to Judge Grande and tell her exactly what had happened.

"I don't think my client is going to get a fair trial if this woman appears in the courtroom," I told the judge. "I would ask the court to enforce my agreement with the prosecution."

Grande was sympathetic, but she refused to take any action.

"I guess you have only one choice," she said.

"I guess you're right," I replied.

I put Andrea's name on my witness list.

That night in the hotel, I casually delivered the bad news to her. "You've been subpoenaed to appear as a witness at the trial," I said. "That means you're excluded from the courtroom."

Andrea assumed that the prosecution was responsible, and I did nothing to change her opinion. "I must speak with the judge about this!" she fumed. "I'm being deprived of my rights as a citizen."

"Look, Andrea," I said unsympathetically, "in the first place, you're not being deprived of anything. And in the second place, you're not even a citizen."

The battle did not end there. Andrea was relentless. She began bombarding the judge with notes demanding an audience. Grande finally did agree to see her late one afternoon toward the end of jury selection. Andrea went through her spiel about how she knew more about the case than anyone

else and was therefore indispensable to the defense.
"I'm sorry, but there's nothing I can do," the judge said.
"Your name is on the witness list." Grande gave me a boost by
failing to mention *who* put Andrea on the witness list.
Alan Dershowitz presented me with the same kind of problem. But unlike Andrea, who represented a real threat to the defense, Dershowitz was never more than nuisance.
Alan had been more or less isolated from the case since I became Claus's lawyer. I couldn't keep him away from the trial, but
his performance at the hearing on the Kuh notes convinced me
that he should remain on the periphery. I decided the best thing
would be to sentence Dershowitz to talk to Claus. Claus understood this role quite well and kept both Andrea and Alan fully
engaged in chitchat while I focused on the business of conducting his defense.

In his book, Alan claimed Claus told him on the eve of the
trial that John Sheehan did not want him in the courtroom and
would walk out if Dershowitz showed his face. I can only say
that no one wanted Alan in the courtroom. But none of us, including John, was about to abandon a client at the beginning of
his trial because Alan Dershowitz was sitting in the spectators'
gallery.

"The press was referring to me as the 'legal mastermind,' the
'player-coach,' the 'backbone' of the defense, the 'unseen force
behind Claus's new defense,' the lawyer who 'will direct the von
Bulow defense from his law school office,' and even 'the most
important person in von Bulow's life,' " Alan wrote with charac-
teristic modesty. "There was every reason to believe that I would
be present on opening day. But Claus was terrified of losing
whatever clout Sheehan might provide."

This was about as close as Dershowitz came to admitting that
he played no role in the defense. Alan's account of the second
trial is largely the product of his overheated imagination. The
most fanciful episode he describes is a "summit meeting" near
the end of the trial at which all the defense lawyers are supposed
to have debated whether or not Claus should take the stand.

I had decided before the trial that von Bulow should not take
the stand, and Claus concurred in my decision. He was very

comfortable with the idea that we were going to present a medical defense, and that there was simply no need for his testimony. Claus always liked to tell reporters that he was eager to tell his story in court, but he never communicated any such desire to me.

Alan, by the way, urged von Bulow to take the stand, an action I was convinced could only lead to disaster. Some later thought he did so because Claus's testimony would have provided extremely dramatic material for the book he was writing. However, in *Reversal of Fortune,* Dershowitz claims that in urging Claus to testify, he was only playing the role of "devil's advocate" at Claus's request.

With the trial fast approaching, the prosecution was wrestling with a problem of its own—a sensational new piece of evidence. Two nights before the trial was scheduled to begin, Alexander von Auersperg called Lieutenant John Reise, the Rhode Island state police detective responsible for the investigation into Sunny's death. Reise, whose home was not far from the von Bulow residence, immediately drove to Clarendon Court after receiving the call. He was escorted to Claus and Sunny's bedroom. Opening a decorative box Claus kept on a night table next to his bed, Alexander showed Reise an extraordinary discovery. Underneath some shotgun shells Claus kept in the box, there was a hypodermic needle. The apparently unused needle was still in its plastic sheath.

It was an astonishing discovery, but there was no dancing for joy. Reise left Clarendon Court that night without touching the needle. He returned the next day with prosecutors DeSisto and Gemma to show them the new evidence. The prosecutors gloomily reviewed their options. They could attempt to use the needle as evidence, but that would raise serious questions about the competence of the state police, who had searched the bedroom four years earlier. How could the officers have overlooked such an important piece of evidence in such an obvious place? It also occurred to the prosecutors that the fortuitous discovery of the needle only two nights before Claus's trial would obviously lead to charges that the needle was a plant.

DeSisto and Gemma decided to deal with the problem by

pretending that the needle did not exist. It was not photographed, cataloged, or subjected to a laboratory analysis for the possible presence of drugs. The needle, indeed, was never touched. The prosecutors simply left it in the box and went back to work as if nothing had happened.

The defense was told nothing, and I did not learn of the needle's existence until after the trial was over. DeSisto and Gemma later claimed that there was no need to inform me of the discovery, since the needle was "inculpatory"—or damaging to Claus's case! The extraordinary appearance of the needle remains one of the unsolved mysteries of the von Bulow case.

The defense had a few problems of its own—like finding Providence. Joann, Andy, and I set out for the trial by car on a Sunday night. I was at the wheel, and when I turned off the highway to look for gas after dark, I became hopelessly lost on a maze of back roads in Connecticut. Or was it Rhode Island? I could see the headlines in the local papers: "Smart-Ass New York Lawyer Still Missing—Von Bulow Trial Postponed." Fortunately, I finally found a gas station and made my way back to the highway. We crawled into Providence around midnight.

We all stayed at the Biltmore Plaza, an old hotel a few blocks from the courthouse. I had a corner suite on the thirteenth floor (officially called the fourteenth floor) with a nice view of the state Capitol. The suite contained a bedroom and a large living room that I converted into a conference room and headquarters. I had two large tables pushed together to form a huge desk–conference table. I also set up a speakerphone system in the room. That enabled me to take notes comfortably, or walk around the room as I spoke with our witnesses by phone. Our medical library, replete with such page-turners as *Principles of Neurology* and *Diabetes Mellitis,* was also located in my suite. I had an IBM computer plugged into Lexis—a large database of legal opinions. Andy Citron—using my ID number—pulled up opinions from Lexis for our legal research during the trial. (Andy did it so well and so often that Lexis proposed using me in a commercial after the trial ended.) We also had a photocopy machine, VCR for video play, and cartons and cartons and cartons of transcripts, documents, and correspondence.

We were ready for white-collar warfare.

Jury selection began on Monday, April 13, 1985. The defense team ate a light breakfast with Claus at the hotel then took a car to the courthouse, a large, red brick Depression-era building perched on a hill next to the campus of Brown University. We had to walk up a long, sweeping stone staircase to the entrance of the building, where the media awaited us. I'd already been through a number of high-profile cases, but they were nothing compared to the cloud of reporters, photographers, and camera crews that followed us to the entrance.

Our first day in court got off to an unpromising start. Claus set off the metal detector and was sent back. He emptied his pockets and launched a second assault on the contraption. Once again, failure. Before the assembled multitude, he stripped off his belt, which had a big metal buckle, and threw himself at the machine again. This time, he succeeded. At that moment, Claus looked a little sad and vulnerable.

The trial would be held in a small, high-ceilinged courtroom on the fifth floor. We were given a small judge's library with a conference table and a telephone. It was here that we worked over lunch, phoning witnesses, reviewing transcripts, and discussing strategy.

The hotel and courthouse constituted our whole little world, and in a few weeks it would be a little pressure cooker. During jury selection, however, we had the luxury of strolling through the pleasant old streets near the courthouse at lunchtime. We ate at the faculty dining room at Brown, a benefit provided by the ubiquitous John Sheehan.

Mail soon began pouring into us in care of the courthouse, and our mornings in the little room included a touch of summer camp: a bailiff would come in with the mail and call out our names.

"OK, I've got a letter for Puccio, here are your letters, Claus," he would announce. Hundreds of people wrote to us in care of the courthouse over the course of the trial.

"Dear Mr. Puccio," wrote a woman from Utah.

"I've been watching the trial every day on television, and I want you to know that I think you are wonderful. Unfortunately, my TV set broke a few days ago, and I was wondering if you could send me the money to repair it."

Jury selection went smoothly enough. The prosecution and defense, of course, try to select jurors who they believe to be sympathetic to their case. Actually, I'm happy with jurors who are neutral. I think most jurors have a natural inclination to believe something must have happened for the defendant to be indicted. And so, finding people who are genuinely impartial is a plus for the defense. I think we came up with a reasonably objective jury, but not because I possessed any magic powers.

Books have been written about jury selection, and experts abound, but picking jurors is a crapshoot. It's the one part of the trial where you're really not in control. I think there's something to be said for picking the first twelve people who come through the door, but nobody does it that way. Everybody tries to pick the "right" jurors.

Only one person, of course, can conduct an examination, and I didn't want five lawyers at the defense table popping up with questions. We used the same system throughout the trial: If somebody had a suggestion or a question, it would be written down. I would sort of make my way around the defense table while questioning a witness, and pick up all the notes. It never bothered me that the jury could see I was checking with my colleagues.

We also employed something of a committee system on sizing up prospective jurors. John Sheehan, Claus, and myself would pool our observations about a prospective juror and try to decide if he or she was "good" or "bad" for the defense. Rhode Island is a tight-knit state, and John would sometimes know something about a juror's family, if not about the juror himself. Claus practiced the art of jury selection rather badly. He seemed to have an unerring instinct for the wrong jurors. On one occasion, Claus seized on the idea that an apparently nondescript middle-aged woman would make an ideal juror.

"I must have this woman," Claus whispered dramatically. "It is my life that is at stake here."

Moments later, Claus's ideal juror emotionally announced to the courtroom that she believed our client was guilty as sin. She practically had to be carried away.

We arrived at a jury of fourteen: nine women and five men. Two of the jurors would serve as alternates and be dismissed just prior to the start of deliberations.

I had anticipated that the trial would be largely a repeat of Claus's first go-round, and that proved to be the case. The prosecution got under way as it had before with the testimony of Sunny's maid, Maria Schrallhammer. Maria repeated the damaging testimony about Claus's apparent indifference to Sunny's first coma and her discovery of the infamous black bag.

Maria had been hired by Sunny's first husband, Prince von Auersperg, and retained a liking for the safari guide. I asked Maria if she didn't hope that the prince and Sunny would be able to patch up their marriage. She denied any such feeling, a little too quickly, I believed.

"No, that's wrong, because it was a beautiful family, it was beautiful—two beautiful children, it was just a fairy-tale family."

A "fairy-tale family." I filed this phrase away for use in my final argument to the jury.

"It was almost like a picture book, isn't that correct?" I asked. "Almost like a storybook it was so beautiful, isn't that right."

"It was like a picture, when the two [of them] would go out to parties, or when we had parties at home," she replied.

"And you were very unhappy when the storybook was destroyed by their divorce, isn't that correct?"

"Well, sure, I was unhappy for the children. They loved their home."

"And the person you blamed for that is Mr. von Bulow, isn't that correct?"

"Never, that's not correct, Never. I never blamed him for that."

The answer was delivered emphatically, in a mechanical tone of voice. I was confident the jury also knew who Maria blamed for shattering the "fairy tale."

There was no way I was going to shake Maria's story about Claus casually lolling about in bed next to his semicomatose wife, thumbing through a book while the maid repeatedly entered and exited their bedroom throughout the day. But I gently tried to suggest the absurdity of her scenario while briefly leading her through the story again on cross-examination. Despite her concern over Sunny, Maria admitted, she managed to down lunch and dinner without difficulty during this day of crisis. And apart from her urgings to Claus, she made no effort to summon help for "Mrs."—as she called Sunny.

But all this was just preliminary sparring, as far as I was concerned. Maria Schrallhammer had been regarded by many observers as the most important witness for the prosecution at the first trial. But I was confident the medical defense I planned to present would considerably diminish the impact of her testimony. If no crime had been committed—if the jury did not believe there was any insulin—her description of Claus's behavior prior to the first coma would have very little significance.

Maria's black bag testimony was another matter, however. She had described finding a bottle marked INSULIN among the contents of the black bag. Her "What for, insulin?" remark was a hit of the first trial. But this time around, we had the benefit of notes made by Richard Kuh, the attorney hired by the family to investigate Sunny's death before the police became involved.

Kuh's notes revealed that Maria had made no mention of insulin—or syringes—when she was questioned about the contents of the black bag. Indeed, she even told Kuh that the labels on the bottles in the black bag had been "all scraped off." It was only after the family received the results of a lab test that indicated insulin was present on a needle found in the bag that Maria began to claim she had seen a bottle marked INSULIN.

Q. Now, did you ever tell anyone that the labels . . . in the black bag were, and I quote, "All scraped off?" Did you ever tell that to anyone, yes or no?
A. No.
Q. Maybe I didn't ask the question carefully enough. Let me ask you again.
A. No, I didn't understand that question.

Maria was in some ways a clever witness. Her grasp of English weakened when tough questions were posed.

Q. I'm sorry. Did you ever tell anyone that the labels were all scraped off, the labels on whatever you saw, whatever you say you saw in the black bag? Did you ever say that to anyone?
A. The labels were scraped off?
Q. Yes.
A. I don't remember that.

I was making some progress. Maria had gone from a flat denial to a memory lapse. I pressed further, and Maria conceded that she had not mentioned insulin or syringes to Kuh during their first interview.

"Well, I was not concerned about the syringe and the insulin," she said. "I never knew that insulin is something so significant for people. I only knew insulin is for diabetes, and since there was no diabetic in the house, I was not concerned about the insulin."

Maria's memory also cleared up enough to recall that she had told Kuh about the labels being scraped off the bottles she saw in the bag. But she continued to insist she had seen a bottle marked INSULIN.

When I asked Maria how she could tell Kuh the labels were scraped off without mentioning she saw a bottle marked insulin, language difficulties reappeared.

"I don't recall because I really don't understand in the way you mean it," she said.

I was very pleased with the cross-examination. I was confident that on the one issue that really counted—Maria's discovery of the insulin bottle—her testimony had been seriously damaged.

By the end of Maria's testimony, on Monday, April 27, I had settled into a routine that would last throughout the trial.

At the end of the day, the legal team would walk back to the hotel and go up to the conference room in my suite, where we'd try to unwind a bit. I'd usually have soda and a cheese plate or fruit brought up. John Sheehan would pour a drink from a bottle of Absolut vodka that was always kept in the room. During the course of the trial, Claus became very angry about the expense of Sheehan's vodka. One night, while Joann, Andy, and I were working on the case, Claus showed up at my suite in his bathrobe carrying a large bottle of cheap vodka. As the three of us looked on in amazement, Claus poured the cheap stuff into the Absolut bottle and walked out! Sheehan wasn't fooled. He didn't, of course, know that Claus had switched vodka on him, but he immediately remarked that there was something "wrong" with his Absolut. (I never asked Claus any questions about the source of his money for his defense, but he later told others that J. Paul Getty, Jr., had financed his long legal struggle. This included the money for bail following his conviction, Claus's appeal, the second trial, and a nasty civil suit with his stepchildren that followed the second trial. Claus, of course, had worked for Getty's father. The son believed fervently in his innocence and was certainly as responsible as anyone for von Bulow's eventual acquittal.)

Over drinks, we'd switch on the TV and jump from channel to channel to see how the trial was being played that day on the news. We'd talk about the events of the day, and then Claus would go off to prepare for that night's social event. He and Andrea were hardly stay-at-homes. They dined with journalists and various society types throughout the trial.

I generally had an early dinner with Joann and Andy, so we could get back to the hotel and resume our work. But on a few occasions, I did go out with Claus. More often than not, a Claus admirer in the restaurant would send over a bottle to the table. Anyhow, on one occasion a bottle of champagne arrived, and Claus began bowing and scraping in the direction of the donor. The guy eventually got up and came over to our table.

"Mr. Von Bulow, I wasn't sending the bottle to you. I wanted to pay my respects to Tom Puccio," he said.

It turned out the guy's name was Puccio—the owner of a high-end marble company called Puccio Marble. He had been following my career throughout the years and wanted to make my acquaintance. I sort of treasured the moment, but Claus continued to lead me in the free champagne sweepstakes by about two hundred to one.

Most nights, I would be back from dinner and deep into work before Claus was even ready to begin his evening. He and Andrea would drop by about seven-thirty to tell me which writer or blue blood they were dining with. Claus would be looking his elegant best. Andrea, as always, would be dressed to kill, and I would always offer a small prayer that her gown was not one of Sunny's.

I would spend the night reviewing transcripts, discussing strategy, and getting our witnesses ready to testify. Frequently, this involved lengthy telephone conversations with experts about complex medical testimony. It wasn't possible to interrupt these guys every five minutes to say, "What do you mean?" So I tape-recorded all the conversations and listened to them again before calling the expert back with specific questions. There were times when I was completely exhausted, and would fall asleep while listening to a cassette.

I would be up at 5:30 or 6 A.M. Some mornings I'd remain in bed for an hour listening to the tape recording I had fallen asleep over. I would also read through *The New York Times, Daily News, New York Post,* the *Providence Journal,* and the *Boston Globe.* I believe that reporters often react to courtroom events in the same way as jurors, and the papers give me a rough feel for what I'm doing right or wrong. Some reporters are sophisticated, but others think just like the average member of the jury. And if those reporters aren't getting your message, if they don't know where you're going, then maybe you'd better rethink your strategy.

I also believe that even sequestered jurors are affected by media coverage. Even if they haven't seen a TV news show or read a newspaper, they're in contact with friends, relatives, and court personnel who have. (I got into the habit of tossing the papers into a pile, and by the time the trial ended, there was an enormous stack of newspapers along one wall—kind of like rings on a tree.)

About eight o'clock, I'd meet with Joann, Andy, and Claus in the conference room. Claus's nights were not completely devoted to wining and dining. He would return to his hotel room after dinner and sit down in front of a typewriter to write up his suggestions and ideas for the trial. These proposals were always politely presented to me the next morning. I have to admit I almost always ignored them.

After the morning meeting at the hotel, we would walk to the courthouse, past the CNN van that was always parked just outside. CNN is an established news network now, but in 1985, it was still a struggling operation that many cable companies were reluctant to carry. Nevertheless, it devoted a lot of time and money to televising big chunks of the trial. Having a TV camera in the courtroom was a novelty at the time, but after the first few days, people forgot the camera was there and got down to business in the usual way.

(The CNN van also served as a hangout for Andrea Reynolds. Having been barred from the courtroom thanks to my scheming, she would watch the trial from the truck. Andrea claimed to have used disguises to evade the press during her trips from the hotel to the van—wigs, glasses, or heavy clothing to make herself look fat. Now, Andrea did not strike me as particularly publicity averse, and I never saw her in disguise myself. But this may only mean that like the media, I was fooled by her clever camouflage.)

The prosecution's second witness was Alexander von Auersperg, Claus's twenty-five-year-old stepson, who had testified at the first trial about discovering the black bag in a closet at Clarendon Court about a month after his mother's second coma.

Claus and I had never agreed about how to handle Alexander. He regarded the young man as the central player in a conspiracy to frame him for Sunny's comas. From our first meeting on, Claus urged me to go after Alexander on the witness stand, exposing him as a rich, spoiled, shiftless drug addict. But once again I ignored my client's advice. Alexander had emerged as a sympathetic figure at the first trial, and I saw no percentage in alienating the jury by coming down hard on him. More importantly, nothing in Alexander's testimony weakened the medical defense I was planning.

Press accounts of my cross-examination of Alexander focused

on the revelation that, during the weeks following Sunny's collapse into coma, von Auersperg and other family members had discussed giving Claus a cash payment if he would withdraw any claims to Sunny's estate. It appeared that money, as well as concern for Sunny's well-being, was high on the family agenda. But I scored much more significant points by getting Alexander to admit he had thrown away some of the drugs discovered during his search of Clarendon Court.

Still, Claus was bitterly disappointed when his stepson left the witness stand with his reputation unscathed. I've been told that to this day, Claus is still angry about my gentle treatment of Alexander.

With Alexander out of the way, the prosecution turned to the most crucial part of the case—a parade of medical witnesses. And it was here that the state sprung one of its few surprises—a claim that Claus and Sunny had engaged in a struggle at Clarendon Court prior to her second coma. The prosecutors trotted in three physicians who had treated Sunny at Newport Hospital and testified about various scratches and bruises that they had observed on Sunny's body. The implication, of course, was that Claus had forcibly injected Sunny with insulin on the night of December 21, 1980.

Nothing about a struggle had been introduced as evidence at the first trial, and I objected to just about every question prosecutors Mark DeSisto and Henry Gemma asked about the cuts and bruises. In particular, I wanted to keep the physicians from making any conclusions about how Sunny had gotten the injuries. One of the physicians, Dr. Jeremy Worthington, was prepared to testify that Sunny's scratches and bruises had been caused by a struggle.

The jury was sent out of the courtroom as we argued the issue before Judge Grande. It was here that John Sheehan produced one of the sharpest bits of cross-examination during the entire trial. I sometimes permitted John to conduct a cross-examination, and he never disappointed. In this case, he strode up to the witness stand and rolled up his left sleeve to show Worthington some scratches on his arm.

"Is that from a struggle?" Sheehan asked.

"I cannot say, sir," replied the doctor.

"Well, how did I get my scratches?"

"I don't know."

"Yet you do know how Mrs. von Bulow got hers, is that what you're saying to me?" John asked triumphantly.

"No, I do not know how she got those scratches," Worthington conceded.

That was the end for the struggle theory. (Sheehan, by the way, had scratched himself with a nail file.) I argued that this was hardly the time to permit Dr. Worthington, a neurologist, to make his "maiden voyage" as a medical expert. Judge Grande agreed, ruling that the neurologist lacked the experience and background necessary to render such an opinion. Worthington's testimony was kept from the jury.

It was a very bad beginning for the prosecution's medical case. And there would be more hard times ahead. I had already laid plans for a pair of very unpleasant developments for the state.

Joann Crispi made a big discovery during one trial weekend, when she and Andy were holed up in the conference room of my New York law firm. (We generally returned home on Friday evenings, but got little time for relaxation.) Joann was reviewing the medical records from Newport Hospital, where Sunny was treated following her first coma. These records had already been scrutinized and picked over by more than twenty-five medical experts for the prosecution and the defense, not to mention a small army of lawyers and police investigators. The hospital records had also been introduced into evidence at the first trial and shipped into the jury room during deliberations. It didn't seem possible that they could yield anything new, but Joann made an extraordinary discovery. She was poring over the indecipherable notes of a nurse who attended Sunny, when the meaningless scrawl that had danced before her eyes at least a dozen times suddenly became clear.

The nurse noted that Sunny had not only regained consciousness a few hours after arriving in the hospital following her first coma but was strong and clear-minded enough to sit up in bed and write on a pad.

Joann immediately recognized the significance of the entry. At the very time Sunny should have been in the deepest part of an insulin-induced coma, according to prosecution expert George Cahill, she was awake and alert!

She immediately phoned me with the good news, but a celebration was premature. We had to find the nurse and have her confirm the accuracy of the entry. That turned out to be a little more difficult than I anticipated. Sunny's first coma had occurred more than four years previously, and we discovered that the nurse had not only left the hospital, but Rhode Island as well. I hired a private investigator who learned her new address in Florida by interviewing some of her former neighbors.

The next day, I spoke to her by phone. We were fearful that the nurse might say she was mistaken, or simply didn't recall what had happened. But she was very emphatic in confirming that Sunny was sitting up in bed and writing at the time noted in the hospital records. Incredibly, the nurse had never been interviewed by anyone from the prosecution or asked to explain the meaning of her notes on Mrs. von Bulow.

This gave me the ammunition I needed to ambush one of the world's foremost endocrinologists and the prosecution's star witness. I was very eager to ask the distinguished Dr. Cahill about this energetic letter writing in a supposedly comatose patient.

But first, I had another surprise in store for the prosecution, in the form of Dr. Janis Gailitis, the chief of medicine at Newport Hospital. Dr. Gailitis, who had treated Sunny following both comas, had been an effective weapon for the state at the first trial. But now I hoped to turn him into a booby trap.

During our pretrial preparations, I made ample use of a provision in Rhode Island law that permits the defense to subpoena documents prior to trial. I not only got a raft of documents that way but also a face-to-face look at the prosecution witnesses who delivered them. In some instances, I was able to strike up a conversation. That's what happened with Dr. Gailitis. He showed up at the courthouse with copies of his records, and we chatted amiably for a few minutes. I could see that he was friendly.

"Do you think we could interview you?" I asked.

"No problem," Gailitis replied.

The interview was far more fruitful than we ever could have imagined. Dr. Gailitis told us that he believed Sunny's first coma was not caused by an insulin injection but rather by vomiting that cut off the flow of oxygen to her brain. While Gailitis had no special expertise in endocrinology, his opinion was bound to carry weight with the jury, since he was the physician who had personally treated her during both comas.

And there was more. Dr. Gailitis said the prosecution knew of his diagnosis and had advised him not to testify about his opinion unless he was specifically asked. The good doctor also said his damaging diagnosis had been omitted from an interview that he gave to the Rhode Island state police.

Gailitis's testimony created a sensation. At the morning session, he was a prosecution witness. At the afternoon session, he testified for me outside the presence of the jury. Prosecutor Mark DeSisto was thrust into the awkward role of angrily cross-examining his own witness. But Gailitis stuck firmly to his story. I moved for the dismissal of the first attempted murder charge against Claus based on the testimony, and Judge Grande ordered a hearing to determine if the prosecution had deliberately withheld information vital to the defense.

Grande ultimately denied my motion, but the whole affair was a severe embarrassment for the prosecution. The hearing also electrified the press, which was turning out every day hoping for a soap opera drama to unfold. Gailitis's allegations fully satisfied the three national TV networks and the great army of reporters from other news organizations.

Stephen Famiglietti, the hero of the first trial, and one of his assistants, Susan McGuirl, were hauled into Judge Grande's courtroom to answer Gailitis's charges. I gave them both a rough going-over, but they vehemently denied that Gailitis had informed them of his diagnosis. And both testified they would have informed the defense if he had done so.

Judge Grande concluded that there had been no effort to conceal Gailitis's diagnosis from the defense. But she permitted him to testify to the jury that he believed Sunny's first coma had nothing to do with insulin. He did on Friday, May 10. The trial had now run two weeks, and I had every reason to believe that things were going our way.

The third week of the trial featured the prosecution's all-important effort to prove that Sunny's comas were caused by insulin injections. Their star witness was Dr. George Cahill of the Harvard Medical School. Prosecutor Henry Gemma led Cahill through a recitation of the physician's extensive credentials. Just how impressive they were quickly became evident when Gemma asked Cahill if he was board certified in his specialities of metabolic disease and endocrinology. Physicians are required to pass a demanding examination to obtain certification in their specialties.

"No, I'm not," Cahill testified, "and the reason is that when the exam was first put together in the early seventies . . . I made up the questions. . . . Therefore, I couldn't take the exam, obviously, since I put it together."

Cahill went on to explain that he was director of the prestigious Joselyn Research Laboratories and had written several hundred articles on blood sugar, including the chapter on blood sugar control, diabetes, and hypoglycemia (a condition that causes an abnormally low blood sugar level in the body) that appears in all three of the major medical textbooks used in the United States.

He used four sugar cubes to show the jury the importance of sugar as the fuel for the brain. Sugar stored in the liver is released to replenish the sugar used up by the brain. As sugar is used up by the brain, the insulin level in the bloodstream falls, which is a signal to the liver to release more sugar. This simple explanation brought Cahill to the heart of the case: If additional insulin is introduced into the system, it sends a false signal to the liver that there is no need to release sugar. The brain slowly starves, and the victim becomes jittery, forgetful, and may even pass out. In extreme cases, the result can be an irreversible coma, which is exactly what the prosecution was asserting.

Cahill testified that he had spent thirty to forty hours reviewing Sunny's medical records. Gemma then led the doctor through a recitation of the blood sugar and insulin levels that were recorded for Sunny at various times during her hospitalization for the two comas. Cahill also testified about the glucose injections that Sunny received in an effort to raise her blood sugar level. He dismissed the drugs and alcohol found in her body as possible causes of the coma.

His conclusion that both comas were induced by "exogenous" insulin—insulin by injection—was fairly simple and easy for the jury to understand: Cahill said the large amount of glucose needed to bring Sunny's blood sugar level back to normal could not be explained in any other way. But he hedged when Gemma asked him about the cause of the second coma.

"I'd say the probability there was insulin or exogenous insulin was part of the total event," Cahill testified.

Part of the total event? Cahill hadn't equivocated like that during the first trial. Obviously, he'd lost a little bit of the overwhelming self-confidence he'd demonstrated then.

Gemma concluded his examination by almost casually asking Cahill about an insulin reading of 216 that was recorded for Sunny following her second coma. An insulin level of 216 is extremely high, and the prosecution referred to the reading repeatedly during the first trial.

"Did you need the 216, Doctor, in order to form your opinion?" Gemma asked.

"No," Cahill answered.

DeSisto and Gemma had anticipated, correctly, that I would launch a full-scale assault on the reliability of the test used to determine Sunny's insulin level. They sought to outmaneuver me by asserting that the test was of no importance in reaching a conclusion about the cause of her coma. Perhaps they believed my attack on the test might tend to undermine the credibility of all the medical evidence presented by the prosecution in the eyes of the jurors.

I thought they made a major error. A much better strategy would have been a vigorous defense of the test. My task would have been much, much harder if the jury believed Sunny's insulin level was as high as the test suggested.

I began my cross-examination of Cahill by probing his apparent equivocation about the cause of the second coma. I first got him to concede that he was only "90 percent" sure that the second coma was caused by an insulin injection. The learned doctor already looked a little uncomfortable. I started pressing.

Q. You have concluded that it's exogenous insulin, in other words, insulin by injection, on the second coma?
A. You said exogenous, sir . . . It could be exogenous, it could be endogenous [insulin manufactured by the body]. You have asked me my opinion initially, you didn't ask me about the other 10 percent.

"This is not a crapshoot," I angrily shot back. "I'm asking you for an opinion."

It's almost always a mistake for a witness to spar with the lawyer questioning him. The cross-examination was already moving my way. I focused my questions on Cahill's 10 percent zone of uncertainty.

What, besides an injection of insulin, might have caused Sunny's insulin level to rise?, I wanted to know. Cahill again became breezy and authoritative. He testified that "worm medicine used in the tropics" and a rare Jamaican fruit called salpighia would do the trick. I even helped him out a little bit.

Q. Is this Jamaican fruit readily available? Could I go out and buy it, buy it in Newport?
A. No.
Q. Buy it in Providence?
A. Highly improbable.

[Under my questioning, Cahill also said there were some rare chemical compounds that would raise the body's insulin level.]
Q. I think that you're telling us is that you really have to scour the world and search your imagination to come up with something other than regular insulin, is that right?
A. Correct.
Q. There is nothing that is sold that would do it, is that right?
A. Correct.

I then took Cahill on a short side tour with some questions about a test that was not performed on Sunny before returning to lower the boom.

Q. Now, Doctor, have you heard of sulfonylureas?
A. Yes, sir.
Q. Can you tell us what those are?
A. Sulfonylureas are drugs which in the mid-1950s began to be used for diabetics. We are still not certain today exactly how they work, but one of their actions is to . . . put out more insulin and, therefore, lower blood glucose.
Q. Now, will you agree with me that sulfonylureas can be purchased in drugstores quite easily, Doctor?
A. Yes, sir.
Q. You're not talking about Jamaican fruit here?
A. Yes.
Q. And you're not talking about worm medicine or anything like that. You're talking about a pill that someone could take very simply?
A. Yes, sir.
Q. And no test was done here for sulfonylureas, is that correct?
A. It was done, I believe, on the first admission.
Q. I'm talking now only about the second admission.
A. Correct.
Q. So, no test was done for sulfonylureas, is that correct?
A. Correct, to my knowledge.
Q. Would you like to look at the records?
A. I don't have any reference to it. My guess is you are correct.
Q. If you don't have any reference to it after thirty hours of study of the records, can I easily assume there was no test of sulfonylureas done, is that right?
A. Uh-hum.
Q. You cannot say to a reasonable degree of medical certainty that insulin by injection was involved, can you, rather than sulfonylureas, is that right?
A. No. When she was given . . .

Cahill was interrupted by an unhappy Henry Gemma, who was on his feet asking Judge Grande to allow Cahill to "explain" his answer. It was Gemma, of course, who had interrupted Cahill's answer! The judge refused to intercede.

It was time to go for the kill.

Q. Now, at this point, Doctor, you have changed your
testimony because you can't testify that to a reasonable degree
of medical certainty there wasn't sulfonylureas, is that right?
A. Yes.

Cahill's composure was headed south. There was now anger
in his eyes. He'd been badly embarrassed by an amateur. I next
switched to a passage in the *Cecil Textbook of Medicine,* an authoritative reference book. During the course of my cross-examination, Cahill had routinely conceded that alcohol and aspirin—two of the drugs found in Sunny's system—lower the blood
sugar level. But he denied that propranolol, a drug Sunny used
that is also known by the brand name Inderol, had this effect.

I now read him a passage from *Cecil* that said propranolol was
also responsible for hypoglycemia, or low blood sugar. Cahill
again equivocated and hardly covered himself in glory when I
asked him if it was true that he could not give me a "Yes" or
"No" answer to the question of whether he agreed or disagreed
with the statement in *Cecil.*

"How tall—excuse me, sir, the answer is no, I can't give you a
clear answer," he said.

I don't know how height got into Cahill's answer, but with the
state's top witness in a state of confusion, it was now time to state
my own theory for the cause of Sunny's coma.

Q. Now, will you agree, however, that at the time of the second
admission, Mrs. von Bulow had those very three things in her
system, which this medical volume says lower blood sugar: A.
She had alcohol. B. She had Inderol and C. She had salicylate.
Is that right?
A. No. Can you refresh me on the alcohol level, sir?
Q. Well, I'm asking you first, Doctor, did she have alcohol in
her system?
A. Can you refresh me on what level it was?
Q. Can you answer my question?
A. I'll have to look at my notes.
Q. Well, regardless of the level, did she have alcohol in her
system?
A. No. The answer on alcohol is no.

Not only was Cahill the expert asking for my help with the medical records, he had mixed up the comas. Tests had shown alcohol in Sunny's system following the second coma.

Q. Now, taking all these things together, a combination of the three, propranolol, salicylates, and alcohol, would all of those substances acting together, if taken by Mrs. von Bulow the night before, have lowered her blood sugar?
A. I really don't know. I don't—no experience on all three drugs. In a panel of normal individuals to see whether one person should have a particular idiosyncrasy, I don't know.

With significant damage done to Cahill's explanation of the second coma, I moved on to Sunny's first coma.

I produced another leading medical textbook, *Harrison's Principles of Internal Medicine*. This seemed to have the same effect on Cahill as waving a red cape at a bull might have. Perhaps the sight of an amateur waving a textbook brought his expert blood to a boil.

When I asked Cahill about the textbook's reputation in the medical community, his voice dropped so low that the judge could not hear the answer.

JUDGE GRANDE: You really must keep your voice up, Dr. Cahill. It's physically straining for the court reporter and members of the jury to constantly try to catch what you're saying as you drop your voice.
CAHILL: I'm sorry, it's so difficult for me to answer inane questions.
JUDGE GRANDE: I think, Dr. Cahill, that was an extremely inappropriate comment. Members of the jury, you will disregard the gratuitous characterization by the witness.

Having the conduct of the state's most important witness rebuked by the judge in front of the jury was a bonus I couldn't have imagined. Knowing when to end a cross-examination is crucial, and after some further sparring with Cahill about the facts of the first coma, I decided it was time to go for the jugular by moving on to the nurse's notes. I had Cahill testify that Sunny's blood sugar level had plunged from forty-one to twenty at 11 P.M. on the night of her first admission to Newport Hospital.

Q. Is there any question about her being in a hypoglycemic coma at that time?
A. She was comatose and she was hypoglycemic, yes, sir.
[With Sunny at or near the deepest point in her coma, according to Cahill's testimony, I dropped my bombshell.]
Q. At the time you say she was in this hypoglycemic coma, it's a fact, is it not, that she was sitting up in her bed writing on a pad; isn't that right?
A. I was unaware of that, sir.
[Cahill was clearly surprised. I pressed my advantage.]
Q. If I were to tell you that Mrs. von Bulow were sitting up in her bed writing on a pad at the time her blood sugar was 20, you would change your opinion about this coma, wouldn't you doctor?
A. I would—

Gemma tried to give Cahill some breathing space by objecting, but Judge Grande ordered the prosecution witness to answer.

A. Would I change my opinion of the coma? She wasn't comatose if she was sitting up on the bed writing on a pad.

Exactly. I next had Cahill read the nurse's notes on Sunny's condition from 10 P.M. to 1 A.M.
Cahill tried to put the best face on things by picking up on the fact that the nurse had indicated that Sunny was still groggy.

Q. Will you grant me this, that if she was sitting up in bed writing on a pad, she was out of the coma, you'll grant me that, won't you?
A. By definition, yes, but she was still delirious; semicomatose would be the best description.

I stated what I thought to be obvious—that Cahill was simply unaware of the fact that Sunny had emerged from the coma.

Q. Doctor, you thought that she was in a coma for 24 hours until I just pointed it out?
A. I never said that, sir.

I pressed Cahill again. This time, he appealed to the judge.

A. Your honor, can I ask the court where I state she was in a coma for 24 hours?
JUDGE GRANDE: Doctor, you can ask me if we can have a 15-minute recess, and I'll say yes.
CAHILL: I don't remember having made that comment.

Prosecutor Gemma made an effort to patch things up with a few friendly questions to Cahill after I had finished, but the damage was done.

Cahill was followed to the stand by Dr. Robert Bradley, a colleague at the Joselyn Research Institute. Bradley seemed to provide all the assurance that Cahill was lacking by testifying that he was "100 percent certain" that insulin was the cause of the first coma and "99 percent" certain that insulin caused the second coma. Bradley held his ground on cross-examination. But it didn't matter. His "100 percent" gambit sounded ludicrous.

Still, I was very happy with the progress of the case. Dr. Gailitis, the Newport physician who had treated Sunny, had testified that her first coma had nothing to do with insulin. He had also accused the prosecution of withholding this information from the defense. And the state's chief medical witness had performed miserably on the stand.

If any group was unhappy—besides the prosecution—it was the media. A trial that was supposed to have been a tabloid editor's dream was starting to turn into a course on endocrinology, just as I'd hoped it would. But now the focus of the trial shifted to something far more to the media's liking. It was time to fight the Battle of Alexandra Isles.

10

DIVINE PROVIDENCE

THE PROSECUTION desperately needed Alexandra Isles.

Isles, of course, had given damaging testimony against Claus at the first trial. Jurors said her testimony was an important factor in their decision to find von Bulow guilty. Now she was more crucial than ever, to supply a motive for the alleged attempted murder and shore up the state's faltering case.

But Claus' ex-lover was nowhere to be found, and she relayed word through various intermediaries that she had no intention of repeating her performance in a second trial. According to her lawyer, she had left the country and would not return to testify. Rumor had her hiding out in Ireland, where her mother lived. In Rhode Island, the prosecutors announced the state had launched an international hunt for their elusive soap opera star.

If Isles failed to turn up, Mark DeSisto and Henry Gemma wanted Judge Grande to allow them to read the jury her original testimony, or show the videotape of her appearance in the first trial. But in order to convince Grande to do so, they would have to establish that the state had spared no effort to find her and bring her back to Rhode Island.

Naturally, I objected. I pointed out that Isles had not been cross-examined at the first trial. Presenting that testimony at the retrial, I argued, would give the prosecution an unfair advantage. (Of course, Claus's defense had passed up the chance to question Isles of its own volition. But now, I hoped Claus's crazy decision to be a "gentleman" and spare his beloved the pain of cross-examination might be turned to our advantage.)

The videotape of Isles's testimony was something to behold.

The cameraman, evidently swept away by this tale of money, romance, and infidelity, kept cutting back and forth, from shots of Isles to shots of von Bulow. It looked like one of Isles's cheesier "Dark Shadows" episodes, and I knew the judge would not permit it to be played before the jury. The quality of the videotape reduced the prosecution to requesting that just the audio portion be played.

I still objected and followed up with an attack on the state's efforts to find Isles, which I said were slipshod and halfhearted. My campaign was utterly successful. It almost turned out to be a major mistake.

John Sheehan had argued all along that I should permit the prosecution to read Isles's testimony into the record. This idea was appealing—there was no way the droning monotone of a middle-aged court reporter could possibly match the actual appearance of the beautiful, mysterious Alexandra Isles. And once the reading took place, there was no way the prosecution could produce Alexandra herself, if the actress chose to resurface.

"We don't know what else she might say if she shows up," John added.

That was true. The danger with a girlfriend is that she could say almost anything. If Alexandra decided, on a whim, to testify that Claus promised to inject Sunny with insulin and leave her on the bathroom floor until her temperature dropped to eighty-six degrees, the jurors might well believe her. They'd have no trouble accepting that Claus shared intimate secrets with his lover, and they would not expect the pillow talk to have outside corroboration. A credible performance by Isles could be highly damaging.

John was not the only member of the defense team with thoughts about Alexandra Isles.

"She will return," Claus predicted. "She will make the most dramatic entrance possible." As it turned out, Claus knew Isles better than any of us.

Rhode Island lacked subpoena power outside the United States, and there was no way Isles could be compelled to return. She would have to come back voluntarily, a possibility that appeared more likely as the trial wore on.

Even in absentia, Isles was the star of the trial as far as the press was concerned. The *Providence Journal* quoted state police Lieutenant John Reise, the officer in charge of the von Bulow investigation, as saying Claus had written letters threatening his ex-lover, which might have discouraged her from testifying. Claus denied the charge, and no letters were ever produced. Von Bulow was also rumored to have paid Isles to stay away from the trial—a charge that was totally false.

Theater critic John Simon, an ex-boyfriend of Isles's, told the *Journal* and the *New York Post* that he had recently been in contact with our missing witness. Simon was quoted as saying that Alexandra feared that I might try to portray her as a "loose woman" if she returned to the stand. I liked this story just fine and was happy that copies of the *Post* article were given to reporters covering the trial.

"If Simon can get in contact with her, so can the prosecution," I said just prior to a hearing Judge Grande convened on the extent of prosecution efforts to track Isles down.

I hauled the state attorney general, Arlene Violet, into court to explain why Rhode Island had failed to ask federal law enforcement agencies like the FBI for help in finding Isles. The state's efforts really had been pretty pathetic. Judge Grande had agreed to subpoena Isles to testify two months before the trial began, but the state simply left the subpoena with a doorman of the Manhattan apartment building where, as I pointed out to the court, Isles no longer lived.

I also got in contact with a former FBI official named Tom Biamonte, who I knew from my days as a federal prosecutor. Biamonte had served in Europe for the FBI and knew the ins and outs of dealing with foreign police departments. (Ironically, Tom had been an FBI nemesis of mine during my investigation of Joseph Stabile, the corrupt FBI agent I had investigated as a federal prosecutor. Tom became a believer in me, however, when Stabile pleaded guilty.) I put Tom on Isles's trail, and he quickly came up with several likely addresses for the missing witness. At that point, I stopped his search. After all, if we actually did find her, she might come back, which was the last thing I wanted.

Biamonte testified for us at the hearing, and he was a terrific witness. He explained how the state should have been able to get a fix on Isles's probable whereabouts by taking a few elementary steps such as phoning the Dublin police—which is exactly what Tom had done. A day later, I won what was thought to be the most significant legal victory of the trial. Judge Grande ruled that Claus's "profound constitutional right" to confront and cross-examine Isles outweighed the state's wish to present her uncontested testimony from the first trial. While it was true the state had no power to compel Isles to return to the United States, Grande ruled that Rhode Island should have been more diligent in its efforts to track her down and ask her to return voluntarily.

Grande's ruling had but one tiny loophole. She gave the state three more days to find Isles and told me to be ready to go forward with von Bulow's defense when the trial resumed following the long Memorial Day weekend.

I left Providence in a great frame of mind. Everything seemed to be going well, inside and outside the courtroom. I felt we'd done a good job, overall, in reducing the impact of the prosecution witnesses. At one point, the *Boston Globe* published a comparison of the testimony at the first and second trials. The newspaper concluded that while the witnesses gave essentially the same testimony, they were blocked from adding "embellishments" that often stick in the minds of jurors.

One such "embellishment" came from Maria Schrallhammer. At the first trial, the maid had testified that years ago she had seen Claus give Sunny vitamin shots with a hypodermic needle. We stopped her from saying it at the second trial. And Dr. Richard Stock, Sunny's personal physician, was prevented from testifying that he believed her first coma was caused by insulin, as he had at the first trial.

"Puccio has used objections as often as diners use knives and forks, and at times it seems the lawyers at the defense table are in a race to see who can lodge an objection to prosecution testimony first," a reporter covering the trial wrote.

Practically all of these developments spelled boredom for a hungry press. "We probably put five million people to sleep last week," complained a Providence TV reporter. He was referring to complicated medical testimony that included what I thought to be a sparkling cross-examination of Dr. Cahill.

Some journalist clutched at straws: "Several old high society friends of [Claus and Sunny] are listed on the defense witness list and they could add some zip to the trial."

Fat chance.

Claus told me he had lunched with a British journalist who complained about the deadliness of the testimony.

"This is so boring," she told Claus. "I wish I'd married somebody rich so I didn't have to sit here."

"Well, that's exactly what I did, and that's the only reason I got to sit here," von Bulow replied.

Another victory involved the lovely Andrea Reynolds. I realized I'd finally neutralized her for good when I read in *Time* magazine that she was comparing me to Dracula. "The jury likes Gemma and DeSisto," she volunteered. "They don't like Puccio. They draw away from him when he approaches the jury box. You can tell by their body language."

All in all, I felt pretty confident. But as I was preparing to leave for a few days of well-deserved rest in New York, I noticed that Claus appeared dejected.

"What are you so down about?" I asked.

"I know my Isles," he replied.

"What do you mean?" I countered.

"She'll be here. I know it," he predicted.

"You've got to be kidding!" I said.

"No. The trial is building to a dramatic climax. She'll be here."

I didn't pay any attention to him. I spent a great weekend in New York. I went to Central Park on Monday morning, Memorial Day. It was a day of brilliant sunshine and comfortable temperatures. I returned to my Brooklyn apartment happy and relaxed, only to be confronted by a blinking light on the telephone answering machine. I had always hated these things with a passion, but I had broken down and purchased one during the trial. I pushed the button for my messages, and the tape went on and on. It seemed like every reporter in the Western Hemisphere was looking for me. "Urgent . . . Call me . . . Urgent . . . Call me."

I switched on the TV. My timing was perfect. There, on the screen, was Logan Airport in Boston, mobbed with reporters. The camera panned to a plane and followed a woman as she got off. There to greet her were my two good friend and colleagues, Henry Gemma and Mark DeSisto. They ushered Alexandra Isles into a car and sped away. As Claus had predicted, the thirty-nine-year-old Manhattan socialite had made a dramatic reappearance. She had arrived only a day before Judge Grande's deadline was to expire—not exactly a photo finish but close enough to make headlines worldwide.

Oh boy, I thought to myself. I packed my bags, and rushed back to Rhode Island to figure out what the hell I was going to do. I got a call from the prosecutors shortly after I arrived in my hotel room. They announced the obvious: Alexandra Isles had returned to testify.

Our strategy session in my suite that night was not exactly the height of gaiety. There would be no nightclubbing for Claus. He was stretched out on my bed in a deep, dark funk.

The first crucial decision I had to make was whether to talk to Isles in advance. Through her lawyer, I was invited to interview the actress before she testified on Tuesday morning. The offer was made in the name of even-handedness: Alexandra would make herself available to both the prosecution and the defense.

Now, if I were teaching trial practice in a law school, I would write TAKE THE INTERVIEW! in big, bold letters on the blackboard. It's almost always to the advantage of the defense to be able to interview a prosecution witness. But I let instinct take over at this crucial juncture and turned down the offer. An interview, I figured, cuts two ways. Isles and her lawyers could learn a great deal about defense strategy through the kind of questions I would ask. I also knew that Isles had expressed concern about how she'd be treated in my cross-examination. I wanted her to remain as nervous as possible. If her imagination took flight about how fearsome I might be, so much the better. As a further volley in my psychological warfare, I tried to keep her off balance by initially signaling that I would be happy to talk with her, and then postponing a meeting.

I also had to develop a strategy for the cross-examination. It was clear to me that while Isles may indeed have wanted to help Clause at the first trial, she was now out to kill him. I intended to portray Isles as a woman motivated by vindictiveness and jealousy—the kind of person who would send love letters and photos of herself and her lover to the lover's wife at Christmastime.

As I feared, Isles had come up with some new and damaging memories since her first appearance on the witness stand. The prosecutors informed us she now recalled a telephone conversation she had with Claus shortly after the first coma. Isles said Claus told her that he had a long argument with Sunny on the night before Sunny was stricken. Claus told her Sunny drank heavily and had taken a sedative (Seconal) before going to sleep. The next day, when Sunny lay in bed unconscious, Claus told Isles, he "watched her and watched her. And finally when she was on the point of dying, he said that he couldn't go through with it, and he called and saved her life."

This neatly supported Maria's account of Claus's behavior during the first coma and hardly portrayed Claus as the Husband of the Year. Nevertheless, her story was consistent with the defense contention that insulin played no part in the coma. I was pleased with the part about Sunny's consumption of drugs and alcohol before her collapse. Isles's testimony also suggested that Claus ultimately did the right thing by phoning for help.

She also had additional recollections about the runaround she was getting from Claus. She told of discovering that a Manhattan apartment where Claus was supposedly living apart from Sunny had no phone. But when she dialed the Fifth Avenue apartment, Isles said, a maid informed her that Mr. von Bulow would be home that night. That was okay with me, too. Once again, Isles had Claus looking like a jerk. But the anecdote underscored her possible motive for wanting to hurt her ex-lover on the witness stand.

I had two pieces of ammunition unavailable to the defense at the first trial. The first was an interview Isles gave to a *New York Post* gossip columnist in which she said Claus wanted her as a mistress. This was a far cry from the wildly romantic relationship Isles claimed to have had with Claus. She liked to describe herself as a woman blinded by love, but she certainly didn't sound that way in the *Post*. I also had a copy of a letter she had written to Claus following his conviction in which she begged von Bulow to continue their relationship.

There was an air of glamour about Isles at the first trial, but this time she came on like the girl next door. She wore no makeup and a simple skirt and blouse. Her thick dark hair was primly pulled back.

Once again, Isles recounted, in a soft, wounded tone, her version of the events that led up to Sunny's coma: Her urgent discussions of marriage with Claus before Sunny's first and second comas and, of course, the telephone conversation in which Claus supposedly told her he watched Sunny reach the brink of death before deciding to save her. It provided the prosecution with the motive they desperately needed: Claus, desperate to keep her love, had attempted to kill his wife.

Nobody denied the basics of Isles's story—that she and Claus had had an affair that von Bulow was eager to keep secret from his wife. It was my job, however, to make the jury doubt that the affair was as intense and romantic as Isles claimed. Basically, I wanted the jury to believe that Claus had been having a relatively meaningless fling with Alexandra, and that he had no intention of leaving Sunny for her. Not the greatest guy in the world, granted. But a man with no motive to do away with his wife.

I went right at her on cross-examination by reading a quote attributed to her in the *Post* article.

" 'I believe Claus loved me, to whatever extent he is able to love. Claus would've wanted me to be his mistress, to have paid my rent and bought my clothes and taken care of all my bills, but it never happened. You see, I have a trust fund from my grandmother.' "

She then ducked my question about the accuracy of the quote.

"I don't recall saying any of that," she testified. The answer was not only evasive, it was implausible. It hardly seemed likely that the *Post* reporter had invented a trust fund from her grandmother.

I switched gears by asking Isles to admit the obvious: She had pressured Claus to tell Sunny about the relationship to pave the way for their marriage. She danced around the question by saying that confronting Sunny with the truth was not of much importance to her. I now moved into a line of questioning that I hoped would do some real damage.

Q. Well, there came a time in early December [1980], did there not, when you had some items delivered to the apartment occupied by Mr. and Mrs. von Bulow at 960 Fifth Avenue, is that right?
A. That's correct.
Q. And among these items that you had delivered were gifts that Mr. von Bulow had given you, is that right?
A. Uh-hum.
Q. And love letters, isn't that right?
A. I don't know about that. I remember there being—it was a picture of him and I think some other pictures; letters, I don't know.
Q. But in any event, these items you had delivered to Mr. von Bulow's apartment had something to do with the relationship between the two of you, isn't that right?
A. Yes.

I came straight to the point, bluntly asking Isles if she believed delivering these items to the Fifth Avenue apartment would reveal her relationship with Claus to Sunny.

"I didn't believe it and that's not why I returned those things. I believe that in a house like that where there are many servants, where I had dropped things off before, it would be put into his room and she wouldn't be aware of it."

"You know, do you not, that Mrs. von Bulow was hospitalized on the evening that you delivered these presents, isn't that right?"

A. I didn't know that.

Q. And did you know, in fact, that she was hospitalized because she had ingested an incredible quantity of aspirin?

After an objection from the prosecution that was overruled, Isles answered: "I know that she did that and that happened. That was in the letter Claus sent to me saying she had a concussion."

I followed that up by pointing out that Isles delivered Christmas presents to Claus at 960 Fifth Avenue on December 19, less than three weeks after Sunny's suicide attempt.

Q. And you delivered these presents knowing full well that these presents would come to Mrs. von Bulow's attention and have an adverse effect on her emotionally, isn't that correct?
A. No.

I thought Isles was weakening. She was adamant in denying that she was trying to reveal their relationship to Sunny. She also seemed to be trying to create the impression that there was something almost casual or routine about these deliveries. I decided to zero in.

Q. But also, it's a very serious thing, isn't it, for a girlfriend to deliver presents to the home of a man who's still married. Isn't that something that's serious to you?
A. It wasn't my intention that she would see them or be hurt.
Q. But you know it could have had that effect, isn't that correct?
A. I didn't think about it because I imagined the way the apartment was and that things wouldn't—that she was not a housewife that would pick things up at the front door.

I didn't believe for a moment that the jury would buy this lame explanation. It was time to move on. I asked Isles about her letter to Claus after the first trial.

Q. You said you wanted to continue the relationship with him, isn't that right?

A. Were those my words?

Q. Something to that effect—you wanted to be with him, you wanted to spend time with him, you were jealous of other people who were spending time with him. Isn't that right?

A. Perhaps.

Q. As a matter of fact, he didn't want to continue the relationship with you after that trial, isn't that correct?

A. I don't blame him.

Q. As a matter of fact, he didn't want to continue the relationship after the last trial even though you did, isn't that correct?

A. I didn't really want to either.

Q. But you said in the letter you wanted to, didn't you?

A. Yes. Part of me wrote that letter.

Q. You didn't really mean it when you said it in the letter, is that what you're saying now?

A. No, that's what you're saying.

Q. Well, you're saying that you wrote a letter saying that you wanted a continuance—

A. Have you ever been in love? I doubt it but you do some crazy things.

With that rather personal exchange, I thought it time to end the cross-examination. Overall, I thought I had greatly minimized the impact of Isles's dramatic reappearance. I felt the jury would believe that only a callous and vindictive woman would send Christmas presents and mementos of an adulterous affair to the home of Sunny von Bulow. And I think I also established that her actions may very well have contributed to Sunny's aspirin overdose.

Isles was one of two "motive" witnesses for the state. The other was G. Morris Gurley, a family financial adviser who had testified at the first trial about what Claus could expect to collect in the event of Sunny's death. The defense received another boost when Judge Grande ruled that Gurley would not be permitted to testify. She accepted my argument that the state's case had failed to establish any factual basis for the belief that Claus may have been motivated by money.

I wasn't able, of course, to wipe all suspicions about money from the jurors' minds. In his opening statement to the jury, Mark DeSisto had suggested Sunny's fortune was the motive for Claus's alleged crime. Moreover, virtually all of the jurors had read something about the first trial, where the money motive came up repeatedly. (All but one of our jurors knew von Bulow had been convicted the first time around.)

Still, the specifics of Gurley's testimony would have been damaging to Claus. He was prepared to say that only two weeks before she slipped into her first coma, Sunny had signed a new will granting Claus a $14 million inheritance in the event of her death. This fact, combined with a prenuptial agreement that cut Claus off from Sunny's fortune in the event of a divorce, might have been very persuasive—particularly if the jurors bought Alexandra Isles's contention that Claus wanted to leave Sunny and marry her. And if permitted, Gurley would have testified that Claus listed no income on his tax forms between 1974 and 1979. (The most that Claus reported earning between 1967 and 1979 was $33,000.)

Finally, it was our turn at bat.

In Rhode Island, the defense has an option. It can deliver an opening statement at the beginning of the trial, or at the beginning of its own case. I decided to delay my opening to guard against the possibility that the prosecution might present some surprises. Now it was time for me to lay out the defense theory of the case. I don't believe in putting the victim on trial as a defense tactic. I wanted to paint Sunny as somebody who had lost her way in life, as indeed she had. I portrayed her as a woman who was beset by a host of personal problems, not the least of which was Claus's affair with Alexandra Isles. I said her aspirin overdose, three weeks before the second coma, was a suicide attempt.

Most important of all, I assured the jurors the defense would show that insulin was not the cause of either coma. This was a criminal trial without a crime.

My first witness was Dr. Leo Dal Cortivo, the chief toxicologist for the Suffolk County, New York, medical examiner's office. He testified that Sunny had taken a "massive overdose" of aspirin on December 1. He also had something to say about the alleged murder weapon—the insulin-encrusted needle found in the black bag. Dal Cortivo testified that if the needle had been used for such an injection, it would have been wiped clean when it was withdrawn from the skin. No insulin should have been found on the outside of the needle.

Dal Cortivo was followed to the stand by Dr. Kurt Dubowski, a toxicologist at the University of Oklahoma. Dubowski testified that his analysis of Sunny's hospital records showed that she had taken a large quantity of aspirin, barbiturates, and alcohol prior to her second coma. These three substances, alone or in combination, could have raised Sunny's insulin level.

My British expert, Dr. Vincent Marks, followed them to the stand and testified that neither coma was insulin-induced. The endocrinologist said the first coma was caused by a cutoff of oxygen to the brain, as Dr. Gailitis had suggested, and that the second coma was caused by hypothermia induced by alcohol.

Then came our much-courted witness, Dr. Arthur Rubenstein, chairman of the Department of Medicine at the University of Chicago. Rubenstein testified that laboratory tests showing insulin on the needle in the black bag and a high insulin level in Sunny's body following the second coma were meaningless.

Rubenstein spoke with great authority. He was instrumental in developing the so-called C-Peptide test used to measure Sunny's insulin level. This was the famous 216 figure that Dr. Cahill had emphasized in the first trial but tried to downplay in his second testimony.

The insulin level had been tested three times by a national testing laboratory, twice in Boston and once in California. Each test reached wildly different results. The lab in Boston turned the job over to the lab in California because it had been unable to reconcile the conflicting results of its two tests, which suggested Sunny's insulin level was either an extremely low .8 or an astronomically high 350.

The California lab came up with the 216 figure used by the

prosecution. But Rubenstein testified that the California test was flawed by the fact that it had only been run once. Running the test twice, and obtaining roughly the same result on both tests, would be a powerful evidence of accuracy. Running it once, he said, left only a "hope" that the results were valid.

"I personally have no confidence in any of these values," he concluded.

Next I questioned Rubenstein about the test that had found a high insulin level on the needle that the state claimed was the weapon Claus used to try to kill his wife. Washings from the needle were tested for the presence of insulin and two drugs found in the black bag—amobarbital and Valium. The lab ran three tests on the washings and came out with values of 2,700, 3,400, and 4,500 for insulin. But Rubenstein testified that the numbers should have been roughly equal to put any faith in the accuracy of the test.

He again concluded that the test results were meaningless.

Rubenstein was followed to the stand by Dr. Daniel Furst, an associate professor of medicine at the University of Iowa. Furst was an expert on aspirin, and I had called him to buttress my contention that Sunny had attempted suicide at the beginning of December.

The order in which I presented my witnesses was not to my liking, but there was little I could do about it. I had chosen to go with top authorities in each field, rather than "professional" experts at my beck and call. As a result, the order of appearance was dictated by their availability rather than a logical progression. I intended to make up for any confusion this might cause in the minds of the jurors in my final argument.

Based on the aspirin level in Sunny's blood, Furst estimated that she had swallowed sixty-five tablets, which he described as an "incredible overdose."

The cross-examination of the medical witnesses was largely ineffective. The prosecutors were understandably weighed down and confused by the complexity of the testimony. This was evident when Henry Gemma tried to cross-examine Furst by referring to a formula used by Dr. Kurt Dubowski, the defense toxicologist, to estimate the amount of aspirin in Sunny's blood. I permitted Gemma to ask a few questions about the Dubowski formula before stepping in.

PUCCIO: Your Honor, I have an objection to this examination. I also think that there is some confusion. Mr. Gemma is talking about a different witness. He is talking about Dr. Dal Cortivo, not Dr. Dubowski. In any event, we object to this kind of examination.

JUDGE GRANDE: Mr. Gemma?

GEMMA: Doctor, when I asked . . .

JUDGE GRANDE: Are you prepared to respond to what Mr. Puccio said?

GEMMA: Your Honor, I do believe I was incorrect. It was Dr. Dal Cortivo who testified, not Dr. Dubowski, to this fact, yes, so I would rephrase the question and use Dr. Dal Cortivo's name in place of Dr. Dubowski.

My next witness was Dr. Harry Lebovitz, professor of medicine at the Downstate Medical Center in Brooklyn. A noted endocrinologist in his own right, Harry had already done von Bulow a great service by analyzing Sunny's medical records and leading us to other experts who greatly strengthened our case.

Harry testified that neither coma was caused by insulin. The first coma, he said, was caused by the cutoff of oxygen to Sunny's brain. The second coma was induced by "severe hypothermia, possibly aggravated by barbiturates and alcohol."

Next up after Harry was another endocrinologist, Dr. Ralph DeFronzo, an associate professor of medicine at Yale. I had asked Harry to find us an "antidote" to the tall, patrician Dr. Cahill of Harvard. And he came up with DeFronzo, a short, unassuming Italian from Yale. The Yale man proved to be one of our most important witnesses.

DeFronzo's specialty was "glucose metabolism," or the rate at which sugar in the bloodstream is absorbed by various tissues in the body. DeFronzo was the codeveloper of the test used to measure the rate of glucose consumption.

During Sunny's hospitalization following her second coma,

she was given large doses of glucose in order to raise her blood sugar level. But DeFronzo said that a large amount of the glucose was not absorbed by her tissues. His eye-glazing medical testimony was very important to the defense. He calculated Sunny's rate of glucose consumption at "6.02 milligrams per kilograms of body weight per hour." That was slow, said De-Fronzo. If Sunny's insulin level was 216, as the prosecution claimed, her rate of glucose consumption should have been at least twice that high.

Using an entirely different approach from the one adopted by Dr. Rubenstein, DeFronzo was able to cast serious doubt on the assertion that Sunny's second coma was caused by an insulin injection. He concluded that it was triggered by severe hypothermia and drugs, including alcohol and barbiturates.

I next asked DeFronzo to analyze Sunny's first coma.

Q. And doctor, did you notice that shortly after Mrs. von Bulow entered the hospital, she started to wake up?
A. Yes. I think this is extremely important, that her glucose value [blood sugar level] at the time she was starting to wake up dropped from 41 to 21 milligrams per deciliter. It would be incredible if, while this lady's glucose value is dropping, that she could be waking from a hypoglycemic coma; that would defy all medical laws. If hypoglycemia [low blood sugar] is responsible for the coma, while the glucose value [blood sugar level] is getting even lower, there is no way she can be waking up.

Again, DeFronzo had taken a different approach from my other medical experts and convincingly argued that Sunny's first coma could not have been insulin-induced.

He calculated Sunny's rate of glucose consumption for the first coma, which was near normal. Again, her rate of glucose consumption should have been much higher if she had received an insulin injection. DeFronzo concluded that Sunny's first coma was caused by a cutoff in oxygen to her brain.

I was elated with DeFronzo's testimony, even though it received hardly any mention in the press. This was understandable, given the complexity of the medical testimony. Still, if I was right in believing that trial reporters reacted much like jurors, I'd have to work hard in my final argument. I felt we'd produced more than enough evidence to win an acquittal. The final challenge was to set it all out for the jurors, so they'd see it as clearly as I did.

The summation is the most important part of the trial for a defense lawyer. Many cases are won and lost in summation. If you're a prosecutor with videotapes of the defendant committing the crime, fingerprints, and a signed confession, you probably can get away with a lackluster summation. But a defense lawyer has no such luxury. If he gives a bad summation, he's going to lose.

Some lawyers think you have to relentlessly hammer your message into the minds of the jurors on a daily basis. That way, the theory goes, by the end of the trial the jury will be brainwashed into seeing things from your point of view. There's another school of thought that believes in carefully getting all the points you want to make into the trial record, and then pulling it all together in a summation, which fully unfolds the defense view of the case for the first time.

My approach falls between these two extremes, but I tend to emphasize the importance of the summation. Jurors aren't always paying attention to the testimony of witnesses, and no one witness tells the whole story. All trials are disrupted by delays, postponements, and legal arguments that are heard outside the presence of the jury. The trial record is like a jigsaw puzzle. Somebody has to put all the pieces together, and a defense lawyer who does it skillfully has taken a big step toward winning the case for his client.

Cases are decided on not just evidence but also on the inferences one draws from the evidence. A persuasive advocate shows the jurors inferences they might not have drawn themselves. The jurors knew that Sunny von Bulow emerged from her first coma only a few hours after entering the hospital, and they knew that fact was a major embarrassment for the prosecution's key medical witness. But did they realize that Sunny's quick recovery also implied the maid may have greatly exaggerated the severity of Sunny's condition? It was my job to make sure jurors did think about inferences like these.

Preparation for the summation is ongoing throughout the trial. You don't suddenly sit down and read the trial record at the end of the case, as if you're cramming for a final exam. You reread the trial transcripts periodically to keep fresh in your mind what has been said, and by whom. And you constantly think summation—how will this or that fact or witness "play" in your final argument. I also keep a summation folder. Each time I get an idea about summation during the trial, I scribble it down on a scrap of paper and toss it into a folder. At the end of the von Bulow defense, I found some good ideas in the small mountain of scrap paper I had amassed.

I don't prepare an outline or a narrative. I just make up a list of key points I want to make, and I may shuffle them back and forth depending on the order I want to present them. I also bring my notes to the podium with me when I address a jury, but to tell the truth, I hardly ever use them. They are with me more as a crutch or security blanket than anything else.

There is always a central theme or themes that I return to again and again and again. In von Bulow, the theme was very simple: no insulin injection. I began with a brief, friendly introduction about their role as jurors and described the charges against Claus as "monstrous" and "incredible." I then quickly moved to the heart of the case.

"I'm asking you to keep your eye on the ball, and the ball here is insulin injections."

I then delivered a brisk summary of the highlights of the testimony from my medical experts. It's crucial to keep in mind that complex testimony has to be reduced to terms a jury of lay people can easily understand. And it has to be done without patronizing them.

I did this by lining up my endocrinologists: Vincent Marks, Harry Lebovitz, and Ralph DeFronzo and pointing out the similarities in their opinions. The first coma was caused by hypoxia—the cutting off of oxygen to Sunny's brain. The second coma was caused by hypothermia aggravated by drugs and alcohol.

I also enlisted the aid of Dr. Gailitis, who, as I pointed out, testified for the prosecution. Unlike experts who relied on medical records, Gailitis was an eyewitness. "You have the person on the scene, the person with direct knowledge, with the experience, with the background, giving you a photograph of what took place in that room on that day, and what did he say was the cause of the coma that happened before his very eyes? Hypoxia."

I weaved in the testimony of the defense experts with attacks on the prosecution experts: Dr. Cahill and his colleague from the Joselyn Research Institute, Robert Bradley. In doing so, I zeroed in on Cahill's failure to recognize Sunny had quickly emerged from her first coma.

I pointed to DeFronzo's testimony that it would defy "all medical laws" to have Sunny awakening from a "hypoglycemic coma" (one caused by low blood sugar) at the very time her blood sugar level was at its lowest point.

"George Cahill didn't know she was waking up; Dr. De-Fronzo did," I said. It was thus with all my experts. They were smarter, quicker, on top of all the facts.

I reminded the jurors of Cahill's weak and waffling performance during my cross-examination and then turned to Dr. Bradley, who had been ludicrously unshakeable.

"It's quite embarrassing for an expert of [Cahill's] stature not to notice that Mrs. von Bulow was up and writing on a pad, so, what do you do when your leading expert is embarrassed? Well, one of the things that you do is call back to the Joselyn Institute, see who's on the bench, and say, 'Send in Bradley. He's Mr. 100 Percent.' "

My voice was sarcastic and I thought I caught a glimmer of a smile in the eyes of some of the jurors. I hoped they agreed with me that Bradley was a backup quarterback trying to make up for the starter's poor play by expressing a degree of certainty that simply wasn't justified.

I finished my medical presentation by referring to the testimony of Dr. Arthur Rubenstein, who had effectively cast doubt on the reliability of the lab tests that found insulin on the needle in the black bag and an insulin level of 216 in Sunny's blood-stream. I also forcefully pointed out that the prosecution had run away from a finding that should have supported its case. "Is there any wonder why Cahill and Bradley don't rely on the 216? The 216, I submit to you, and I hope I don't sound a little bit too flip, is a joke. It's a joke to the layman, it's a very, very bad joke to the endocrinologist."

It was time now to switch gears. I had used the phrase "no insulin injection," or variants of it, eighteen times during my discussion of the medical testimony. But I wanted to do more than just knock down the state's insulin theory. I wanted to offer a plausible explanation of what did happen to Sunny.

"Nobody here is accusing Mrs. von Bulow of being an alcoholic," I said. "That's not necessary, but what we are saying to you is that alcohol is involved in this case." I reminded them of Dr. Stock's admission that Claus had complained of Sunny's drinking during a visit to his office in May 1976, more than three years before her first coma. I asked what motive von Bulow could have "other than the fact that he was concerned about his wife and thought the family doctor of twenty-five years ought to know about it." I then pointed to the use of Valium and barbiturates written by Stock from 1977 to 1979 to show that Sunny had ready access to these drugs.

I then switched to the state's key nonmedical witnesses, Maria Schrallhammer and Alexandra Isles.

I talked about the maid's intense devotion to Sunny and her resentment of Claus as the man who had shattered the "fairy-tale romance" between Sunny and Prince Alfred von Auersperg. I also asked the jury to consider the impact Claus's affair with Alexandra Isles must have had on a woman who regarded Sunny as "the most important person in her life." In particular, I asked them to consider how Maria must have reacted to Isles's cheeky appearance at the Fifth Avenue apartment to deliver Christmas gifts to the man of the house.

I returned to Maria's account of the first coma and asked: "Do you believe the maid was in there, back and forth, shaking Mrs. von Bulow? Mrs. von Bulow was moaning and moaning and Mr. von Bulow was sitting in bed reading a book, do you believe that? There's no doubt that Miss Schrallhammer wants to say something that hurts Mr. von Bulow and she may have good reason in her mind. That doesn't make it a fact."

I next attacked Alexandra Isles, who I described—accurately—as Claus's girlfriend on the side. I reminded them about Claus's phantom apartment, the empty flat without a phone where he was supposedly living apart from Sunny.

"What does that sound like? Doesn't it sound like a man who is stringing someone along, someone who doesn't want to leave his wife, but doesn't want to leave his girlfriend either?"

The juiciest prop in the case was the black bag. I told the jury that Claus and Sunny were sharing the drugs in the black bag. But I zeroed in on the most crucial claim about the black bag: the maid's testimony that she saw a bottle marked INSULIN and needles and syringes in the black bag around Thanksgiving of 1980, about a month before Sunny's second coma.

"If, in fact, she saw a bottle that said 'insulin' and needles and syringes, bells would have gone off, bells would have gone off and the whole world would have known at that very moment." Surely, Maria would have told Sunny of this shocking discovery. "It defies credibility to believe that she wouldn't have gone to Mrs. von Bulow if she thought her husband was trying to do her harm," I said.

I then pointed to the notes taken by the family lawyer, Richard Kuh, and Maria's own testimony on cross-examination that she did not mention insulin to Kuh during her interview with the lawyer a month after Sunny's second coma. "She doesn't say a word about an insulin bottle, she doesn't say a word about syringes, she doesn't say a word about needles. I submit to you, ladies and gentlemen, if she in fact saw those things back on Thanksgiving 1980, that is the very first thing she would have done when she spoke to Mr. Kuh, she would have said: 'This is what I saw.' "

The timing here was crucial. I wanted the jury to remember it was only after the Kuh interview that the family received a laboratory report that indicated a high level of insulin in Sunny's blood.

This, as I pointed out, was "the now famous, incredibly wrong, totally invalid 216."

"That's where the insulin story began. . . . The very next interview of Maria Schrallhammer, she's talking about insulin."

I then talked about the night of December 1, 1980, hours after Alexandra Isles had delivered to Claus and Sunny's apartment a bag filled with mementos of her affair with Claus. I brought up the fact that Sunny had been on a crash diet at that time, and that she was also worried about her daughter, who had moved to Europe following her marriage.

"She's in the middle of what her doctor described as semistarvation crash diet, her daughter has gotten married and left the country, her husband is in love with another woman, and that woman delivers to her apartment a shopping bag full of mementos of that love affair in a fit of pique. Can you blame her? Can you blame her for what she did that evening? Can you blame her for taking sixty-five aspirin tablets?"

I wanted the jurors to realize that we were not blaming Sunny for the tragedy that befell her. But I also wanted them to see how easy it would have been for Claus to ignore his wife's plight. Instead, he dialed 911 and rushed to Maria's nearby apartment to get her help.

"If he wanted her to die, this was the golden opportunity," I said.

The prosecution never did deal adequately with the aspirin episode. Why would Claus rush her to the hospital following a serious aspirin overdose and then try to kill her with an insulin injection three weeks later? It was a hole in the state's case that "you can drive a two-ton Mack truck through," I told the jury.

I wound up my summation by moving point by point through some of the other weaknesses in the state's case. I asked the jurors if they believed von Bulow would have left the black bag sitting around Clarendon Court if it actually contained the "murder weapon." And I reminded them that if the needle had been used as the "murder weapon," it should have been wiped clean by Sunny's skin—not encrusted with insulin. I also reminded them that the test that identified insulin on the needle was as flawed as the "216" test.

I ended with a simple plea.

"We ask for justice and we are confident that we will get justice at your hands. Thank you."

I had spoken for about two hours and fifteen minutes. The trial resumed with the prosecution's closing argument. That was another one of the quirks in Rhode Island law. Normally, the defense gets the last word and the luxury of responding to whatever the prosecution says in its closing argument. In this case, it didn't make any difference. I thought Mark DeSisto followed me with a strong and forceful summary of the state's case, but there were just too many holes and weaknesses in the prosecution's presentation.

Judge Grande sent the jury out to deliberate at 11:33 A.M. on Friday, June 7, 1985. During about four hours of deliberation that day, they asked for a rereading of medical testimony, which I took to be a favorable sign. My job was done. There was nothing more to do except wait around Providence and act confident with the press, which is exactly what I did.

The deliberations continued through the weekend. One of the two alternate jurors, who were discharged when deliberations began, showed up on a New York TV station. She had doubts about Maria Schrallhammer's testimony. She wondered aloud why the maid hadn't questioned Mr. or Mrs. von Bulow about the black bag. The juror also dismissed Alexandra Isles "as an actress."

"He saved his wife. He still cared for her. There was still feeling there," she said of Claus.

The jury sent Judge Grande a note on Sunday reporting that it was making "substantial progress" toward a verdict.

"To tell you the truth, I wouldn't be surprised if they've already reached a verdict and want to sleep on it," I told a *Washington Post* reporter. "Of course, when they're still out next week, you can remind me I said that."

It turned out to be one of my better predictions. On Monday morning, June 10, 1985, some two months after the trial had begun, the jury reached a verdict. We received word in the little courthouse room where we'd spent our lunch hours during the trial. I was reasonably confident of victory, but it was still a moment of drama and tension.

Claus was at his most elegant in a custom-made blue-gray suit. We quietly walked into the courtroom together and sat down at the defense table for the last time. The jurors walked slowly past us on the way to the jury box. There's an old, but very fallible, courthouse rule that if the verdict is guilty, none of the jurors will look the defendant in the eye. Not one of them cast even a glance in our direction.

The doors to the courtroom were locked and Judge Grande ordered the court clerk to read the charges to the jury foreman, a social worker named Robert Rocchio. What had the jury decided on the charge that the defendant on December 27, 1979, committed the crime of assault with intent to murder?

"Not guilty," Rocchio replied.

Claus had shut his eyes and bowed his head.

And what did jury say to the second charge of attempted murder on December, 21, 1980?

"Not guilty."

There were tears in Claus's eyes when he turned to shake hands with me and John Sheehan. I heard applause and muffled cheers among the spectators. I also heard the sound of a woman weeping a few feet behind me. It was Andrea Reynolds, who had finally made it into the courtroom. She rushed up to Claus and kissed him on the cheek.

"May I come with you, darling?" she asked.

"My daughter comes first," Claus responded.

11

LOST IN NEW HAVEN

IF CLAUS VON BULOW was a shining example of what happens when things go right for a defense lawyer, the Stanley Friedman case provided exhibit A for what can happen to an attorney when things go wrong. It's the one case in which I wasn't able to do anything for my client. Friedman was convicted on every count and sentenced to twelve years in prison. I lost every motion in the case except one, and the motion I won I wish I'd lost—a motion by the prosecution to disqualify me as Friedman's lawyer.

Stanley Friedman was the head of the Bronx Democratic party, and he was one of the most powerful politicians in New York City. A party boss of the old style, he'd never been elected to public office. But he had far more power than most of the people who had. A congressman might make the headlines, but Stanley made the congressmen. Not to mention the judges, city council members, and state legislators.

He was caught in the middle of a huge public corruption scandal, which was gradually destroying the political careers of some of New York's best-known politicians, from Ed Koch to the former Miss America Bess Myerson. Before it was over, the long-running municipal soap opera would spawn dozens of subplots. But Stanley was unfortunately cast from the beginning in one of the star roles—the supposedly crooked pol who sells city contracts for a share of the ill-gotten gains.

The nub of this very complicated case involved the Parking Violations Bureau, the city agency responsible for collecting parking ticket fines. New York, which has far more cars than places to park them, gives out a *lot* of tickets. The PVB, in an early and unfortunate example of "privatization," was farming the work out to private collection agencies.

As the Decade of Greed ground along, the taxpayers of New York were discovering that the PVB was a little graft factory. Collection agencies hired to make motorists with overdue tickets pay up were expected to fork over cash bribes to get this lucrative business from the city. Stanley Friedman, it was charged, had used his considerable political clout to steer a $22.7 million contract for a handheld parking ticket computer to a company that bribed him with a share in its new stock offering.

It was the sort of case that, at an earlier point in my career, I could easily have wound up prosecuting. When I agreed to defend Stanley, I know it must have shocked some people. The lawyer who sent seven crooked congressmen to jail was going to try to keep Bronx boss Stanley Friedman out!

The switch from prosecutor to defense attorney never bothered me because my mission always was the same: to excel as a lawyer. I was not the kind of lawyer who believes his job is simply to fight for the side of righteousness—to put away the bad guys or defend the helpless innocent victim. I've always found that attitude admirable, but a little dangerous. The law is a game of rules, but once you start thinking that God himself wants you to win the case, you're more likely to be tempted to break them.

I didn't think God had an opinion about the Stanley Friedman case, one way or another.

It doesn't come down to me choosing to be a prosecutor and then deciding to investigate crooked politicians. I became a federal prosecutor as a result of a chance interview with the lawyer who was about to become the U.S. attorney in the Eastern District. Thereafter, my role as a corruption fighter evolved gradually, with one case leading to another. The conviction I obtained against Joseph Stabile, the crooked FBI agent, was really a case I would have preferred to duck. Abscam emerged from a low-level investigation into stolen art and securities. You handle every case as it comes, and you do your best.

Defense work is just as serendipitous, if not more so. You don't know who will walk through the door, or what their problem will be. I didn't get up one morning and say, "I want to defend politicians," any more than I made a career decision to prosecute politicians. My decision to represent Friedman flowed naturally from events. It was a big case, an exciting case, a new challenge.

The chain of events that led to Friedman's downfall began in Chicago in 1985, where an FBI informer named Michael Burnett worked for a collection agency that did business in the Windy City and New York. Burnett reported to the Bureau that his boss, Bernard Sandow, was boasting about paying off politicians in both cities.

Burnett tape-recorded a dinner meeting at which Sandow talked bribes with Geoffrey Lindenauer, the deputy director of the New York City Parking Violations Bureau. Subsequently, the FBI confronted Sandow with the evidence against him and turned him into a government informer.

Neither man's evidence took the FBI very far up the New York City political food chain. And Burnett's cover was blown in December, when a magazine published a story about the Chicago end of the investigation, including Burnett's role as informer. Lindenauer, and anyone else involved in the PVB bribery scheme, now knew that they were the targets of a federal probe.

The investigation might have come to a grinding halt had it not been for a bizarre development back in New York. In the early morning hours of January 10, 1986, two police officers in Queens stopped a car that was weaving erratically along the Grand Central Parkway. The driver was Donald Manes, the borough president of Queens. Like Friedman, Manes was a powerful behind-the-scenes power broker. Unlike Stanley, he was well known to the public and was considered a possible future candidate for mayor.

Manes did not look like a future mayor that night. He was semiincoherent, and bleeding badly from a deep cut on his wrist. His explanations of how he got in that condition made no sense at all. The story sent shock waves through the city. There was speculation that Manes had been slashed by a prostitute. Mayor Koch opined that his portly friend had been driven haywire by a liquid diet. The truth, of course, was that Manes had attempted to commit suicide. He was deep in PVB corruption, and the story out of Chicago had terrified him into believing the FBI was hot on his trail—though in truth the investigators had not even begun to focus on him.

The Manes scandal turned a low-profile behind-the-scenes investigation into the hottest New York City story since the police corruption scandal fifteen years earlier. A turf war immediately broke out between my old friend U.S. attorney Rudy Giuliani, and the Manhattan district attorney, Robert Morgenthau. Both men were understandably eager to seize the leading role in a municipal scandal that was already producing a blizzard of headlines.

The government was soon able to "flip" Lindenauer into a witness for the prosecution. He implicated Manes and Stanley Friedman in a bribery scheme with a company called Citisource—a firm that had obtained a contract to build a handheld computer for PVB traffic agents. The government charged that Friedman and Manes each received a large block of Citisource stock for using their political clout to get Citisource the contract. Lindenauer was also awarded a large block of stock for his efforts.

My law firm, Stroock & Stroock & Lavan, represented Citisource, which needed a lot of representing. The city had canceled the computer contract and filed a civil suit against the firm to get its money back. Because the case already had criminal overtones, one of my law partners asked me to sit in on meetings to discuss strategy in the civil suit.

Stanley Friedman, who had represented Citisource in its dealings with the city, attended these sessions. He was a middle-aged man who looked the part of a cigar-smoking big-city pol. Like most politicians I've known, he was very personable. Unlike many politicians I've known, he was also a very intelligent guy, and not easily excitable. He was not the type of person a prosecutor could panic into a guilty plea. In a case that would have more than its fair share of semihysterical personalities, Stanley was a rock.

At the time, Stanley had not yet been indicted, but the pressure was clearly growing. Eventually, he dropped by my office and asked me to represent him.

I can't say I was surprised to see him. Hadn't *Time* magazine called me one of the top criminal-trial attorneys in the country? I was still on my post–von Bulow high, sure that there was no case so hopeless that it would not succeed under my magic touch.

"I've done a lot of checking on you, and I've been told you're terrific—if you're interested in the case," Stanley said. "I have one question for you: Are you interested?"

I was interested, and that was the whole conversation.

FRIEDMAN, then fifty, was the only child of a Bronx taxi cab driver and his wife. He grew up in the Hunts Point section of the borough and attended public schools. He set off for City College in 1954 with the idea of becoming a dentist. But Friedman switched his major to government because his science class schedule was interfering with basketball practice. After graduating from City College, he went to Brooklyn Law School. It was during law school that Stanley joined the local Democratic club in the Bronx and launched a twenty-five-year political career.

Friedman had the sort of personality that thrives on grass-roots politics. He delivered campaign literature door-to-door and cataloged the complaints and problems of citizens who had no heat, hot water, no job, or a clogged sewer. The same citizens would receive a letter at election time reminding them of the service that had been rendered.

In 1964, the Democratic organization gave Stanley a job: He was named an assistant district attorney in the Bronx at a salary of $5,750. Sixteen months later, he moved into his first real political job as counsel to the majority leader of the city council. From there, Stanley moved through a raft of municipal jobs, building up a network of friends and political allies along the way. He was a legislative lobbyist for former Mayor Abe Beame, and later one of Beame's deputy mayors.

When Ed Koch defeated Beame in 1978, Stanley went to

work for the law firm of Saxe, Bacon & Bolin, the firm where the late Roy Cohn was a partner. During the same year, with Koch's support, Friedman became chairman of the Bronx Democratic organization. From 1978 to 1986, Stanley was a force to be reckoned with in New York City politics.

Friedman was an excellent client. He was bright, well prepared, and a total realist. With some clients, it's necessary to explain carefully the consequences of a certain move. But I never had to explain anything to Stanley. He was deeply involved in his own defense. There was never any talk of a plea bargain or negotiations with the government. Stanley was innocent, and we were going to trial. It was that simple.

Being a realist myself, I immediately began to prepare for Stanley's indictment. In March 1986, Geoffrey Lindenauer, the former PVB official, agreed to cooperate with the government. He pled guilty to getting $410,000 in bribes from various collection agencies for Manes, himself, and others. Lindenauer told federal investigators that Friedman and Manes had been given blocks of stock in Citisource for using their political clout to steer the contract to the company.

Three days after Lindenauer entered the plea, Donald Manes committed suicide by plunging a knife into his chest in the kitchen of his Queens home.

Manes had been a popular, well-liked politician. His death shocked the city. It was also a bad break for Stanley Friedman. At the time, Stanley was not the central figure in the case in terms of day-to-day media blasts. But with Manes's death, Friedman went to the top of the list.

In April 1986, about a month after the Manes's suicide, Giuliani obtained a federal racketeering indictment against Friedman and four other men. They were charged with turning the Parking Violations Bureau into an "enterprise for plunder."

"You're all alone in the spotlight," I told my client.

"Yeah, I know it," Friedman replied.

WHILE THE FRIEDMAN CASE was heating up, I was also representing the head of the city's Health and Hospital Corporation, John

McLaughlin. John, who ran the city's sprawling public health system, was also a lawyer. His legal problem at the time he retained me involved a dispute over his handling of a former client's trust fund. In the summer of 1985, John was indicted on charges of stealing money from the trust fund and forced to resign from his post at HHC. His case was totally unrelated to the municipal corruption probe. But suddenly, as the scandal heated up in early 1986, Manhattan DA Morgenthau began pursuing a new charge: that McLaughlin had accepted a bribe (in the form of cheap stock) from a California consulting company that had gotten an HHC contract. The charge was baloney, but John was instantly, and unfairly, propelled into the role of featured player in the corruption scandal. And I was suddenly the lawyer defending *two* of the scandal heavyweights.

These developments put me squarely in the middle of an ongoing turf war between the legendary Bob Morgenthau and upstart Giuliani. Stanley Friedman was the prize, and I was his lawyer.

The two of them had already waged a pitched battle for Lindenauer's services. Giuliani had obtained a throw-the-book-at-him federal indictment of Lindenauer in February as part of the effort to get the PVB's deputy director to cooperate with the government. On the day Lindenauer was to be arraigned on federal charges, Morgenthau's men slapped Lindenauer with a subpoena to testify before a state grand jury.

The two prosecutors eventually worked out a deal to divide the spoils: Giuliani would prosecute Manes and Morgenthau would prosecute Friedman. Lindenauer would testify against both.

Manes's subsequent suicide again upset the law enforcement apple cart. With only one first prize left, there could be only one real winner. Giuliani and Morgenthau now laid claim to Friedman. Since both men planned to prosecute Stanley, the all-important question was: Who would go first? Obviously, the first prosecutor would get the lion's share of the case, and in the event of a conviction, the second prosecution would be nothing more than a footnote.

I was not a disinterested bystander, however. I was rooting for

Giuliani. If Rudy went first, I knew, he would request an adjournment because he wasn't prepared to go to trial immediately. That was important to me, because I was due in court soon to defend John McLaughlin. I knew it would be a long, difficult trial, and I wanted at least a few weeks' hiatus before Stanley's trial began.

And I wanted to take the federal charges first, because I felt it offered Stanley the best protection. Under the principle of double jeopardy, you can't be tried twice for the same crime. But the United States and New York State were considered two "separate sovereignties" that theoretically could both prosecute. It depended, however, on who prosecuted first. New York had a law that a defendant can't be tried twice on the same *set of facts*. Thus, if we won the federal case, the state case would have been crippled. The reverse wouldn't be true. If Morgenthau went first, Stanley could still face a similar federal prosecution later.

The jurisdictional dispute was finally resolved by Whitman Knapp, the federal judge assigned to Giuliani's Friedman prosecution. Knapp, a seventy-seven-year-old patrician, had been chairman of the famed Knapp Commission, the special panel that had exposed the shocking extent of police corruption in New York City in the 1960s and early 1970s. He had also worked for two of Bob Morgenthau's illustrious predecessors in the Manhattan DA's office: Tom Dewey and Frank Hogan.

I sat through several stormy meetings with Knapp, rooting for Rudy but basically not much more than a spectator. It was the Giuliani and Morgenthau show. Their mutual disdain was obvious. But it was nothing compared to the acrimony between Morgenthau and the judge.

Morgenthau was a giant in law enforcement, one of the greatest federal prosecutors of all time. The son of Henry Morgenthau, FDR's secretary of the treasury, he also had a long and distinguished career as a state prosecutor.

Perhaps for that reason, Knapp seemed eager to take on Morgenthau. His manner was absolutely imperious. I think Knapp could have shown Morgenthau a little more respect and consideration, but he didn't. He was trying to take Morgenthau down a peg, and he didn't do it in the nicest way.

Late one afternoon in June 1986, just before the McLaughlin trial was scheduled to begin, Knapp summoned us to his chambers in the federal courthouse in Foley Square in Manhattan. It was the typical suite for a federal judge. Knapp had a big prison-industries desk and a long, rectangular, government-issue conference table surrounded by chairs with leather seats and brass fittings. Everything in the room was a good knockoff of expensive furniture.

Knapp sat at the head of the table. I sat across from him. Giuliani and Morgenthau took seats opposite each other. Knapp's law clerk, a blond kid who looked a bit like an Ivy League football player, came into the room and handed the judge a stack of papers. The judge then passed around to us copies of a written opinion he had prepared.

"I've reached a decision in this case," Knapp announced, "but I haven't filed it with the court and I haven't signed it. I thought I would give you the opportunity to look it over. Perhaps it will stimulate some discussion, and there won't even be a need to issue this decision."

It was an extraordinary moment. It was as if Knapp had given us the power to read tomorrow's newspaper. The only thing I'd ever seen like it was the day the chief judge of the Rhode Island Supreme Court had summoned John Sheehan and me to his chambers in order to move the von Bulow case from Newport to Providence.

Everybody left Knapp's chambers to read Knapp's ruling.

The opinion gave Giuliani everything that he wanted. It also contained a stinging attack on Morgenthau, accusing him of trying to manipulate the case for his own ends. That was true enough, but Giuliani and I had behaved in exactly the same way.

After reading the ruling, we again gathered in the judge's chambers.

"Well, Bob, what do you think?" Knapp said to Morgenthau. "Maybe we can resolve this in another way."

A deal was immediately cut: The McLaughlin case would go first, then there would be a hiatus, after which Rudy Giuliani would bring Stanley Friedman to trial.

Knapp then collected all the copies of his opinion back and handed them to his clerk, who left the room.

While this back room maneuvering took place, I was absorbed with the day-to-day business of getting ready for the McLaughlin and Friedman trials. Preparation for Friedman was complicated by the fact that there were four other defendants: Lester Shafran, who was head of the PVB; Marvin Kaplan, the chairman of Citisource; Michael Lazar, a former New York City transportation commissioner; and Marvin Bergman, a former law partner of Donald Manes. (Bergman's link to the case consisted of only a few shreds of flimsy evidence. He never should have been indicted with Stanley and the others in the first place, and Knapp ultimately decided to sever his case from the other defendants.)

I'd never been involved in a multi-defendant case before as a defense lawyer, and I didn't enjoy the process. Although I never had any major problems with the attorneys for the other defendants, I also never felt I had the sort of control I was used to in the courtroom. Often when I wanted the jury's thoughts to move in one direction, I found that one of the other counsels was sending them off somewhere else. And although it had no effect on my client, I realized that the minor defendants in these monster trials risk being overlooked completely until the time comes for the jury to come up with a verdict. Certainly Bergman would not have had a fair shake if the judge had allowed his case to remain lumped with the others' cases.

Those problems came later. But my discomfort with the multi-defendant format constrained me from the beginning. There was, for instance, the question of whether to hold the trial in New York. The publicity had been absolutely horrendous. A juror would have had to be living in a cave for the last year to avoid forming an opinion about Friedman. And if he came out of his cave long enough to glimpse a few headlines, he'd still believe Stanley Friedman was the reincarnation of Boss Tweed.

As a result, I made a decision that would come back to haunt me: to move the trial from New York to New Haven, Connecticut. I commissioned a public opinion poll that confirmed what we already knew: It would be extremely difficult for Stanley and his codefendants to get a fair trial in New York City. I made a motion that the trial be held elsewhere, and Giuliani readily agreed.

Before the trial actually began, I realized the move was not such a great idea. For one thing, trying the McLaughlin case in Manhattan that summer convinced me that New York juries aren't all that bad for municipal corruption cases. But by then it was not simply a matter of changing my mind. Other people were involved. The other defense lawyers had been preparing for an out-of-town case. To tell them I'd changed my mind would, I felt, be treating them a little like flunkies. I didn't want them to think I expected them to jump at my every whim. That would have destroyed the professional relationship that had to exist for us to have any chance of prevailing.

We went to New Haven, Connecticut, a small city in a state that likes to call itself the Land of Steady Habits. A place where, I came to believe, the citizenry regarded political corruption as a crime only slightly less serious than mass murder.

ALTHOUGH I HAD wanted Rudy Giuliani to win the fight with Robert Morgenthau and try the case, it was not because I thought Giuliani would be an easy adversary. I had known Rudy for years and was very well aware of what an aggressive prosecutor he could be. As I've said, we had quite a bit in common—our Italian roots, our relatively humble upbringing, our special position as only children in very child-centered households. Neither of us were exactly party animals, but we were social friends as well as professional colleagues. Our paths had crossed dozens of times in the relatively small world of New York law enforcement. We were probably equally ambitious, though I never shared Rudy's obsession with politics. We both also had strong egos and a love of courtroom litigation. Only one of us, however, regarded his career as one long moral crusade.

The prosecution, as I came to discover, was willing to do almost anything to win the case. This kind of high-stakes, high-profile case can wind up generating animosity between the prosecution and the defense. But there are usually established limits beyond which neither side will go in pursuit of victory. In this case, they seemed to ignore the boundaries.

Early in the investigation, Giuliani dispatched agents to the headquarters of the Bronx Democratic party with a "forthwith" subpoena for party records. This was a demand to produce the records immediately, a very rare thing and a move that is easily contestable in court, because you have to show a judge that there is some valid reason for having instant access to the records. I suppose Rudy was fearful that the records would be destroyed, though in that case a search warrant would have been the way to go.

In any case, I sent an assistant up to the Bronx to assist in the task of getting the records together. She was going through the records with a woman who worked for the party when the agents at the scene threatened to arrest her for obstructing justice!

I immediately called the assistant prosecutor in Rudy's office who was handling the matter.

"Are you out of your mind?" I asked. "She is my associate in my law firm. She is up there to help—not obstruct justice."

The assistant was apologetic.

"Rudy ordered me to do it," he said.

I then called Rudy, who blamed the assistant.

It was laughable, but I guess it should have given me some insight into what was to come. Later, the government made a bid to have me removed from the case by arguing that my representation of another (minor) figure in the municipal scandal created a conflict of interest. Judge Knapp brushed this effort aside, saying that the government simply wanted to get me out of the case.

Hard on the heels of Giuliani's effort to have me disqualified as Stanley's lawyer came the Great Bugging Episode.

The government's star witness, we knew, was going to be Geoffrey Lindenauer, the former PVB official who had made a deal with the prosecution. Naturally, we were intensely interested in material that might impeach Lindenauer's credibility. One of the things we did was to compile a list of people who might have information about Lindenauer. A prime candidate was Dr. Jerome Driesen, a Queens psychiatrist who had been a close friend of Lindenauer's.

Lindenauer, who had no professional background in psychology or psychiatry, had styled himself as a psychotherapist. His "mentor" was a psychologist-charlatan named Jacob List, who was subsequently convicted of income tax evasion.

When List's institute folded in the late 1960s, Lindenauer carried on with his own Institute for Emotional Education. Using bogus doctoral degrees that he purchased for $250 each from a small Canadian divinity school, "Dr." Lindenauer counseled patients and, by his own account, occasionally had sex with them. The "institute," indeed, seemed to thrive on sex between staff members and their unlucky patients.

It was at the institute in 1970 that Lindenauer met and befriended Dr. Jerome Driesen. In fact, Lindenauer thought so much of Driesen that he awarded his friend the institute's "Award for Excellence" in 1972. During the same year, Lindenauer and his mother (an "associate professor of natural science" at the institute) spent $50,000 in a successful fight against a bill that would have required state licensing of psychotherapists.

Donald Manes's wife, Marlene, also frequented the institute. Within a few years, Manes and Lindenauer were fast friends. Following the financial collapse of the institute in 1976, Manes put Lindenauer on the city payroll. Within eighteen months, Lindenauer was deputy director of the PVB. From this position, he served as Manes's bagman. By Lindenauer's account, he and the borough president collected more than $500,000 in bribes from companies doing business with the PVB from 1979 to 1985.

Lindenauer completed the circle by recruiting Driesen as *his* bagman. Driesen, dressed in a fur coat, would tool around town in a Rolls-Royce picking up payoffs for Lindenauer. This did not mean therapy was ignored. Driesen also lent Lindenauer the use of his office at night, so the deputy director of the PVB could continue his sideline as a psychotherapist.

By his own account, Driesen was then a cocaine addict whose

heavy use of the drug ultimately damaged his memory. He also picked up quick cash by testifying as an expert witness for the city about 250 times. As one might imagine, Driesen lied about his qualifications as an "expert." He also took bribes to recommend unqualified applicants for city jobs.

When I targeted Driesen as a possible source of damaging information about Lindenauer, I didn't know many of the details of this most colorful story. I got help contacting Driesen from Harold Borg, a Queens lawyer who defended low-level hoodlums. I had gotten to know Borg during my days as a young federal prosecutor in Brooklyn when Harold often handled the defendants in truck hijacking cases. (These cases were almost always straightforward. There were never any conferences about the possible cooperation of a defendant. And the lawyers for these young John Gottis never appealed to you not to indict their clients.)

I asked Borg if he knew anybody close to Lindenauer, and he said he knew Driesen very well. Borg said he had used the psychiatrist as an expert witness in several cases. He agreed to set up a meeting with Driesen to discuss Lindenauer.

I told Borg I could offer Driesen a little information in return for his help. Inviting someone to a meeting like this is a little like asking to be a weekend house guest. There's no quid pro quo, but you really should bring a little present to show you appreciate the other person's trouble. Instead of a bottle of wine or box of cheese, I brought a nugget of information. Stanley Friedman had heard from a reporter that Driesen had been secretly indicted by a state grand jury in Queens for offering Manes a bribe to get a state license for a psychiatric hospital in Queens. Certainly, this was the sort of thing Driesen would want to know. I hoped in return he'd tell me something about Lindenauer that would impeach his credibility.

The meeting was set for 10 P.M. at Driesen's office on the East Side of Manhattan. I was not feeling particularly energetic when I arrived. After a tough day in a Manhattan courtroom on the McLaughlin case, I went to a cocktail party hosted by one of my law partners. A few glasses of champagne later, I moved on to the Hotel Carlyle, where I met Harold Borg for a sandwich. We then walked to Driesen's office on East Eighty-second Street.

Driesen's office was located in one of those dull, white-brick apartment buildings that used to be known as "stew palaces" because they were stuffed with airline flight attendants. I was ushered into a dark, dingy office with schlock-modern furniture and dirty white carpeting.

Harold introduced me to Dr. Driesen, a tall, balding man with glasses who looked like a slender Phil Silvers. Driesen was extremely nervous and fidgety. It was a very hot night, and Driesen began to sweat profusely as soon as we began to talk. I guess a warning bell should have gone off in my mind when the sweating Driesen got up and turned *off* the air conditioner.

The room had been bugged, and I was totally oblivious to the fact. As my friends later gleefully pointed out, the famous Abscam prosecutor who had snared seven congressmen was secretly taped by the FBI. I had to admit I was no more aware that a tape recorder was rolling than Angelo Errichetti and Senator Harrison Williams. But, as W. C. Fields used to say, you can't cheat an honest man.

This is what had happened: Unknown to me, the FBI had made a case against Driesen for sharing PVB bribes with Lindenauer. In response, he had agreed to cooperate with the government. At our overheated meeting on East Eighty-second Street, he was cooperating like crazy. His office was bugged by the FBI, with Rudy Giuliani's approval.

The alleged target was Harold Borg—the FBI claimed it had learned he had access to the secret Queens grand jury testimony in the Driesen case. But the meeting itself disclosed what really must have been running through the FBI's mind.

I sat on a couch in Driesen's office during what proved to be a frustrating thirty minutes. The psychiatrist's line of chatter was confused, incoherent, and at times, boring.

DRIESEN: I was down in the Bahamas.
PUCCIO: So you came back early.
BORG: That's where the collect call from. I didn't mind Bermuda, but the Bahamas.

DRIESEN: I didn't call collect.
BORG: You called my house collect.
DRIESEN: I didn't call collect.

And so it went. The combination of heat, a long, hard day and the champagne caused me to nod off on a few occasions during the meeting. Fortunately, the FBI had used only audiotape for the meeting, so my siesta was not apparent to those who later read the transcript.

I told Driesen I'd been informed he was under indictment in Queens. (*The New York Times* had already reported that an indictment had been returned, but the newspaper did not identify Driesen by name.)

The psychiatrist repeatedly demanded to know how I could really be sure he was under indictment. This was, of course, an invitation for me to produce grand jury minutes or a copy of the indictment—"proof" of what I was saying. When it became clear that nothing of the sort would be popping out of my briefcase, Driesen took the direct approach by simply asking for the indictment!

When I finally began to ask Driesen a little bit about Lindenauer, he became evasive.

PUCCIO: Are you familiar with List, Jacob List?
DRIESEN: I know of List. I never met the man.
PUCCIO: Do you know if Lindenauer was a disciple of Lists's?
DRIESEN: Yeah, I read that in the uh, that was in, that was on page three of the *Post* uh . . .

This was strange indeed. A professional psychiatrist who had been Lindenauer's friend for fifteen years was citing a *New York Post* story!

I tried again.

PUCCIO: Well, I believe that Lindenauer's got some severe emotional problems, and if that's true, I'd like to know about it.
DRIESEN: I don't understand what you're asking me. You're

asking me to what? I uh, to say that he has severe emotional problems?
PUCCIO: If the guy does I'd like to know about it.
DRIESEN: And if he doesn't, he doesn't.
PUCCIO: If he doesn't, he doesn't.

A minute later, the psychiatrist tried it again.

DRIESEN: . . . You want me to say he's crazy in other words.
PUCCIO: Yeah, if he were.
DRIESEN: If he were. And if he were not?
PUCCIO: Tell me that too.

I decided to leave no doubt in Driesen's mind.

"Just so we understand each other," I said. "Whatever you tell me is going to be the truth no matter what, right?"

Near the end of the meeting, Driesen made a final impassioned speech which, in effect, asked me to break the law by producing grand jury testimony.

". . . Get me, tell me, questions. Give me the questions. Give me the answers. Give me the uh, uh. What does an indictment have? It has numbers on it. Give me the numbers on the indictment . . ."

Driesen wasn't exactly eloquent, but he certainly deserved an "A" for effort by trying to get me to commit two crimes: obstruction of justice (for handing over grand jury materials) and suborning perjury (by urging him to lie about Lindenauer).

I didn't suspect a thing. All I knew was that the meeting had been a total bust. And Harold Borg, who had gone to the trouble of setting it up, was a little bit angry with me for being rude enough to doze off in front of the good Dr. Driesen.

Borg and I went home. Back in Driesen's office, the psychiatrist was talking over the meeting with an FBI agent.

DRIESEN: Whoever said he's not a sharp guy, Puccio? Did you see us pussyfooting in there?
FBI AGENT: Yeah.

DRIESEN: What does he want me to say? And, you know, he wants me to say he's crazy.

At that point, the FBI turned off the tape recorder.

When, Rudy later told me that he had agreed to the FBI plan to tape-record me, this did not seem like the same guy I'd known for the past twenty years. Maybe one of the reasons I found it so shocking was that Rudy had been involved in the final stage of a massive FBI investigation of me many years previously. Back then, the story had a much different ending:

While I was the chief of the Criminal Division in the Eastern District in the 1970s, I sent a witness in an important narcotics case to Florida for a removal hearing. (A removal hearing is the federal equivalent of an extradition hearing.) We wanted to bring a defendant from Florida to New York. The job of the witness was to identify the defendant as the man we wanted.

My witness and the defendant's lawyer got together in the hallway of the courthouse where, according to my witness, the lawyer offered him a bribe to change his testimony. My witness was instructed to play along by telling the lawyer that I lived high on the hog and could use an extra $50,000.

I launched a major investigation using agents from the Drug Enforcement Administration. The lawyer we were investigating, however, went to the FBI, where he told agents that a high-ranking Justice Department official (me) was trying to extort a huge bribe from his client.

The result (for not the first time) was dueling federal law enforcement agencies. Neither side, of course, knew what the other was doing. The investigation went on for months. We were getting fantastic tape recordings in our obstruction of justice investigation as details for the delivery of an enormous sum of money to me were worked out. The FBI, of course, was absolutely rapturous about *its* fantastic tape recordings of the same meetings.

Finally, the day for the big bribe arrived. I had already designated a DEA agent to act as my "bagman" for the cash. There must have been fifty agents from each side working on the big sting.

The FBI duly informed the Justice Department in Washing-

ton that the head of the Criminal Division in one of department's largest offices was about to accept a bribe. Rudy was then
the deputy to Harold "Ace" Tyler, the number two man in the
Justice Department.

Giuliani burst into laughter when he heard the grim news. He
picked up the phone and called David Trager, who was then the
U.S. attorney in the Eastern District.

"Dave, I'm calling because we have a huge investigation that
is about to culminate," he said. "Is Tom Puccio investigating
somebody in Florida?"

I had, of course, kept Trager informed of the progress of my
own massive probe.

"Yes, it's a very big investigation," Trager replied.

"Well, there's another agency on the other side of the investigation," Rudy reported.

Both probes, needless to say, were immediately terminated.

As I said, Rudy and I go way back. We had remained friends
following our days of playing "good cop" and "bad cop" with
"Prince of the City" detective Bob Leuci in the early 1970s.
(Rudy, you'll remember, wound up being portrayed in the movie
as Leuci's saintlike federal protector. I was his cold-hearted tor-
mentor.) Rudy went into private practice in New York after leaving the Justice Department in 1976, but he soon became bored.
He campaigned hard to get a federal judgeship that became vacant while Democrat Jimmy Carter was in office. I tried to help
him out by phoning Attorney General Benjamin Civiletti and
boosting Rudy's candidacy. It didn't work out, but following Ronald Reagan's election in 1980, Rudy returned to Washington as
associate attorney general, the number three position in the Justice Department. After the Abscam investigations, when I was
inundated with invitations to speaking engagements, I always
knew where to find a stand-in for invitations I couldn't accept.
Rudy loved the idea of jumping in and speaking before whatever
Rotary group or ladies auxiliary came down the pike.

When the U.S. attorney's position in Washington, D.C., became vacant in 1981, Rudy became my booster and biggest
backer for the post. But even Rudy's clout in the Justice Department wasn't enough to put the fox (me) in the chicken coop.

When Rudy returned to New York as the U.S. attorney in 1983, I played the role of peacemaker between him, my friend Jack Newfield, and Wayne Barrett of the *Village Voice.* The *Voice* had written stories about Brooklyn Congressman Charles Schumer. Schumer had been a state legislator prior to going to Washington, and the *Voice* reported that Schumer had illegally used state employees as campaign workers. The Eastern District was set to indict Schumer on federal charges, but Giuliani vetoed the prosecution, saying it was a state rather than a federal matter. Needless to say, Jack and Wayne were angered by Rudy's decision. We had a long dinner at an Italian restaurant, where Rudy and the *Voice* writers worked out their differences. I attended Rudy's 1985 marriage to his second wife, Donna Hanover.

We were not exactly blood brothers, but our relationship remained amicable until the Friedman case.

I left Driesen's office unaware I had experienced anything but a dull and fruitless encounter with a very weird psychiatrist. I *was* surprised when Driesen's name appeared on Giuliani's list of government witnesses. Why, I wondered, would the prosecution want somebody as flaky as Driesen on the stand?

But I didn't dwell on the matter. I was deep into my defense of John McLaughlin, the former city hospitals head dragged into the municipal corruption quagmire. The trial came to an end on August 28. John was acquitted of bribery and the other major charges Morgenthau had filed up against him. But he was convicted of misappropriating a small amount of money by allegedly overcharging a client for travel expenses.

McLaughlin had done fairly well, especially given the gravity of some of the charges against him and the widespread impression that he was linked to a municipal corruption scandal that had stirred up everyone in town. But I was downcast at the verdict. I couldn't accept a client getting convicted, no matter how trivial the charges.

The gloom, however, was lifted when a buoyant John McLaughlin appeared at my home on the night of the verdict with a bottle of champagne and demanded we go out for a celebratory dinner. I can assure you that it's not very often that a defendant who has been convicted becomes the person who does the cheering up! (John was facing six months in prison, but thanks to a successfull appeal and lots of legal maneuvering, I was eventually able to keep him out of jail entirely.)

McLaughlin's gesture sent me off to New Haven in the best possible mood. I was ready to do for Stanley Friedman what I had done for Claus von Bulow and—more or less—John McLaughlin.

The Stanley Friedman who went on trial in Connecticut was not exactly the same guy familiar to the regulars at New York political gatherings. I had done what I could to change him back into the Long Island dentist he might have become if the City College basketball team had had a less demanding schedule. Stanley shaved off his goatee and gave up smoking cigars (until he was three or four blocks from the courthouse). The greatest makeover in the world, of course, couldn't have changed the man himself. From head to toe, he was still a political boss from the big city.

The trial got under way on September 22, 1986. It was widely heralded in the press as a clash of the legal titans: me versus Rudy Giuliani. In his three years as U.S. attorney, Rudy had won a reputation as a tough, crime-fighting prosecutor in the mold of Tom Dewey. His office had successfully prosecuted several important cases against the Mafia, and he was already looked upon as a potential candidate for mayor or governor. I, of course, was the guy who sprung Claus von Bulow and masterminded Abscam. But our confrontation was no more than a sideshow that had no real impact on the outcome.

The case against Stanley was very strong. The charges fell into two categories: (1) taking a bribe, in the form of $1 million in Citisource stock that was held in his name but was to be shared equally with Lindenauer and Manes; (2) paying Lindenauer and Manes a $35,000 bribe from Datacom, another computer-service company that Stanley represented. The president of Datacom, Joseph Delario, had denied paying any bribes, but as the trial opened, the government was trying to turn Delario into a cooperating witness.

The other defendants faced similar charges. As chairman of

Citisource, Marvin Kaplan was accused of paying the stock bribe. Michael Lazar, the city's former transportation commissioner, was accused of funneling bribes from Datacom to Lindenauer from 1979 to 1982. Manes's former law partner Marvin Bergman was charged with delivering bribe money to Lindenauer from a collection company. Finally, former PVB director Lester Shafran was accused of accepting bribes from a collection agency.

The defense set up headquarters in the Colony, a small hotel within walking distance of the federal courthouse on the New Haven Green.

Jury selection was agony. The defense had a combined total of twenty-four peremptory challenges, but with five defendants and five lawyers, it proved exceedingly difficult to reach agreement on which potential jurors to exclude. We had hired a jury selection expert to assist us in finding sympathetic jurors. But our inability to decide among ourselves resulted in a situation in which the expert made the decisions rather than serving as someone who helped us to do the picking.

In a multi-defendant case like this, you have to establish some form of democracy when you're making challenges. After long and agonizing discussions that went nowhere, we'd turn to the hired expert, and he'd go with whatever opinion he'd held from the beginning. For all our efforts, we might as well not have been in the courtroom.

The lawyers in the Friedman case spent a lot of time together, and a lot of time in preparation, but we didn't spend enough time discussing how we should proceed. A good retreat—a day or two of soul searching and discussion—would have been very useful. We needed more discipline and a unified approach. I'm not being critical of the other attorneys in the case, by the way. As the lawyer for the lead defendant in the case, it was my responsibility more than anybody else's to pull things together.

Multi-defendant cases are so common these days, I almost think they should offer a course on them in law school—Psychodynamics of the Mass Defense. Mob cases, of course, often feature enough defendants to form a zip code. But coordination is never a problem. If the boss is on trial with the underboss and a few capos, the boss's lawyer calls all the shots or somebody gets killed. I've been told by some mob lawyers that they can't even make an objection unless it's been cleared up the line.

Needless to say, this approach wasn't possible in the Friedman case.

It was in a meeting in Judge Knapp's chambers during jury selection that Giuliani informed Knapp (and me) that my June meeting with Jerome Driesen had been tape-recorded by the FBI. He was making the disclosure, Rudy said, because the government planned to call Driesen as a witness.

Of course I was stunned. Giuliani claimed that the meeting was bugged because there was an ongoing investigation of Harold Borg. This was a total crock. I think the FBI meant to knock me out of the case by putting me into some kind of compromising situation. I was well aware that this was a high-stakes case, but I never imagined they'd do something like this.

I complained bitterly to Knapp about the government's tactics, arguing, quite reasonably, that it had been part of an effort to set me up.

Later, outside Knapp's chambers, Rudy got me alone.

"I've got to tell you I really had no choice," he said. "I had to do this. It was one of the worst moments of my life, waiting for them to get back and tell me what happened at the meeting."

What was I supposed to say?

"Don't worry about it," I told him, and walked away.

Later, I was told that Rudy believed I'd somehow been tipped off that the meeting was going to be tape-recorded. If that's so, he must have been less relieved to discover my innocence than irritated I had outwitted him. I do think he was afraid that the bugging could cause serious legal problems. I suspect that's the real reason he decided to bring the matter to Judge Knapp's attention before the trial started. He was afraid that if he didn't do so, I might have turned the whole episode into grounds for an appeal.

THE TRIAL got started in earnest with opening statements on September 30. I threw everything I had into an attack on Lindenauer, calling him a liar and a manipulator who had manufactured the charges against Friedman following Manes's suicide in order to get himself a favorable deal with the government.

"Stanley Friedman was picked by Geoffrey Lindenauer to fill the empty chair filled by Donald Manes," I said. "He was the perfect victim."

My opening statement went over well, and things only seemed to get better in the days that followed. The transcript of our meeting in chambers with Judge Knapp soon became public. The news that Giuliani had bugged the lead defense attorney produced headlines in all the papers. The publicity about Rudy and me tended to take the edge off the appearance of the state's star witness, Geoffrey Lindenauer himself.

Lindenauer took the jury through a career of bribe taking that began in 1979 when he went to the home of Michael Lazar to pick up a $500 cash payment. At the time, Lazar was representing Datacom.

"Michael reached into his bathrobe pocket and gave me a plain white envelope with the money," Lindenauer testified. The witness moved from this account of a casually delivered bribe to other tales of wrongdoing.

He claimed, of course, that he, Friedman, and Manes had agreed on a three-way split of a large block of Citisource stock to be held in Friedman's name. According to Lindenauer, Manes chose Friedman to hold the stock because he trusted him. Lindenauer was surprised at Manes's choice, since the Queens borough president and Friedman were then engaged in a heated political feud.

And he added what can charitably be described as colorful details: At one meeting in Friedman's office, Lindenauer told the jury, he asked Stanley exactly how many shares Friedman would be holding for them. Lindenauer said Stanley wrote 57,500 on a piece of paper, held up the paper to show him the figure, and then burned the paper in an ashtray on his desk.

Lindenauer moved smoothly through two days of gentle questioning by David Zornow, one of Giuliani's assistants. I couldn't wait to get at Lindenauer on cross-examination. Given Lindenauer's past history, I decided to come quickly to the point.

PUCCIO: Is it a true statement that you engaged in lying, deceit, and manipulation?
LINDENAUER: Yes I did.
PUCCIO: On many, many occasions?
LINDENAUER: Yes I did.
PUCCIO: Did you lie to people?
LINDENAUER: I have lied to people.
PUCCIO: Have you defrauded people?
LINDENAUER: I did.
PUCCIO: Have you manipulated people?
LINDENAUER: I have not told people the truth.
PUCCIO: What do you understand manipulation to mean, Mr. Lindenauer?
LINDENAUER: That's a difficult . . . I don't know.
PUCCIO: You don't know what manipulation means. Is that your testimony?

I could see that Lindenauer was already on the ropes. Things got even better when I asked him when his meetings with Stanley Friedman had supposedly occurred.

He had testified that Manes surprised him by having Stanley hold the stock, since the two were locked in a bitter battle over the Board of Education. I was able to bring out the fact that this political quarrel took place a month *after* Citisource had already gotten the contract from the city, and a good year after Lindenauer claimed the stock split with Stanley had already been arranged.

I pressed him for the dates of other meetings he had testified about. But Lindenauer, much to my satisfaction, was suddenly in a fog.

"So much was happening that the dates really are jumbled," he tried to explain. Lindenauer also suffered numerous memory lapses, responding with "I don't recall" answers on more than three dozen occasions. At times, the witness glanced at the judge, hoping, it seemed, that Knapp would somehow bail him out.

I also hammered away at Lindenauer's dubious past, though Knapp blocked me from questioning him closely about his strange career as a psychotherapist. Food seemed as much a part of Lindenauer's life as sex therapy. He is very chubby, as was his political partner in crime, Donald Manes. This prompted an official from one of the collection companies to give them the code names of "Fat number 1" (Manes) and "Fat number 2" (Lindenauer). I had noticed that Lindenauer's bribe taking was often executed during a meal paid for by the briber.

"Did you ever pay for a meal in your life?" I sarcastically asked.

"Many meals" was the indignant reply.

I would have happily thrown the kitchen sink at Lindenauer if there was one handy in the courtroom. I was followed by Gerald Lefcourt, the lawyer for Marvin Kaplan. Gerry did a great job of skewering Lindenauer.

"Mr. Lindenauer, do you have a problem with your memory?" Lefcourt asked at one point.

"I don't recall any problem with my memory," Lindenauer replied with a straight face.

The courtroom dissolved in laughter.

It was with good reason the defense felt confident when the day drew to a close. The government's star witness had been badly shaken.

But Lindenauer made a comeback. With five defendants in the case, there were five lawyers to cross-examine him. As I've said before, the key to cross-examination is knowing when to stop. But that isn't easy, or even possible, in a multi-defendant trial. Each lawyer had an individual responsibility to his own client. Each lawyer must confront the "If my guy's convicted and I didn't cross-examine the key witness how will I look?" dilemma.

Lindenauer remained on the stand for another week. He was batted around so much that even I began to feel a little sorry for him at the end. The greedy, corrupt bagman and fixer wound up looking like a poor slob by the time the defense finished with him.

Nevertheless, we were heartened by the way the case was moving. I think we shared a false sense of optimism during the first couple of weeks in the trial. Generally speaking, the newspapers were making the defense look great, and I think that helped me to delude myself into thinking that the trial was going better than it actually was. Stanley was popular with the press and knew several of the reporters covering the case personally.

I fell into a routine similar to the one I followed during the von Bulow trial. I would get up at five-thirty or six and read the newspapers, which Stanley had already dropped off at the door to my room. We would gather for breakfast at the hotel, and then walk to court. By the time we reached the middle of the New Haven Green, we'd have picked up a crowd of reporters, cameramen, and photographers. We would work through the lunch hour or eat at a nearby restaurant.

At 5 P.M., we'd walk back to the hotel and usually have dinner right away. At night, I frequently worked alone—reviewing transcripts and other material in my room.

As I said, I was absolutely sure that I was on the road to another major acquittal. But there were signs of trouble, which I was able to overlook in my hyperconfident state. For one thing, it was almost immediately evident that Judge Knapp hated Stanley. I suspect that the role the judge played as New York City's number one guardian of public morality during the Knapp Commission hearings made him antagonistic to a politician accused of corruption. At one meeting in chambers during the trial, Knapp seemed surprised that I (no slouch in the field of keeping public officials honest) was representing a man like Stanley Friedman.

Not that the defense was Knapp's only target.

The judge was capable of exploding with anger—yelling and screaming—and two minutes later forgetting the whole thing. One of the extraordinary things about being a lawyer is finding yourself in front of judges who are capricious, whimsical, and unpredictable. These men and women wield enormous, virtually unchallenged power, and a lawyer can only try mightily to make the best of the situation.

Knapp's behavior was so extreme, I sometimes felt as if Rudy and I were two prisoners writhing under the whip of an out-of-control jailer. On one level, Giuliani and I were opponents, locked in a deadly serious battle, with another human being's fate hanging in the balance. But there were moments in the courtroom when all that was overridden by our mutual misery. Giuliani and I used to look at each other and roll our eyes. We knew Knapp was like a pendulum swinging back and forth every day. One day Giuliani would get hit, and the next day it would be me. There was no rhyme or reason to Knapp's behavior. The basic weakness of the Friedman defense was simple: There was too much evidence against him. Lindenauer was not the world's greatest witness, but the government was now ready to trot out people who could support Lindenauer's version of events.

For example, Robert Richards, the former president of Citisource, testified that Lindenauer told him Citisource's chances of getting the handheld computer contract would be "dead" if Stanley did not get his stock. He also claimed that codefendant Marvin Kaplan, the chairman of Citisource, told him Friedman wanted to own 25 percent of the company. Richards also recalled a meeting at which Stanley purportedly referred to Lindenauer as a "pig." None of this tied Stanley directly to a bribe, but neither was it helpful to the defense.

A major blow came when the government granted immunity from prosecution to Datacom president Joseph Delario and three other company executives. Delario had already testified before a federal grand jury that he never paid a bribe to anyone. Giuliani had threatened to indict him, but Delario sat tight and refused to make a deal with the government. With the trial winding down, Giuliani offered him a deal he couldn't refuse: freedom from prosecution in exchange for his testimony against Stanley Friedman.

Suddenly, Delario had a whole new story. He claimed that Friedman had demanded $35,000 in "good-faith money" to be paid to Manes and Lindenauer. This was on top of a scheme in which Datacom would pay one percent of its receipts to Stanley from a PVB contract.

It was a terrible blow to our case, although of course I wasn't prepared to admit it. One of the absolute rules of defense work is that you must always tell reporters things are going great— even if fourteen nuns have just taken the stand to identify your client as the man who pulled the trigger.

"We're as optimistic as we were the first day," I announced to the press.

But things weren't going well at all. It was clearly going to be necessary to call Stanley as a witness. It was the first time I'd ever put one of my clients on the witness stand. It was a move I'd never even contemplated in the von Bulow case.

I had tentatively decided before the trial began that Stanley's testimony would be necessary. The only thing that would have derailed that decision would have been the collapse of the government's case. Giuliani had presented a coconspirator case in which the witnesses are also participants in the crimes. The only way to meet this coconspirator testimony is to put Stanley on the stand.

There was no defense case, as there was in the von Bulow trial when we had experts and other witnesses lined up to support our contention that no crime had been committed. In New Haven, it was all up to Stanley.

I led the clean-shaven, cigar-free Stanley through a brief discussion of his background and had him firmly and categorically deny each of the charges against him. He told of meeting Marvin Kaplan in 1982 through his wife, who had known Marvin for years. He had agreed to represent Citisource as a legal client, and in exchange for his work, he received stock in the company.

The government had made a point of noting that Friedman had received the stock in three blocks of 50,000 shares each, an arrangement consistent with the prosecution's contention that it was to be divided with Manes and Lindenauer. Stanley explained the three-way division by saying that he planned to give the stock to his wife and two of his children.

Moving on to the alleged Datacom bribe, which Stanley was supposed to have split with Manes and Lindenauer, we tackled the fact that legal fees paid to Stanley by Datacom were funneled through a company owned by Marvin Kaplan. The prosecution claimed this method of payment was devised to conceal bribes. Stanley had another explanation. Datacom was owned by the Lockheed Corporation, he said, and Delario didn't want to have to explain the payment of a large fee to a "political person" to his corporate bosses at Lockheed.

These were not explanations that the jury—or the judge for that matter—found convincing. During a session in his chambers, Judge Knapp wasted no time in characterizing Stanley's testimony as "highly improbable."

We were gathered together in private to argue about Giuliani's upcoming cross-examination. I had asked the judge to restrict his questioning to matters directly related to Citisource-Datacom. Rudy, I knew, wanted to ask Stanley about other aspects of his business, such as his work as a lobbyist for the taxi industry.

Friedman was a man who had spent his life building up capital in the political favor bank. The huge network of government contacts who owed him favors or good will were his major asset. When someone hired him as a lobbyist-lawyer, they naturally expected him to dip into the favor bank on their behalf.

In the shadowy, deeply pragmatic world of Bronx politics, this was all totally acceptable. Certainly Stanley saw nothing wrong with his method of operation. But the jurors from the Land of Steady Habits were likely to feel otherwise, and Giuliani was eager to paint a very detailed portrait of my client's way of doing business.

Of course I was very eager to keep the cross-examination as narrow as possible. Knapp, in his typical manner, was bouncing from one side to the other. He didn't think Giuliani should wander off into unrelated matters. But on the other hand he didn't think he should make me happy by restricting the questioning.

KNAPP: I can't tell the United States attorney how to try the case. I know how I would if I were doing this, I wouldn't do all this bullshit.

PUCCIO: If you wouldn't do all this bullshit, I don't think you should permit him to do it.

KNAPP: I'm not trying the case. I wouldn't do it because it is illegal. I think it is a waste of goddamn time.

PUCCIO: I think it's highly prejudicial to my client.

KNAPP: With the highly improbable story that your client told, I think that should be what we're talking about, not this bullshit. But that's neither here nor there.

The judge's remarks might have been grounds for a mistrial, but no one, including Stanley, was eager for a sequel.

"The prospect of hearing two months of evidence over again in New Haven struck fear in the hearts and nausea in the stomach of attorneys, court personnel and reporters," wrote a *New York Times* columnist.

If I was ready to throw the kitchen sink at Geoffrey Lindenauer, Rudy Giuliani was prepared to toss the stove, refrigerator, china, silverware, and coffeemaker at Friedman. He took a shotgun approach to questioning Stanley that I did not feel was very effective. His strategy of asking Stanley about everything under the sun became very tedious.

It did, however, produce one hideous moment—the kind of exchange that causes defense attorneys to wake up in the middle of the night, sweating. Discussing a $10,000 fee Stanley received for a lobbying effort, Rudy asked incredulously if Friedman had gotten all that money for making just two phone calls.

"I think it was just one phone call," my client said smugly. I was sure the jurors, some of whom probably made no more than $25,000 for a year's work, were thrilled to hear that.

Returning to the real issue at hand, Giuliani hammered away at the fact that Stanley disclosed the existence of his Citisource stock to only one public official: Donald Manes.

It was the central weakness in our case. Stanley had no independent corroboration for his story. Jurors with doubts about Geoffrey Lindenauer could turn to the testimony of other witnesses. But the jurors were asked to accept Stanley's account on faith alone. Faith in a guy who was proud he could earn $10,000 by making a single phone call.

My strategy for a closing argument was pretty standard: I attacked the credibility and motives of the key witnesses against Friedman. I also argued that the dear departed Donald Manes had been a liar as well.

"Joe Delario, the best I could call him is 'multiple-choice Joe'," I said in a reference to the fact that Delario's trial testimony was directly contradicted by his testimony before the grand jury. "The government brought this liar into your midst to save a drowning Geoffrey Lindenauer."

It was, I said, "Stanley Friedman, head-to-head, against the dregs of the earth."

Jury deliberations went on for three days. As always, it was an agonizing time for the defendants and their lawyers. While we waited, one of the defendants, Michael Lazar, celebrated his fifty-eighth birthday. We gathered at a private club in New Haven for a celebration. Despite the tremendous tension everyone was under, the defendants all retained their sense of humor. Lazar was presented with gifts that included a new bathrobe—a memento of Lindenauer's claim that Lazar pulled a envelope containing a $500 bribe from his bathrobe pocket.

These guys were all self-made men whose careers and reputations were hanging in the balance. I found their calm and camaraderie moving, particularly since I think we all had a pretty good idea of what was to come.

On November 25, Friedman and the other defendants were found guilty. Judge Knapp gave Stanley twelve years in jail, a sentence that was grossly unfair and far more severe than the sentences meted out to defendants convicted of similar crimes. (And when the Feds finished with Stanley, Bob Morgenthau was still waiting in the wings. He charged Friedman with bribing state National Guard officers to purchase Citisource's handheld computer. This pointless exercise resulted in Friedman's conviction on state bribery and conspiracy charges. Despite the Draconian prison sentence, Stanley never tried to make a deal that would have given him a lighter sentence in exchange for giving up one or more of his many political allies.)

I left New Haven a sadder and wiser attorney. Naturally, for a long time afterward, I went over the case in my mind, looking for things I could have done differently.

In retrospect, it's clear that Stanley and I were an unhealthy marriage. My client was absolutely convinced he had done nothing wrong. A machine politician's morality is different from an average citizen. To Stanley, going back on your word was a huge sin. So was testifying against a fellow politician. Taking money for political favors was no sin at all.

Another lawyer might have told him that the jurors would see things differently. But at the time, I was convinced there was virtually no case in the world that I couldn't win.

At a later point in my career, I might have looked at the evidence and decided the case was unwinnable. I might have told Friedman: "Look, Stanley, you've got to take a plea to a lesser charge. You've done a lot of great things in your life. Let's hope you get off with a light sentence."

But I don't think Stanley would have accepted that advice. My best consolation, in looking back over the case, is that Friedman would have insisted on a trial, no matter what. If I wasn't prepared to deliver one, he'd have found another lawyer who could. And I do not think another lawyer could have given him better representation.

Stanley went off to jail, still sticking to his own code and refusing to cooperate with the prosecutors who were eager to keep the municipal corruption investigations going. He was finally released in 1991. His friends in and out of city government gave him a welcome-home party, but he's been barred from having anything to do with his old life in politics.

I went on with my career. And Rudy Giuliani, of course, wound up mayor of New York City. Some of the politicians who went to Stanley's welcome-home party also had seats on the dias for the inauguration.

I remembered a moment during the trial when Stanley and I were standing on the steps of the courthouse. We watched as Rudy Giuliani, wearing a top coat and gloves, walked up the steps and greeted several people who had come over to him.

"This guy will never be a politician," Stanley said. "You never shake hands with your gloves on."

12

BIG JOHN

PEOPLE OFTEN ASK me if I get emotionally involved with my clients, the way the defense attorneys do on television. The answer is—very seldom. You want to get them acquitted or solve their problems, of course. But like doctors, a lawyer can't afford to get too attached to individual clients. It's too draining, and it could hamper your judgment. Besides, I'd be the first to admit that I've defended a few people even Mother Teresa couldn't warm up to.

Once in a while, of course, all this goes out the window. That's the way it was with John Mulheren.

Mulheren was someone I really grew to care about. He was a thirty-eight-year-old stock trader when I met him, father of five adopted kids, husband to an absolutely terrific woman, friend to Bruce Springsteen, Jesse Jackson, and about two-thirds of the continental United States.

He was also locked up in a mental hospital, charged with driving around with a car full of guns and threatening to kill Ivan Boesky, Wall Street's most notorious financier.

"The worst part about this is that people are going to think I'm crazy," Mulheren told his wife, Nancy, when she rushed down to the New Jersey jail where he was taken after his arrest.

"John," Nancy replied calmly, "people already think you are crazy."

My involvement with the case began with a phone call from a man named Charlie Minter. Minter was a successful Wall Street trader. I had once represented a friend of his (Jay McLaughlin), and Minter had seen me in action in court.

"I have a friend named John Mulheren," Minter said. "The

guy is in desperate straits, and he has no confidence in his lawyer. I'm going to suggest he talk to you."

Soon I found myself sitting in a hired limousine, on a two-and-a-half-hour ride to the Carrier Foundation, an upscale mental hospital in New Jersey. It was a warm Saturday night, and I met Mulheren in the cafeteria of the red brick maximum-security unit at the hospital. The building, which looked as if it could be part of a pleasant college campus, was named Edwards Hall.

"We call it Crazy Eddie's," Mulheren told me.

He was an imposing guy, about six foot two, with a furrowed brow and thick, bushy eyebrows that reminded me of John L. Lewis, the old labor leader. He was dressed in a sports shirt and a pair of chinos. As I would soon come to learn, casual dress was one of Mulheren's trademarks—equally appropriate, as far as he was concerned, for a boardroom, a mental hospital, or a federal courtroom.

John had been held for more than a month behind the barred windows in Edwards Hall when we spoke, and I think he was heavily medicated. But he seemed lucid and completely rational to me. Still, there was a faraway look in his eyes that told me he marched to a different drummer.

Seated next to Mulheren was his wife, Nancy, whose love and loyalty held her husband's life together. The Mulherens had been college sweethearts. Nancy, who got her degree in psychology, told people that she had embarked on a lifetime career with a single patient.

We talked for about an hour—mainly about my background and career. John didn't attempt to discuss the charges with me, which was fine. I don't like to deal with the facts at a first meeting. But Mulheren was certainly in a fix. He faced federal and state charges for the Boesky threat, as well as a pending criminal indictment that would charge him with numerous security law violations.

"I'm not part of the attorney old-boy network, and I don't play ball with prosecutors," I told him. "If you hire me, it's because you really want to fight the charges."

That was music to Mulheren's ears. John, who tended to see

things in black and white, saw himself as a totally innocent man. Anything less than an all-out battle against the government was unthinkable to somebody with his outlook on life.

"Tom, I want you to go get those bastards in New York," he said.

I learned later that John was the son of middle-class Irish Catholic parents, one of six children born in the Bronx and raised in Red Bank, New Jersey. His father, John Sr., was a mild-mannered advertising man, easygoing and very religious. John's mother was tough, strong-willed, and the family disciplinarian.

Young John attended high school at the local Christian Brothers Academy. At fourteen, he informed his pious father that he was rejecting the "mumbo jumbo" of the Roman Catholic Church. "If I happened to be born in Africa, I'd be worshipping rocks," he announced. "So how can Catholicism be the one true religion?"

"You obviously don't have the gift of faith," his pious father understated.

Even then, people called him Crazy John. He sometimes went for days without sleeping, a loner who had no use for male companionship but claimed to have eight or nine girlfriends at a time. His favorite TV show was "The Millionaire," and his ambition, from early in life, was to make an enormous amount of money. He was everybody's most unforgettable character.

John arrived at Roanoke College, a small, sleepy southern liberal arts school, in the fall of 1968. He made his entrance on a Harley-Davidson motorcycle, dressed from head to toe in black leather. Another student, watching him march across campus in his leather pants, called out "Hey Slick!" and the nickname stuck. Even his professors called him "Slick"—if they were lucky enough to see him. Mulheren seldom attended classes. He'd borrow notes from other students and use his photographic memory to absorb every cough and comma.

He was, in his own way, brilliant. He was also a manic-depressive, although nobody had yet given a name to the disorder that made Mulheren such a fascinating, and exhausting, companion. John jumped from one obsession to another. He lived in an off-campus apartment with an enormous, heavily scarred tree trunk he used to practice knife throwing. He went to a local bowling alley near campus and remained there for days, until he'd mastered the sport. He also took up painting, archery, and rocketry. He would passionately embrace a new pastime every two or three months, and then move on. Everything was incredibly intense. He spurned normal student pastimes, refusing to drink, watch sports on TV, or hang around with the guys.

"The reason I stay with you is because you don't bug me," he told Nancy, the love of his life.

Like most of the students at Roanoke, he was apolitical in a hotly political era. He expressed himself through pranks, like stealing the Mustang owned by the dean of students and parking it in various parts of the campus. His crowning achievement was the construction of a large concrete obelisk that still stands on campus. John claimed he had mixed 4,000 .22-caliber bullets into the concrete to ensure that it could never be torn down.

After graduation, the newly married John and Nancy Mulheren moved to New York, where John fully intended to make a fortune on Wall Street. Without realizing it, he'd picked a career where his manic-depression would be an enormous advantage. Certainly, he never tried to soft-pedal his eccentricities. Nancy told me that once, early in their marriage, he decided he wanted to rent a gorilla suit to wear to work. His wife insisted they couldn't afford the fifty-dollar rental fee, but John went ahead anyway. He stuck a *Wall Street Journal* under his arm and took the subway to work in his gorilla suit. That night, Nancy discovered the costume hanging from the back of their bedroom door. She pointedly ignored it until John approached and meekly asked: "Don't you at least want me to try it on for you, honey?"

Soon, John could afford all the gorilla suits he wanted. His climb on Wall Street was meteoric. He took an entry-level job as an assistant trader at G.A. Saxon, a small brokerage house, and quickly began making money for the firm.

From the beginning, he enjoyed a considerable advantage over his competitors. He was tremendously intelligent, especially when it came to math. John could work out the risk-reward ratio of a given trade with mathematical precision. He even developed computer programs to deal with complicated stock trades. But his talents weren't merely intellectual. The manic side of his mental disorder seemed to give him the tremendous confidence needed to withstand the pressure of literally gambling millions of dollars on a single financial transaction. He also seemed to possess a "sixth sense"—an instinctive ability to make the right decision on a trade.

A couple of years out of college John was making $100,000— then $250,000. He moved on to Merrill Lynch, where he set up and headed an arbitrage department for the brokerage house. (Arbitragers speculate in the stock of companies involved in takeovers through merger or acquisition.) By 1976 he was making $4 million a year—more than Donald Regan, the chairman of Merrill Lynch who went on to serve as secretary of the treasury under Ronald Reagan. He was twenty-seven years old.

John's career moved in four-year cycles. After a stint at Merrill Lynch he started his own trading firm, then went on to Spear Leeds & Kellogg, another brokerage firm, where he prospered even more as the stock market madness of the 1980s took hold. Along the way, he and Nancy adopted five children, three of whom had learning disabilities.

By his own account, John lost track of how much money he was making, but it increased to $10 million and then $15 million a year. In 1986, *Financial World* magazine put John Mulheren on its list of top-ten Wall Street moneymakers, estimating he earned $25 million a year. John, who shunned the press, refused to be interviewed for the article, telling *Financial World* he wanted to "get back to sleeping at my desk."

He was making a new fortune every few weeks, but he was literally incapable of holding on to money. Any cash John put in his pocket would quickly disappear. If a shirt caught his eye, he'd immediately buy twenty shirts just like it. If John gazed out his office window and took a fancy to the hot dog cart on the street below, he'd send somebody out with $5,000 in cash to buy it on the spot. Finally, Nancy put him on a strict allowance. One of Wall Street's most promising young traders left home for work each morning with five dollars in his wallet. If he ran out of money, he'd literally beg on the streets for more. John once talked a clerk at the Fifty-ninth Street subway station into giving him a token to get home—and returned later to give the clerk a $1,000 reward.

Spontaneous acts of generosity were part of his character. John liked to gamble in Atlantic City for relaxation. If he finished the night in the black, John would give away his winnings, surveying the teeming masses at the slot machines until his internal radar would fix on one lucky low-roller. It's safe to assume his targets never knew the identity of the tall, burly man who walked up and handed them $10,000 in chips.

John contributed enormous amounts to charity. His alma mater got $2 million—perhaps another reason besides the bullets that his obelisk is still standing at Roanoke College. He bought fire engines for the local fire department in his hometown of Rumson, New Jersey. The local police got bullet-proof vests. He formed a foundation to fix up the homes of the poor in Monmouth County. He gave money to friends, family members, acquaintances, and the former bartender who had taught him to surf as a kid. Stories of John's generosity abounded, but most of his giving was done anonymously. It's no exaggeration to say that anyone who asked Mulheren for help got it.

In 1984, when he was at the peak of his success, he decided to retire. John left Spear Leeds, and simply went home. He spent his time jet skiing, working out, and developing a friendship with rock star Bruce Springsteen, who lived nearby. His hiatus lasted about a year. Then John decided to unretire. With a new partner, Israel Englander, he put together his own trading firm—Jamie Securities. His name was still magic on the Street, and he had no difficulty putting together a group of wealthy investors to finance the new company.

He also resumed a friendship with Ivan Boesky, whom he had known since 1976. There's a well-known story about their first meeting: The Mulherens met Boesky and his wife for dinner at Café des Artistes, an expensive Manhattan restaurant. As John and Nancy watched, Boesky ordered every entree on the menu. When all eight dishes arrived, he sampled each one and then directed the waiter to remove the seven he wasn't going to eat.

In his own way, Boesky was as much a character as Mulheren.

They were two unique individuals, but where John was gregarious, open-handed, and likable, Boesky was cold, inscrutable, and personally unpopular. That may have been what drew Mulheren to him. John was stubborn and contrary, and if Wall Street was bad-mouthing Boesky, Mulheren was bound to take the opposite position and leap to his defense.

The famous dinner at Café des Artistes, at any rate, was the beginning of a long relationship. John and Ivan often talked on the phone about stocks, as did others in Wall Street's small circle of high-powered arbitragers.

Like other people in the financial community, John would come to regret the association. Wall Street was shaken on November 14, 1986, when it was announced that Ivan Boesky had pled guilty to insider trading, agreed to pay an astonishing $100 million fine, and promised to cooperate with an ongoing government probe of wrongdoing on Wall Street. The impact of these developments soon rippled down to Mulheren. Boesky had actually had very little to say about John when he began talking with the government, but Michael Davidoff, Boesky's chief trader, implicated Mulheren in a series of "parking" deals.

"Parking" stocks was not an important violation of securities laws, and Mulheren was a decidedly secondary figure in the government's widening probe of Wall Street's excesses. Nevertheless, the pressures on John increased as 1987 drew to a close. He had lost millions of dollars in the October stock market crash, and now the government was pursuing him, with a federal grand jury looking into his dealings with Boesky.

John hired Otto Obermaier, a prominent Manhattan lawyer, to represent him. But his problems were medical as well as legal. He'd stopped taking lithium, a drug that curbed the highs and lows of his manic-depression, because of a stomach disorder. He began to think about committing suicide.

His breakdown came to a climax nine weeks before my first meeting with him in the hospital cafeteria. For his family, and especially Nancy, they'd been nine weeks of pure agony. It began on the day Obermaier informed John that the government was prepared to indict him for security law violations. The evidence had been provided by Boesky and Davidoff.

Obermaier suggested a deal: Mulheren could plead guilty to a single charge and avoid jail. John exploded in rage at the very idea of pleading guilty to anything and stormed out of the meeting. "This is just like the McCarthy era," he told Nancy when he arrived home. "They're going to take everybody down." He stalked into the solarium, a lovely circular room filled with white wicker furniture. He got on the phone and—it seemed to Nancy—called everybody in creation to complain about what was happening.

During their eighteen years of marriage Nancy had become accustomed to life with a manic-depressive—the sustained bursts of high energy followed by briefer periods of black depression. But this time John was worse than she had ever seen him. After getting off the phone, Mulheren retreated to a room upstairs where he popped the movie *Ivanhoe* into a video recorder. When the film finished he rewound and watched *Ivanhoe* again. This continued throughout the night. Nancy hoped that John would eventually "crash," but by morning his mania had grown even worse.

"I'm just going to have to take matters into my own hands," John said ominously. He began to rant incessantly about Davidoff, telling Nancy (falsely, as it turned out) that he had staked out Davidoff's home the previous day. Nancy summoned John's father and his business partner, Israel Englander, to their home in Rumson. Neither was able to calm him.

Mulheren's wild threats terrified his father, who envisioned John Jr. spending his life in jail for murder. "Let me kill him for you," John Sr. said desperately. "I'm much older than you."

Nancy heard John announce that he would leave the house at 4 P.M. It was a familiar refrain—he often framed important matters in terms of deadlines. He had proposed by telling her: "Either you marry me in two weeks or I never want to see you again." ("Okay, I'll marry you," she had replied.)

Good to his word, Mulheren changed his clothes and headed out of the house at the stroke of four.

"I have to do this," he muttered.

Though it was mid-February the day was bright and beautiful. Nancy watched from a window as her husband paused to say good-bye to their children, who were playing under a large tree in the front yard. She picked up the phone and called the police. By the time John drove away from the house, they were waiting for him at the end of the long driveway.

The Rumson police were among the numerous recipients of Mulheren's generosity. The officers knew John well and had no desire to arrest him. But their attempts to reason with him failed. He refused to go home, or to a hospital. Matters were not helped by the fact that his car was loaded with guns.

The cops finally arrested John and took him off to the local lockup. Nancy and John Sr. rushed to the jail, where they found Mulheren making things worse for himself. His previous diatribe had been directed at Davidoff, but now, Nancy noted, John was raving about Boesky. She wondered if her husband had decided to switch targets because the mention of Michael Davidoff produced nothing but blank stares from the local police.

Mulheren's arrest created a sensation on Wall Street and elsewhere. John was a gun fancier, but now it was erroneously reported that he owned grenade launchers and machine guns. His beautiful home was described as an "arsenal," even though Mulheren kept no guns in the house because of his children.

Most unfortunately, John's appearance in the headlines also guaranteed he would not be forgotten by my old pal, U.S. attorney Rudy Giuliani. John left Giuliani with little choice but to arrest him for threatening a government witness.

Mulheren was treated to a taste of federal justice. After an uneventful week in the New Jersey lockup ("I was pretty crazy then, so it really didn't bother me," he recalled) John was transferred to the Metropolitan Correction Center, the federal prison in Manhattan.

MCC was booked solid, and since no cells were available, John was taken to a hallway, where he slept on a cot with no sheets. He was refused medication for his manic-depression and taken almost daily to the "bullpen," the waiting area for prisoners scheduled for court appearances. He would be confined to a small, windowless room where he sat on a bench and stared at the walls while waiting for court appearances that never took place. At night, he would be returned to his cot. Besides his mental torment, Mulheren was also dogged by severe pain. On the day before he was arrested, John had undergone a partial root canal. His dental problem, and the agonizing pain it caused, went untreated at MCC.

Mulheren's suicidal impulses—never far from the surface—intensified. He thought carefully about a variety of ways in which he might end his life.

"You become convinced that everybody would be better off without you," he explained.

Other inmates shared their food with John to make up for meals he missed while waiting in the bullpen. They also told him that his treatment was "bullpen therapy"—a calculated effort by the government to break him. These assurances may well have helped this stubborn Irishman to hang on.

Giuliani's office, meanwhile, resisted efforts to have Mulheren transferred to a mental hospital where his manic-depression might be treated. The government also opposed a motion to permit Mulheren to see his own psychiatrist. If Mulheren really was in need of treatment, Giuliani's prosecutors argued, the proper place was the criminal ward at Bellevue, a public hospital in Manhattan. On March 5, a federal magistrate finally ordered Mulheren to be transferred to Carrier, the New Jersey mental hospital where I first met him. But Giuliani's office wasn't finished. The prosecutors appealed the ruling. They were unsuccessful, but the effort kept Mulheren in the MCC for another week.

By Wall Street standards, John Mulheren was already the toughest dude in town when he left MCC. Wall Street cream puffs like Dennis Levine, Martin Siegel, and Boesky had become government informers without much more than a frown from SEC investigators or Giuliani's prosecutors. But Mulheren had refused to talk or cooperate, a stance that won him the admiration of fellow prisoners like Anthony "Fat Tony" Salerno, head of the Gambino family. In jail, like everywhere else, John acquired a following. On the day he was transferred to Carrier, he received an enthusiastic round of cheers and applause from the MCC inmates.

Unfortunately, John's grimmest days were ahead of him. At Carrier, Mulheren was confined to a locked psychiatric ward where the other patients really did seem crazy. A few days after he arrived, Mulheren encountered a woman named "Judy R." (Patients were known to each other only by their first name and the first initial of their last name.) Judy R. had an encyclopedic knowledge of criminal law and was well versed in the details of Mulheren's case. John found this unnerving, to say the least. He was convinced Judy R. had been dispatched by the government to spy on him. (I later learned that Judy R. was a former federal prosecutor with serious mental problems. Her presence at Carrier while John was there was purely coincidental.)

All in all, the transfer to a mental hospital was not turning out to be the improvement his friends had hoped for. Mulheren missed his family terribly, and unlike MCC, Carrier prohibited visits by young children. At night, John heard the demented screaming of his fellow patients. A month in a psycho ward had brought him closer to conceding defeat than the harsh treatment he'd suffered in prison.

Still, Obermaier wasn't eager to help him get out. In fact, he'd adopted a strategy of postponing John's criminal indictment by keeping him locked up. His approach made some sense. Mulheren was in danger of being prosecuted under a section of the federal firearms act that carried a mandatory jail sentence upon conviction. I think Otto was saying: Give me time to try to figure out a way to avoid an indictment here.

But John's condition continued to grow worse at Carrier. Obermaier was still recommending that he plead guilty to a single criminal charge. For perhaps the only time during his long ordeal, Mulheren began to waver.

"Maybe I should plead guilty," he told his wife.

"What, are you nuts?" Nancy shot back. She did not believe her husband would be able to live with himself if he gave in. Her anger with Obermaier was growing. She did not understand how a man confined to a mental institution could be asked to plead guilty to a crime. She, even more than John, was responsible for the decision to seek a new lawyer.

A day after our meeting at the hospital, John decided to hire me as his attorney. Before I decide to take on a client, I've got to be convinced that I can do something for him. I won't take on a client simply for the sake of getting some business. In John's case, it was already clear to me that before anything else, I needed to get him released from Carrier for his own mental health. So I moved to arrange a meeting with Giuliani as soon as possible.

The U.S. attorney's office was located near Foley Square in lower Manhattan. It was part of a cluster of federal buildings that included a courthouse and the jail where Mulheren was originally held. Rudy had a huge, wedge-shaped office with a large desk at one end. It wasn't a very functional space. There was a government-issued sofa and armchair grouped around a coffee table at the opposite end of the office from his desk, and he used that area for meetings. Giuliani would settle into the armchair. The visitor would sink into the sofa. Rudy's aides would pull up chairs on the other side of the coffee table. Thus, all the government's men would be looking down at whoever was sitting at the table.

Defense lawyers sometimes arrived at these meetings accompanied by a horde of aides and associates, sort of like the heavyweight boxing champion and his entourage. Maybe they wanted company on that low-slung sofa. But I preferred to come alone.

Giuliani's basic pitch was: big case, big headlines. Let's see how this plays out. Mulheren is locked up because he's a danger. We'll forgo an indictment as long as he's in jail.

This struck me as particularly odd: It was as if Giuliani and the government were somehow doing my client a favor by keeping him locked up in a psychiatric ward where his mental health was rapidly deteriorating.

"I look at this differently," I told Rudy. "It's not a question of you giving me more time. It's a question of me giving you time. I'm going to move for an immediate trial, so get Ivan Boesky ready to testify by June first."

When I said that, the blood drained from their faces. John had the right to a speedy trial, as Rudy well knew. But Giuliani's office had bigger fish to fry—the prosecutors were at various stages of important criminal investigations of Michael Milken and other major-league Wall Street criminals. The last thing Giuliani wanted at that point was to expose Ivan Boesky, the government's star witness, to a hostile cross-examination.

"Give us a few minutes," Giuliani said.

I stepped into Rudy's outer office and killed time by staring at the photographs on the wall. There was Rudy with Ronald Reagan, Rudy with U.S. Senator Al D'Amato, Rudy with the sanitation commissioner, Rudy with . . .

After fifteen or twenty minutes, Giuliani called me back in. He announced that the government had decided to do me a big favor: Mulheren could go back on the street. The only condition was that John would have to regularly see a psychiatrist.

I was elated. I couldn't wait to get to the phone and tell Mulheren he was a free man. He was astonished and delighted. Mulheren was released that very day (April 27, 1988), and from then on, I became something of a superlawyer in his eyes.

Adjournments always help the government. The only chance Mike Milken had was to press for an immediate trial. That would have terrorized the government. The old saw about delay helping the defense because witnesses' memories fade is patently false. Witnesses, when properly prepared by the prosecution, have great memory. And additional time gives the government the opportunity to dig up new witnesses and evidence. The prosecution always gains by postponement in a case.

Many defense lawyers can be lazy, and many are just too busy to quickly go forward with the trial of a client. Economics also has a lot to do with delay. In one major case, some said, the lawyers were in no hurry to go to trial, since they were billing one or two million dollars a month in legal fees.

Unfortunately, John's release did nothing to ease his legal problems. The government had the option of pursuing the threatening charges against Mulheren *and* indicting him for securities law violations. In fact, that appeared to be exactly what Giuliani was planning to do. He still wanted Mulheren to plead guilty to a single criminal charge. If he refused, the government would throw the book at him by indicting him across the board.

But I was already thinking that I "couldn't lose." I couldn't use John's mental problems as a defense against the securities violations. But if the government chose to press the threatening charge against him, I'd be able to introduce evidence about his manic-depression, and that might undermine the entire case. On the other hand, if Giuliani decided to go with the securities case only, we would at least be rid of the one charge that could have brought John significant jail time.

The first thing I wanted to do was turn John's weakness into a strength. Strong evidence of manic-depression could be a powerful card for the defense. I proceeded as I had with medical evidence in the von Bulow case. I wanted one of the world's foremost experts on manic-depression—someone money couldn't buy. I wanted a man or woman whose credentials were so formidable that they couldn't be questioned or challenged. I conducted a comprehensive search, and the top person in academia seemed to be Ross Baldessarini at Harvard. All I had to do was convince him to get involved in the trial of a stock trader in New York City.

In looking through his credentials, I noticed that Baldessarini was chairman of something called the Mailman Research Center at Harvard. A light went on. I had once represented a multimillionaire named Joe Mailman, the chairman and CEO of Air Express International. I recalled that Mailman's brother was manic-depressive.

Joe Mailman was already in his eighties when I represented him, and very wealthy. He had an apartment in the Hotel Pierre, where our first meeting took place. He must have had $30 million in paintings on the walls. I can remember sitting on a couch, absentmindedly fingering something behind me. The "thing" turned out to be a painting by Renoir! Even though Joe had all the money in the world, he was also the kind of guy who would say to me on a rainy day: "Where did you get those rubbers? There's a guy at Madison and Thirty-seventh Street who can get you the same thing for three dollars."

Joe was traveling when I tried to reach him, but within forty-five minutes he had called me back from a phone booth somewhere in the Southwest.

"Don't worry. I'll take care of it," Joe assured me after I told him the story.

Within an hour, I was on the phone with Ross Baldessarini. The red carpet had been rolled out. I also contacted Ray Adams, a Harvard psychiatrist who had helped me in the von Bulow case. Both experts agreed to meet with John. Within a couple of months, I had very impressive reports on my desk documenting Mulheren's manic-depression.

I set up a meeting with Giuliani to make my pitch. Before going over to Foley Square, I sent somebody to the Cornell University medical bookstore to pick up every book ever written by Baldessarini and Adams. The bill was around $500.

I made my way to Rudy's office juggling my purchases. Once inside, I opened my briefcase and placed the medical reports on the coffee table.

"You'd better read these before you run off and indict him," I told Rudy and his men. In order to give them a feel for who had prepared the reports, I then piled the medical books on the coffee table.

"They're yours," I said, before walking out.

It is rare for a defense lawyer to show the prosecutor part of his case, and I'll tell you right now nobody hands a prosecutor $500 worth of medical books. That was just for effect, and as gimmicky as it was, I think it worked.

Within three weeks, Giuliani decided to drop the threatening charges. It was a relief knowing John wouldn't have the possibility of serious jail time hanging over his head. With the resolution of the gun charges, the case against Mulheren had been reduced to a series of "parking" violations.

Parking was very common on Wall Street. One firm would "park" stock with another firm. It was a practice that enabled the brokerage firm doing the parking to avoid taxes and evade the net capital requirements established by the SEC. The firm holding the stock would be reimbursed for any decline in the value of the securities, but any increase in the stock would be returned to the original owner.

Parking was, then, a sham transaction: It was illegal, but in the past it had not been regarded as a serious crime, or even a crime at all. Once in a while, the SEC would swoop in and order a twenty-four-hour suspension for violation of the rules. But things had changed. In the wake of the wild 1980s boom on Wall Street, parking was being treated as a major offense by Rudy Giuliani.

Still everybody, including Rudy, realized Mulheren was not a big fish in the Wall Street criminal pond. I wanted to get the U.S. attorney's office to drop the charges. I knew it would be tough. Giuliani was under heavy pressures that had nothing to do with the law. He had a group of aggressive young assistants, all eager to bring indictments. Taking a Wall Street bigwig to trial was their day in the sun. For Rudy, letting Mulheren go would mean undercutting some of his own people.

Matters were further complicated by Giuliani's career timetable. He was preparing to leave office and get into politics. I wondered if it would be better to let things slide in hopes of getting a more favorable hearing from his successor. However, the lawyer most prominently mentioned as next in line for U.S. attorney was none other than Otto Obermaier, John's old lawyer.

I decided Rudy was my best shot. I went back for another round on that sofa, and made my pitch. I emphasized John's background, good works, and the fact that everybody from a paralyzed New York City police officer to Jesse Jackson would be willing to take the stand and testify to Mulheren's generosity and decency. The government was going to put a man like this on trial for parking? I think I almost had Giuliani convinced.

The matter came right down to the wire. Rudy left office at the end of January 1989. His last few days were frenzied. He was trying to settle two other well-publicized Wall Street cases against junk bond king Michael Milken and Robert Freeman. His outer office was crowded with defense lawyers as eager as I was to reach an agreement with him.

But the fates were not kind to John Mulheren. At what proved to be my final meeting with U.S. Attorney Rudolph Giuliani, one of his assistants, Bob Gage, dropped a bombshell:

"What about the manipulation of Gulf and Western stock by your client?" Gage challenged.

"I don't know what you're talking about," I replied.

Gage was suggesting that Mulheren and Boesky had conspired to fix the price of G&W stock, a much more serious matter than "parking." This charge was news to me, and ideally, I'd have wanted to take some time to look into the matter.

But Giuliani was leaving the office on the very next day. For me, this was a make-or-break meeting.

"Give me five minutes to call my client," I said. I raced to a phone and called John. He quickly told me the story.

Boesky and Carl Icahn, a major corporate raider, had been toying with the idea of attempting a takeover of Gulf & Western, the media company that controlled Paramount Pictures and the publishing house of Simon & Schuster. Between them, Boesky and Icahn had acquired a little less than 10 percent of G&W's stock, which at some point they decided to sell.

Boesky had a figure in mind ($45 per share) that would make it profitable for him to unload his six million shares. But the market refused to cooperate. Finally, in October, the price of G&W stock hit $44 a share. It was then that Boesky called John Mulheren.

On the phone outside Rudy's office, I listened to John explain what had happened when Boesky called:

"I like Gulf & Western," Boesky said. "I wouldn't pay more than $45 for it, but it would be great at $45."

"I understand," John replied.

My client thought Boesky was doing him a favor. John knew that stocks Boesky liked had a tendency to do very well. So he started eagerly buying up G&W stock. His buying effort pushed the value to $45. It was then that Boesky unloaded 6.7 million shares of G&W stock, stiffing his old friend John Mulheren. He was left holding a large block of G&W stock while Boesky counted his profits. The transaction wound up costing John $67,000. Far from being part of an illegal conspiracy to manipulate stock prices, John Mulheren thought he had been taken.

I made a snap decision to go back into Giuliani's office and regurgitate everything John had told me. Giving this kind of information to the enemy is a very risky thing to do. You simply don't tip your hand to the opposition. But with Rudy about to cast off on his political career, I thought it was my last, best chance to save John.

It didn't work. Giuliani's people had no rejoinder to John's explanation. They had no explanation, for example, of how my client might have benefited from this "manipulation." Still, I could tell they weren't really listening to me. I knew that John was going to have to stand trial.

Giuliani ultimately offered me the same old deal. John could plead guilty to a single criminal charge.

"Take it," one of his assistants urged me. "He isn't going to jail."

"What's the point of this if he isn't going to jail?" I asked angrily. "What are you doing here, processing cases?"

Giuliani left the office in the hands of Benito Romano, a former deputy who returned from private practice to run things on an interim basis. Not surprisingly, Romano followed the recommendations of the assistants who were working on various cases. (Eventually, President Reagan appointed Republican Senator Alfonse D'Amato's choice for U.S. attorney: Otto Obermaier.)

An indictment and a trial were unavoidable. Preparing a client for this kind of ordeal can be very difficult, but John was relatively easy to deal with. He had, after all, hired me to do battle with the government, and that meant a trial in all probability. More importantly, the most traumatic period for John had already passed. He had already suffered arrest, public humiliation, imprisonment, and a harrowing stay in the maximum security wing of a mental hospital.

"We're going to kick their ass," he told me.

It was time for me to start thinking about strategy. Mulheren was facing two kinds of charges: parking and stock manipulation. The Gulf & Western allegations were the most serious, but also the flimsiest.

The parking charges were another matter. There was a great deal of circumstantial evidence that suggested that the stocks in question were not simply part of John's inventory.

After parking transactions are completed, there are payback transactions. The firm holding the parked stock is reimbursed for the cost of carrying the stock and any decline in its value by the firm doing the parking. If the stock increases in value, the firm holding the parked stock passes along the profits to the firm doing the parking.

According to the government, there were a series of transactions in which John held stock for Boesky, and in which John funneled money to Ivan because the stock increased in value while John held it. By the government's reckoning, profits of $600,000 were involved.

John had an explanation: He said that he *purchased the stock from Boesky "at risk,"* which simply meant that any profits or losses produced by the stock were John's and John's alone. (This was no different from any ordinary stock transaction.)

But from the government's point of view, the parking charges were close to being a slam dunk. In addition to Boesky and Boesky's chief trader, Michael Davidoff, documents seized from John's company by the government indicated that Mulheren's firm, Jamie Securities, had reimbursed Boesky for profits made on stocks the government claimed were being "parked."

John said Boesky and Davidoff were lying. The trouble was, the government seemed to be in the process of acquiring other witnesses by using hardball tactics.

The prosecutors, using the threat of criminal indictment, were pressuring Mulheren's business partner, Israel Englander, to cooperate with the government. The same treatment was being given to Leonard DeStefano, John's accountant, and Edward McCarthy, the controller of his securities firm. I could not be sure who might agree to cooperate, or what might be said about John. If even one of these men caved in to the government pressure, as seemed very likely, we might be faced with serious new problems, and I couldn't even anticipate what those problems might be. (As things developed, Englander and McCarthy agreed to cooperate in exchange for immunity. McCarthy was added to the government lineup, but Englander's grand jury testimony was so equivocal that he was never called as a witness. DeStefano refused the government's offer. His "reward" was to be indicted with John.)

A purely technical defense seemed risky and unpromising. I needed a different approach. My best bet might be to make this dry securities case as emotional as possible. The key to the government's case was Ivan Boesky. I wanted to try the case on the basis of who Mulheren was and who Boesky was—the greatest guy in the world versus the Prince of Darkness. If jurors get that kind of feeling about a defendant and his chief accuser, they tend to find some kind of a hook, however slender, on which to hang an acquittal. That's particularly true when the charges involve a victimless "crime" like parking.

We swung into a heavy research mode, just as I'd done with von Bulow. This time, however, I wasn't interested in becoming an expert on insulin, or even stocks per se. I wanted to know who Ivan Boesky was, how he'd made his fortune, and what sort of deals he'd made to keep it. I hired private detectives, interviewed many of Boesky's former employees, and plowed through the records of his trading company. This is the picture that emerged:

Ivan Boesky grew up in Detroit and attended three colleges without managing to get a degree at any of them. He graduated from a law school that didn't require a college degree and wasn't able to find a job with a law firm. Surprisingly, he did obtain a job as the clerk to a federal judge. This was a very desirable position for any young lawyer—competition for these posts is so stiff that I hadn't even bothered to apply for one following my own graduation from Fordham Law School. Boesky got the job through family connections. Our interviews with former employees disclosed that young Ivan spent his days as a clerk reading the *Wall Street Journal* and making numerous telephone calls to brokerage houses and other financial institutions.

Boesky's subsequent career as a Wall Street genius was equally suspect. He spent seven years in obscurity, moving without distinction through a series of low-level jobs with investment houses while living in a Park Avenue apartment provided by his wealthy in-laws. In 1975, his fortunes shifted when Seema, his wife, received a $700,000 inheritance from her mother's estate. The money was used to found a new arbitrage firm, Ivan Boesky & Company.

Despite an aura of mystery, arbitrage was a fairly straightforward business. The arbitrager speculated in the stock of companies involved in takeovers through merger or acquisition. He would wait until there was a public announcement of the takeover bid, then buy into the stock of the company targeted for the takeover. The individual or firm intent on obtaining the target company would be willing to pay a fat premium for the stock to get a controlling interest. The risk was that if the takeover bid collapsed, the value of the stock could drop sharply, producing a heavy loss for the arbitrager.

This was how risk arbitrage was carried out before Boesky and other practitioners raised the stakes to new levels in the 1980s by buying the stock of target companies before takeover bids were even announced. Such crystal ball gazing could be the result of an arbitrager's analysis of a company's value as a take-over target and a willingness to gamble on that research. Or "risk" arbitrage could be practiced by illegally obtaining inside information about impending takeovers.

During his reign as a supposed financial genius, Boesky appeared larger than life. He operated from a large, white-carpeted Fifth Avenue office adorned with works of art from Etruscan Italy. Ivan stood—always—at the helm of his operation in a black three-piece business suit with a phone in each ear. The helm was a high-tech bank of electronic equipment that included television monitors that permitted him to inspect the Boesky workers toiling on the floor below and a switchboard with 160 phone lines that wired him into the world of high finance. There were video display terminals filled with stock information, a digital clock showing the time around the world, news wires, and stock tickers. Few visitors realized these high-tech props were part of a charade. Maybe, by the end, Boesky didn't even realize it himself.

Ivan loved to tell reporters that intelligence, sweat-of-the-brow research, and hard work were the key to his fabulous success. One frequently repeated story had Boesky's minions obtaining the flight plans of corporate jets so that Ivan could deduce, from the travels of the corporate executives, what deals were cooking. This was completely false, of course. Boesky was working from illegally obtained inside information that enabled him to purchase blocks of stock in companies that were about to become the target of takeover attempts. And with the profits, like a robber baron of old, Boesky was able to buy the status and respectability he craved. He purchased a membership in the

Harvard Club. He made handsome contributions to Princeton, the school his son attended, and to many charitable causes. Boesky was also a very conspicuous consumer. He owned a seventy-five-acre estate in the suburbs north of New York City and was chauffeured about in a pink Rolls-Royce. An interview Boesky granted to a journalist from *U.S. News & World Report* was twice interrupted by his wife, Seema, who walked into Ivan's office to model a fur coat for her husband. His notorious "greed is healthy" speech to graduates of the University of California business school firmly established him as a symbol of the 1980s.

Boesky's turning point, when he surrendered to the Dark Side, probably came in 1982, when he made a bold investment in the stock of Cities Service. The oil company was the target of a takeover attempt by corporate raider T. Boone Pickens. Cities Service executives reacted to the news of Pickens's interest in much the same way villagers in medieval England must have behaved when told Viking ships were offshore. They embraced a "white knight" in the form of Gulf Oil, which promptly launched its own bid for the company.

Boesky saw an opportunity to make a killing and plowed $70 million—most of it borrowed—into Cities Service stock. But when Gulf abruptly pulled out of the deal, the stock plummeted and Boesky was faced with financial ruin.

The man who saved Boesky from disaster was my client, John Mulheren.

John was then the top trader at Spear Leeds, which valued Boesky as one of its biggest customers. When Boesky turned to John in desperation, Mulheren met with his partners at the firm and fashioned a bailout plan. He purchased a large block of Boesky's stock and then worked out an eye-glazing series of trades that reduced Boesky's liability in the event of further losses.

"I don't think Ivan understood what I was doing," Mulheren said of the mechanics of his rescue plan.

Besides saving Boesky, Mulheren wound up making millions for his firm. As John had expected, the Cities Service stock rebounded a few weeks later.

Despite the happy ending, the incident must have shaken Boesky, who nearly lost his shirt. Looking at our research, I could see that the near-debacle convinced Ivan the only way to protect himself against financial ruin was to rely on illegal inside information. Our analysis of his stock market investments after Cities Service clearly indicated Boesky was either psychic or a criminal. When I learned from a helpful college professor that Boesky had purchased an apartment hideaway in Switzerland at that same crucial juncture, I knew even Ivan himself wasn't under any delusions about which of the two he had become.

By the time I began researching Boesky, his only career was that of government witness. The federal prosecutors, I learned later, could hardly believe how quickly he folded under pressure. But even in disgrace, he cast an extraordinary shadow. One of Wall Street's most respected investment bankers, Martin Siegel, admitted he had accepted suitcases stuffed with cash from Boesky in exchange for inside information. Drexel Burnham Lambert, the hottest Wall Street investment house of the 1980s, pled guilty to criminal charges based on information provided by Boesky, and collapsed soon thereafter. Drexel's legendary junk bond chief, Michael Milken, was ruined as well. Even Boesky's plea bargain was the stuff of legends. Newspapers all over the country carried headlines about the fabulous $100 million fine he had agreed to pay for his crimes. As it turned out, the fine, like everything else about Boesky, was less than met the eye.

Naturally, I was eager to dismantle the Boesky legend. It would have been a pleasure even if my client had been a less sympathetic guy than John Mulheren.

In the best of all possible worlds, my work would have been made easy by the plea bargain. But Boesky's unusual deal with the government only required him to discuss matters the prosecutors asked him about. Usually such agreements require the guilty party to come clean about all his wrongdoings. But Boesky's arrangement was different.

I had a sneaking suspicion a few crimes might have slipped through the cracks. So I launched a massive review of Boesky's trading records, which had been subpoenaed by the government. The records, which included millions of documents, were located in two dreary warehouses in lower Manhattan.

My assistants, Andy Citron and Joanne Crispi, headed a team of twenty paralegals who did the research. It was quite a challenge. I recalled reading stories about how Drexel Burnham Lambert had spent millions of dollars photocopying documents subpoenaed by the government. Well, I don't believe anyone from the government actually read all that stuff. But we certainly read our Boesky documents. And it paid off.

A team of paralegals went to a warehouse on Varick Street in lower Manhattan where records from Boesky's trading companies were stored in more than nine hundred boxes. They spent months sifting through the documents. We were helped, to some extent, by Boesky's method of operation. He required all of his key employees to dictate a memo at the end of the workday summarizing everything they had done. The memos were transcribed and hand-delivered to Boesky's mansion. Using those records, our team painstakingly reconstructed all of Boesky's major deals, including every trade involving Boesky and Mulheren. I later brought in professional accountants to further analyze Boesky's business dealings.

A second warehouse holding Boesky documents was located in Greenwich Village. The building was a firetrap that lacked heat and electricity. There were no fire escapes and only one exit. And, of course, the building was loaded with paper. I had already experienced one near-disaster with fire at the Newport courthouse when I accidentally ignited the von Bulow evidence, so this warehouse gave me endless nightmares. Still, we purchased fifty fire extinguishers, fifty Coleman lanterns and hired additional temporary employees to search the records.

A number of the temps, for some reason, were unemployed comedians who had come to the Big Apple seeking fame and fortune. They weren't much interested in law, but they had a limitless inventory of bad stand-up comedy jokes. On the first day, Joann Crispi delivered an impassioned speech to the assembled temps on the importance of fire safety. Her earnest effort was greeted with laughter and merriment. The temps wanted to know if Joann was also an unemployed comedian.

We suspected that Boesky had engaged in much more insider trading that he ever admitted to the prosecutors, but we had no proof. We looked at a number of deals that were not included in his admissions to the government. We found multiple photocopies of a memo from Reid Nagle, a Boesky employee, that was actually marked "Read and Destroy." But Boesky denied wrongdoing in all of them and we were unable to dispute him.

Yet some of our own discoveries at the warehouse were truly tantalizing. It seemed likely Boesky had transferred millions of dollars in assets to his wife. Indeed, we were able to locate a $2.3 million "loan" that Seema Boesky made to her supposedly bankrupt husband.

I also hired private detectives to dig into Boesky's background, but they ultimately failed to turn up anything of use. We wound up with a spate of stories about Boesky's alleged homosexuality, which wouldn't have been of interest to us even if the stories had been more than rumor. We got some meaningless but juicy tidbits, such as the fact that inmates at Lompoc, the federal resort-prison where Boesky served his sentence, had tossed dead rats onto Ivan's bunk as a way of welcoming him. We interviewed inmates who told us that Boesky bribed prison officials, but we were unable to confirm this.

However, our painstaking analysis of the financial documents was much more fruitful than anything uncovered by the army of private detectives who had previously investigated Boesky for Milken, Drexel, and other targets of Boesky's grand jury testimony. We also digested thousands of newspaper and magazine articles about the man whose Wall Street nickname was "Piggie."

By the time we were done, I felt reasonably confident we had done everything possible to prepare for Boesky's testimony. It was now time to do battle:

The trial got under way on May 14, 1990. It was held in a stately, high-ceilinged courtroom in the federal courthouse in Manhattan before a brilliant and respected jurist, Miriam Goldman Cederbaum. The prosecutors were two very young assistant U.S. attorneys, E. Scott Gilbert and Alfred Pavlis. I had no problems with Gilbert or Pavlis, but the judge was a different story. Sometimes, I thought she felt her mission in life was to protect young, innocent government prosecutors from big-shot defense lawyers like me. Also on trial with John was his beleaguered trading assistant, Lenny DeStefano. Lenny was the best-kept secret of the trial. The government had virtually no evidence against him, and his name was rarely mentioned by government witnesses. His indictment was punishment for refusing to cooperate with Giuliani's office. His lawyer, Thomas Fitzpatrick, and I developed a repartee.

PUCCIO: "Now, what's the name of that guy sitting next to you?"
FITZPATRICK: "Lenny . . . Lenny . . . Lenny . . . ???"

John, as always, dressed casually. He wore a brightly colored polo shirt, blue jeans, and loafers with no socks. He looked more like a man ready to leave on an extended sailing excursion than the defendant in a high-stakes criminal trial. John also sometimes acted like a man eager to go on vacation. Early on, the judge asked a group of prospective jurors if a lengthy trial would impose a severe burden on any of them. About a dozen hands shot up. One of those hands belonged to my client, John Mulheren.

He did his best to turn the trial into a social occasion. John occasionally sang during lulls in the court proceedings and chatted amiably with reporters, friends, admirers, and just about anybody else who stuck his or her nose into the courtroom. Despite his happy bravado, Mulheren was under a terrible strain. He would start each Monday fresh and energetic, but as the week wore on, he would become more tense and irritable. In private I knew he was continuing to fight a grueling battle against the thoughts of suicide that bedevil people with his mental condition.

Jury selection was uneventful. In his opening statement, prosecutor Scott Gilbert described Boesky and Mulheren as partners in crime who broke the securities laws for mutual benefit. I focused on the contrast between Mulheren and Boesky, the King of Greed.

"The stench that will be created by Ivan Boesky in this courtroom will not be removed until the trial is over," I warned the jurors.

With the preliminaries out of the way, the government rolled out its big gun: Ivan Boesky. I'd been preparing for this confrontation with Boesky for almost a year, but I didn't have a real feel for the man until he actually took the witness stand. Boesky sat perfectly erect with his hands folded together on his lap. The charcoal-colored suit and candle-white skin might have belonged to an undertaker. The small, cold smile that seemed perpetually stapled to Boesky's face during his years of triumph on Wall Street was gone now, but the smug expression was intact.

Needless to say, Boesky's business suit was perfectly tailored, and every silver hair on his head was in place. I'd been told that when Boesky first met secretly with government attorneys on a sweltering night in 1986, the intense heat and humidity soon prompted the lawyers to shed their suit jackets. But Boesky refused to remove his jacket and kept his tie knotted tightly at the collar throughout the lengthy meeting. You'd have thought he was attending a dinner party instead of a secret debriefing session. I was hoping that Boesky's obvious smugness and his obsession with appearance would work in my favor with the jurors. The contrast between my open-collar, ruddy-faced client and the mannequinlike Boesky couldn't have been more striking. During his three days on the stand, Boesky never made eye contact with John.

Prosecutor Scott Gilbert gently led Boesky through his direct examination. Boesky described a group of alleged parking deals between his trading company, Seemala, and John's firm. He also recounted the Gulf & Western maneuvers.

GILBERT: Did you have any discussions with John Mulheren concerning Gulf & Western?
BOESKY: Yes.
GILBERT: Would you tell us what you said to John Mulheren and what Mr. Mulheren said to you?

BOESKY: Mr. Mulheren asked me if I liked the stock on that particular day, and I said, yes, I still liked it. At the time it was trading at 44¾. I said I liked it; however, I would not pay more than 45 for it and it would be great if it traded at 45. The design of the comment—

PUCCIO: Objection to the "design of the comment." I would ask only for the conversation.

I was determined not to let Boesky deliver a self-serving interpretation of the meaning of these remarks.

Gilbert did not wait for a ruling on my objection or press the judge to allow Boesky to discuss the conversation. Instead, he simply accepted my objection and moved on.

GILBERT: What, if anything, did he [Mulheren] say to you?

BOESKY: "I understand."

Though none of us knew it at the time, this little piece of testimony was a major turning point in the case.

The counterassault on Boesky actually began before I asked him a single question. During a recess, John denounced Boesky as a "liar" in one of his many conversations with reporters covering the trial. This kind of behavior would drive a lot of defense lawyers up a wall. They hate losing control of a client's public statements at such a critical moment. Frequently, they direct their clients to stay away from the press altogether. I never let it bother me, particularly in this case. John enjoyed being the center of attention, and he needed all the moral support he could get.

Not that he was lonely for company. Throughout the trial, he was greeted by a never-ending stream of well-wishers. I'd never seen anything quite like it. The von Bulow case had been more crowded, but the spectators tended to be curiosity seekers who would argue about Claus's guilt or innocence the way baseball fans might argue about Babe Ruth and Willie Mays. But here, the people pumping John's hand were friends who often knew nothing about the facts of the case but cared desperately about him.

It was a pleasure to go to bat for such a man against the likes of Ivan Boesky. I've got to admit I'd been looking forward to my meeting with Boesky for many months. He was, after all, the man who personified the worst of the 1980s—the greed-is-good richie who was the basis for Gordon Gekko, the Michael Douglas character in the movie *Wall Street*.

My first goal was to demonstrate that Boesky had a history of lying. There are far more compelling ways of impeaching a witness than showing the jury that nothing that falls from his lips can be believed.

Q. As you sit here right now, Mr. Boesky, can you think of one lie that you've told under oath?
A. Refresh my recollection, sir.
Q. Well, without my refreshment of your recollection, is it your testimony that you can't think of one lie you've told under oath? Is that your testimony?
A. What is your question, sir?
Q. My question is, without refreshment of your recollection, is it your testimony that you can't think of one lie that you told under oath?
A. I can think of one lie.

Well, that was a start.

The courtroom was jammed with reporters, all of them scribbling down every word. Although he'd pled guilty to a single criminal charge and been sentenced to three years in prison, Boesky had never actually been on trial, or testified in court. I was the first lawyer ever to cross-examine him—to let a jury and the public at large get a glimpse of what the alleged financial genius was really like.

Q. How many times have you lied under oath prior to your appearance in this case, Mr. Boesky?
A. Several times. I cannot tell you the number.
Q. Well, okay, let's start with the first time you lied under oath. When was that, sir?

A. Why don't you refresh my recollection, sir?
Q. I don't have a crystal ball, Mr. Boesky.

I was delighted by these memory lapses. I'd only been questioning Boesky for a few minutes, but he already seemed well on the way to a state of total amnesia. Now I wanted to switch gears for a while before returning to the eminently enjoyable task of ruining Boesky's credibility.

It's very important to leave the jury with a series of memorable images. I try to introduce such lines of questioning near the beginning and end of a courtroom session to capture the jury's first and last impressions. That's why I briefly turned from the lies of Ivan Boesky to a profile that financial writer Connie Bruck had done on Boesky for the *Atlantic Monthly* at a time when Boesky was still widely regarded as a Wall Street genius. Boesky explained to Bruck how he kept his staff alert to the fact that the enormous sums of money they were dealing with were not abstract clumps of numbers: "I tell them, we are talking about 500 million dollars. You are treating it as though it were nothing. Imagine it in one-dollar bills, or better yet, in a pile of silver dollars. I wonder how tall that would be. It would be like Jacob's ladder, wouldn't it? A Jacob's ladder of silver dollars. Imagine— wouldn't that be an aphrodisiac experience, climbing to the top of such a ladder?"

Ivan Boesky sitting on this huge mound of money. "An aphrodisiac." Great stuff. Even though the quote itself wasn't incriminating, I wanted the jury to remember that image. So, while Bruck herself and a score of other writers and journalists listened from the jammed spectators' section, I read the quote and started plugging away at the Jacob's ladder theme. I noticed that Boesky was beginning to become unglued. As I peppered him with questions, he began to cross and uncross his legs, shift in his seat, adjust his jacket, and fiddle nervously with his tie. And we were still in this first half hour of the cross examination.

Q. Did you ever describe an aphrodisiac experience involving money when you spoke to Ms. Bruck?

A. I do not recall my conversations with Ms. Bruck.
Q. I see. So you may have said to Ms. Bruck that having a lot of money was an aphrodisiac experience, is that right?
A. I do not recall my conversation with Ms. Bruck.
Q. Isn't that the kind of thing you would remember, if you described money as an aphrodisiac experience? Isn't that something you would remember?
THE PROSECUTOR: Objection.
THE COURT: Overruled.
Q. Wouldn't you remember that, Mr. Boesky?
A. That's not how I view money, sir. Not then. Not now.
Q. I see.

I naturally wanted to question Boesky very closely about the twenty deals in which we believed he made many millions on insider trading. These were transactions he had never reported to the government. I wanted the jury to see that Boesky had withheld important information, even after agreeing to cooperate with the government. Also, I didn't think it would hurt to show that he was a bigger crook than already advertised. I decided to start with a company I thought would be familiar to the jurors.

Q. And how much did you invest in the Dr Pepper Corporation?
A. I would have to be refreshed.
Q. Well, given us an approximation.
A. I would have to be refreshed.
Q. Did you make any money on your investment?
A. I would have to be refreshed.
Q. You don't know, as you sit here now, whether or not you made money on Dr Pepper?
A. I would have to be refreshed.
Q. Did you receive any inside information in connection with Dr Pepper?
A. No sir.
Q. Are you absolutely sure as you sit here right now that you

received no inside information in connection with your
acquisition of Dr Pepper [stock]?
A. I would have to be refreshed on the list of securities which I
have discussed in the past.

I began to think I could ask this character what planet we
were on, and he'd have no recollection, or lie and claim we were
on Uranus. And so it went for a day and a half. Boesky was on his
way to suffering 159 memory lapses, one of the most impressive
exercises in forgetfulness in the history of American justice.

Boesky's performance was so abysmal that some people
speculated he might have been trying to help my client. But I
think that's baloney. The government's biggest mistake was per-
mitting Bosky to be sentenced before he completed his cooperation. With his jail term out of the way, and nothing hanging over
his head, Boesky had absolutely no incentive to become the kind
of impressive witness the government hoped he would be. His
memory lapses were a way of avoiding a perjury charge and disclosing any information that might be of value to the numerous
investors who were now suing him for fraud. Boesky's testimony
was another example of Ivan taking care of Ivan—or trying to.

When Boesky took the stand, I now realize, he had no idea
what he was getting into. He sounded like a radio commentator
as the prosecution gently led him through his direct examination. When Boesky prepared for his appearance in court, I think
he envisioned himself as some sort of expert witness, lecturing to
the jury. I was a little surprised by his naïveté. Otherwise, things
ran according to plan.

Boesky helped me on cross-examination with an apparently
trivial admission.

Q. While you were at Lompoc prison did you break any laws
of the United States?
A. I think I did.
Q. And tell us what you did.
A. Well, there were a couple of chaps who did laundry there.
And I gave them a few quarters, and they did my laundry.

Boesky said this with an arch tone of voice that helped to create another memorable image: the Lord of the Realm tossing a few coins in the direction of the lowly servants. This, the least of Boesky's crimes, found its way into every account of his testimony. *The New York Times* thought enough of the admission to include it in the lead of its story.

But even for the tabloid papers, the news that Boesky bribed other prisoners to do his laundry paled next to the disclosure I was after next. It involved the famous $100 million penalty Boesky supposedly paid to atone for his sins.

Boesky's deal with the government required him to pay out $50 million in the form of a fine and $50 million to be placed in a fund to repay investors he had ripped off. It seemed an enormous amount of money, and Boesky's lawyers told the judge who sentenced him to jail that their client was virtually bankrupt. But appearances can be deceiving, especially in the case of Ivan Frederick Boesky. The truth was this: Boesky's lawyers had done a great job, but I was left unconvinced.

Q. Mr. Boesky, between the summer of 1986, and the time of [your] sentence in December of '87, did you transfer any assets to your wife or children?
A. I do not recall my financial activities in 1986.
Q. Whether or not you recall your financial activities as you sit here right now, do you recall whether you transferred assets to your wife or children?
A. I have no recollection of my financial activities at this time.

By now, my voice was almost always filled with anger and sarcasm. It was genuine—to know this guy was to despise him. But I also wanted the jury to feel my contempt. And the best was yet to come. As a defense lawyer, I'd learned a few things about the tax laws, and I was suspicious of that $100 million penalty. Who would have believed that you could write off a penalty imposed for illegal conduct as a legitimate business expense? But that's exactly what I thought may have been done in the Boesky case with a wink and a nod from the United States government.

I assumed that it would be easy to get Boesky's income tax returns, but the government fought us tooth and nail on the issue and it was only at the eleventh hour that Judge Cederbaum finally agreed to give me the factual ammunition I needed. Boesky's return revealed, as I had always suspected, that he had taken an enormous tax write-off on the $100 million. The law prevented Boesky from writing off the $50 million portion of the penalty levied as a fine. But, as Boesky admitted under my questioning, he had deducted the $50 million set aside for investors. That saved Boesky a cool $25 million.

"For Ivan Boesky, Punishment Was Tax-Deductible" read the page-one headline in *The New York Times* the following morning. "BOESKY CLEANS UP" screamed the *New York Post.*

Boesky had also gotten the government to agree to accept payment of the $50 million fine in the form of securities rather than cash. I was able to bring out during my questioning of Boesky that these stocks and bonds lost much of their value shortly after Boesky handed them over to the government. Nothing about Ivan Boesky, including the punishment for his crimes, was real.

I had enough information on Boesky to continue torturing him for another week, but one of the most important rules of cross-examination is to know when to stop. I felt Boesky had been completely discredited, and further questioning would only have offered him an opportunity to recover.

Things were going well, but the government now moved into what I thought to be the strongest part of its case: the "parking" allegations. The difficulties faced by the defense can best be illustrated by testimony about Unocal, an oil company.

Boesky had testified that in 1985, he purchased almost two million shares of Unocal, which was then the target of a takeover attempt by corporate raider T. Boone Pickens. But the takeover effort fizzled, and the price of Unocal stock dropped sharply. As a result, Boesky said he lost about $40 million.

Boesky wanted to take a tax write-off on the losses while at the same time retaining control of the stock, which he believed would again rise in value. So, he said, he asked Mulheren to take the stock, promising John he'd be "protected" from any decline in its value.

I wasn't worried about Boesky's testimony—nothing he said appeared credible. But in this case, the government had two witnesses and documentary evidence to back up Boesky's story.

The first witness was Boesky's chief trader, Michael Davidoff. Davidoff testified that he had worked out the details of the Unocal trade with John and a method of repayment for increases in the value of the stock. He said John agreed to return the profits on Unocal stock to Ivan by paying Boesky's trading company vastly inflated floor brokerage fees.

Davidoff's testimony, in turn, was backed up by Edward McCarthy, who had been the chief financial officer at John's trading company. McCarthy had been called before a federal grand jury eight times, and eight times he had denied under oath that there was anything improper or illegal about John's dealings with Boesky. But the threat of a criminal indictment, which would have cost McCarthy his job and a $1.2 million bonus he was due to receive, prompted him to make a 180-degree turn. McCarthy entered into a cooperation agreement with the government and swore under oath that his previous testimony was a lie.

At trial, he testified that John had asked him to maintain separate records on the Unocal stock because it really belonged to "Ivan."

Backing up their testimony were some records seized from John's firm by the government. Among them was a so-called chit sheet that showed the monthly amount of inflated floor brokerage fees being paid to Boesky by Mulheren. The chit sheet also showed that the monthly floor brokerage payments were deducted from a total amount allegedly owed by Mulheren to Boesky. Floor brokerage was the fee one firm paid to another for handling its stock transaction.

John's position was that the difference between the normal brokerage fee and the amount he paid Boesky represented lawful compensation for services Boesky had performed for him.

That kind of behavior wasn't unusual on Wall Street. But the jury would still have to conclude that Mulheren's explanation deserved more weight than the combined evidence from Boesky, Davidoff, McCarthy, and the chit sheet.

I hammered hard at Davidoff and McCarthy on cross-examination, but the prospects were not entirely encouraging. My best hope was our original strategy—that the jurors would tell themselves: "Mulheren's a good guy and Boesky's a terrible guy, so let's overlook this."

The government also presented Martin Davis, the chairman and CEO of Gulf & Western, as a witness. Davis testified about the effort by Boesky and Carl Icahn to take over Gulf & Western and, failing that, to "greenmail" the firm.

He also said that while Boesky and Icahn were circling the company, he received a visit from John Mulheren, ostensibly to discuss an unrelated business deal. According to Davis, Mulheren bad-mouthed Boesky during their meeting and even offered to keep an eye on Boesky for Davis. This kind of behavior would have been completely out of character for John, as the government knew. The prosecutors were clearly hoping to imply that Mulheren was working hand in hand with Boesky on Gulf & Western, without actually offering any evidence of collusion.

I wasn't particularly concerned about Davis's testimony, since he had nothing to say about the alleged "manipulation" that moved the price of G & W stock from 44¾ to 45. I also used his testimony to bring out the fact that Gulf & Western stock briefly sold at $45 on the day before the alleged manipulation, and two weeks earlier. Boesky could have, therefore, easily dumped his G&W stock at $45 simply by following the market closely.

Davis's testimony completed the government's case against John. I had decided to kick off the defense case with testimony from three character witnesses. I've never regarded character witnesses as important, but in this case, things were different. I wanted the jurors to focus on John's personality and decency, and so I presented a string of witnesses that included some of Wall Street's biggest names and investors in his trading company.

Alan Greenberg, chairman and CEO of Bear, Stearns & Company, a brokerage giant on Wall Street, testified to John's honesty.

Samuel Belzberg, a member of Canada's fabulously wealthy Belzberg family, also testified to John's honesty, adding that he had invested $80 million in John's company. (One difficulty in the government's case was the absence of any real victims in the crimes they were alleging.)

My "star" witness was, of course, John Mulheren himself. The decision to put him on the stand wasn't very difficult. He was very eager to testify, and I believed the jury would want to hear his explanation of what happened. I also thought that his basic decency would work its way through to the jurors.

Prior to the trial, I had gingerly raised the possibility with his wife, Nancy, of putting John in a jacket and tie.

"Forget it," she said. That was the beginning and end of my stint as a fashion consultant. My client took the stand in a turquoise sports shirt, jeans, and loafers with no socks.

The direct examination went smoothly enough. I led John through an account of his life and professional career, including his first meeting with Boesky at the Café des Artistes in 1976. John then described the purchase of Unocal stock, which he said was strictly a business transaction. He had agreed, in a very brief phone conversation with Boesky, to buy $10 million of Unocal.

That was followed by a phone call from Davidoff to work out the details.

"OK. I'm going to sell it to you and I might want to buy it back. OK. And you'll be held harmless. You won't lose any money," Davidoff told him.

At this point, John specifically rejected such an arrangement. "You can stop right there. I don't do those trades. If I'm not at risk of the market, I will not do the trade," he told Davidoff. "And he [Davidoff] just hemmed and hawed and said, 'Ok. Thanks a lot. Let's just do the trade.'" (Davidoff, by the way, didn't dispute John's recollection of the conversation. Instead, Davidoff testified that he thought John was only joking.)

John also denied discussing Unocal with McCarthy or telling anyone to maintain separate records on the Unocal transaction.

John explained the other "parking" deals in a similar fashion. In each case, he had accepted the risk of profit or loss on each of the stocks purchased from Boesky.

He acknowledged making inflated floor brokerage payments to Boesky, even though he owed no money to Boesky or his firm. The extra money was payback for trading ideas and other favors, unrelated to any parking deals.

I was reasonably satisfied with John's performance, but things didn't go so well on cross-examination. John turned angry and belligerent. It was as if he at last had a chance to strike back at the government for the previous two years of misery it had inflicted on him and his family. John was heavily medicated throughout the trial, but drugs could not lift the entire burden of the pressure bearing down on him.

The main target of his wrath was prosecutor Alfred Pavlis, a slender, baby-faced young man who looked a lot like the proverbial callow youth.

John seemed intent on showing his contempt for Pavlis and the whole judicial process. At one point, Pavlis produced John's application for employment at Spear Leeds & Kellogg and asked him to identify his signature on the application. John appeared to be giving Pavlis a hard time by saying he wasn't sure he had signed his own employment application.

PAVLIS: That's not your signature?
MULHEREN: I don't think so. I don't know. Most people sign my signature.
PAVLIS: Is it your testimony under oath that that's not your signature?
MULHEREN: I have no idea. Half the time people sign my signature.
JUDGE CEDERBAUM: Why don't you take a closer look at it?
MULHEREN: Have you ever seen my signature, Your Honor?
JUDGE CEDERBAUM: First you look at what is being shown, and see if you recognize it.
MULHEREN: If the question is, does my signature sometimes look like that, sometimes it does, OK?

JUDGE CEDERBAUM: Mr. Mulheren, do you recognize your own signature?

MULHEREN: Often I don't, Your Honor.

Great. John was not only tormenting Pavlis, he was tormenting the judge. Ironically, he was also being completely truthful. A variety of employees were authorized to sign his name, including his secretary. I was able to put her on the stand, where she testified that she signed Mulheren's name to many documents, including the one John had been questioned about by Pavlis and the judge!

Nevertheless, John's attitude was not winning any points for the defense. Mercifully, a midmorning recess interrupted Pavlis's cross-examination.

It was time to shape John up. Outside the courtroom during the break, we had a chat.

"Look, I know you had to get this out of your system, but you're not helping yourself," I told John. "Just answer the questions in a calm, straightforward manner."

John agreed, and the rest of the cross-examination went smoothly enough.

We were now nearing the end of the trial, but there was one more moment of drama. Judge Cederbaum had been wrestling with the question of whether or not to permit the testimony of our final character witness, a New York City police officer named Steven McDonald.

McDonald was a twenty-eight-year-old patrolman when he was shot and paralyzed from the neck down while breaking up a robbery in Central Park in July 1986. The entire city seemed to share the tragedy with McDonald and his pregnant wife, Patti. Needless to say, John Mulheren was one of the first to reach out to help the couple.

Now McDonald was eager to repay John's continuing kindness since the shooting by testifying on his behalf. There were many people ready to do the same, but I thought McDonald to be a great example of a perfect stranger whose life had been touched by John's generosity. He was also far removed from the power and money of Wall Street.

McDonald was confined to a wheelchair and breathed through a respirator. Judge Cederbaum was concerned that McDonald's appearance would evoke too much sympathy from the jury, but she finally agreed to let him testify.

As some jury members wept, McDonald described how Mulheren had visited him at Bellevue Hospital following the shooting.

"The last thing I remember he did on leaving was to place his hand on my head and give me a wink," McDonald testified in a hoarse voice.

"John Mulheren has called me throughout the four years [since the shooting] to see how I and my family were doing through this time."

I rested the defense case after Steven McDonald's testimony.

In his closing argument, prosecutor Alfred Pavlis hammered away at the friendship between Boesky and Mulheren, a relationship I had minimized as part of the defense strategy. The government even rolled out charts to illustrate the alleged closeness of their relationship. As Pavlis spoke, my client and at least one of the jurors appeared to be sleeping.

I hoped things would go better for the defense. My closing argument to the jury lasted four hours and restated the good versus evil theme I had struck throughout the trial. I can't think of another case in which I spent an hour of summation talking about—even quoting—the testimony of character witnesses. But that's how I began my summation, with a recap of the testimony of a dozen people who said John Mulheren was one of the most decent and honest men they had ever known.

"He is the proud father of five children and a devoted husband," I said. "He came with absolutely nothing to where he is today."

The slow rhythm of Steven McDonald's respirator was the only other sound in the courtroom as I spoke.

I once again contrasted John and the "Prince of Darkness," Ivan Boesky.

"Boesky, ladies and gentlemen, is a pile of human garbage. And that is what the government of the United States put up to testify against John Mulheren."

"People who lie and lied and lie more times than they can remember are going to lie before you in this trial," I reminded the jurors.

I concluded by asking them: "Who would you believe?"

The answer, I hoped and prayed, would be Mulheren.

Jury deliberations were nerve-racking, as usual. They had become more and more difficult for me with the passing of the years, and having a good guy like Mulheren as a client made them all the harder.

But nothing could have prepared me for the outcome. The jury convicted John of conspiring with Boesky to manipulate the price of Gulf & Western stock and deadlocked on the parking allegations. In other words, the jurors were unable to reach agreement on what was clearly the strongest part of the government's case while finding John guilty of a crime that was based solely on the testimony of Ivan Boesky. The judge later declared a mistrial on the twenty-six counts on which the jury deadlocked.

(Subsequent press interviews with the jurors only deepened the mystery, since they said they did not believe Boesky or his testimony.)

John proved to be a tower of strength in adversity. As the jury left the courtroom, he immediately walked to his stunned wife and took her hand.

"Don't worry, for God's sake," he whispered. The couple had a shared faith in his innocence that carried them through hard times.

I wasn't lacking in confidence myself. I already had high hopes for an appeal, since the conviction rested on the most tenuous evidence imaginable—Ivan Boesky. (The jury acquitted John's codefendant, Lenny DeStefano, of all charges.)

In November 1990, Judge Cederbaum sentenced John to a year and a day in jail. I was pleased. John would be eligible for parole in two months, and since he had already been locked up by the government for at least that long, it seemed unlikely he'd ever spend a single day in jail.

Work on the appeal, meanwhile, went forward. It was filed with the U.S. Court of Appeals for the Second Circuit. We ar-

gued that the government had failed to prove the Gulf & Western charges and that, indeed, there had been no violation of the
securities law by John Mulheren.

Seven months after John's conviction, the appeals court is-
sued a stinging rebuke to the government's prosecution by dis-
missing the Gulf & Western charges.

The court ruled that the government had failed to prove its
case—by a wide margin. In order to establish that John meant to
manipulate the price of G&W stock, the government was obli-
gated to present some evidence of his intent. But, as the appeals
court pointed out, the closest the government came was the brief
telephone conversation between Boesky and John on the day
G&W stock went to $45 a share.

GILBERT: Did you have any discussions with John Mulheren
concerning Gulf & Western?
BOESKY: Yes.
GILBERT: Would you tell us what you said to John Mulheren
and what Mr. Mulheren said to you?
BOESKY: Mr. Mulheren asked me if I liked the stock on that
particular day, and I said, yes, I still liked it. At the time it was
trading at 44¾. I said I liked it; however, I would not pay more
than 45 for it and it would be great if it traded at 45. The
design of the comment—
PUCCIO: Objection to the "design of the comment." I would
ask only for the conversation.

The court noted that Boesky was never asked the meaning of
his words and that "to hang a conviction on the threadbare
phrase 'it would be great if it traded at 45,' particularly when the
government does not suggest the words were some sort of sinister code, defies reason and a sense of fair play."

The court also noted that I had objected to Boesky's attempt
to explain his remarks and that "the government—for reasons
known only to itself—abandoned further inquiries into Boesky's
state of mind."

The government was entitled to ask what Boesky meant.
What happened was a good example of a veteran lawyer being

able, through experience and instinct, to make an objection that throws an inexperienced prosecutor off balance. It wasn't even a valid objection. It was an attempt to cut off damaging testimony. The government's failure to follow through had cost it the appeal.

John Mulheren paid me a ton of money to defend him, and that one objection, I think, made it worth his while.

The appeals court also took the unusual step of ruling that the jury "must have engaged in false surmise and rank speculation" in order to reach a guilty verdict on the basis of the evidence presented by the government.

To the public, the appeals court ruling seemed to signal total victory for John and serious embarrassment for the U.S. attorney's office in Manhattan.

But behind the scenes, the government had decided to play out a dirty little endgame. The weapon at hand was the twenty-six counts in the indictment that constituted the alleged parking violations against Mulheren. Judge Cederbaum had declared a mistrial after the jury deadlocked on these charges.

Theoretically, the government was free to put John on trial again on these charges, and that's exactly what the prosecutor, Scott Gilbert, now threatened to do. With hindsight, it's easy to see that the government's gambit was an outrageous bluff, but this wasn't so clear at the time.

After so much time and trouble, the very possibility of another trial was disheartening, to say the least. Despite the fact that the jury had been unable to reach a verdict on the parking charges, I still regarded them as the strongest part of the government's case against John. A retrial could produce a conviction and possible jail time for my client.

My own background and experience with the Justice Department did not serve me well in this instance. As a prosecutor, I had never bluffed. If I said somebody was going to be indicted, well, you could take that to the bank. As a result, I probably took the government's threat more seriously than I should have.

The U.S. attorney's office was offering another deal: It was willing to drop the remaining charges against John if he entered into a settlement with the Securities and Exchange Commission.

The SEC had brought separate, noncriminal charges against John on the same matters. But to get an SEC settlement, John would have had to agree to stop working in the securities industry.

This seemed to me to be an attractive offer, and I urged John to give the deal serious consideration. My advice came as a real shock to Mulheren. His wartime consigliere, the man he had hired to battle the government to the bitter end, was advising him to compromise.

"No way," he told me.

John's take-no-prisoners approach to life and his capacity to take enormous risks now served him well.

I phoned Scott Gilbert and told him my client had no interest in making a deal.

About a week later, Gilbert called me back. The government, he announced, had decided against retrying the case. They had been bluffing all along. Subsequently, the SEC threw in the towel and declined to pursue its charges against John.

This, I suppose, is as close as you can get to a happy ending when you take on the federal government. Unlike Boesky, Milken, and other Wall Street high flyers, John never spent a day in jail and was not barred from the securities industry.

John Mulheren now heads a trading company called Buffalo Partners. His office is (literally) located on Wall Street next to the New York Stock Exchange. Lenny DeStefano, his silent, loyal sidekick, is back at his side on the trading desk.

John and wife, Nancy, have adopted a sixth child and are thinking about adopting a seventh.

Afterword

My LIFE AND career have intersected with the lives and careers of many others during my days as a prosecutor and defense attorney. Sometimes the relationship has been relatively brief and has ended when the case was over. With others it continues to this day.

Edward Neaher, the Chadborne partner and later U.S. attorney who offered me my first job, went on to the federal bench where he served with distinction for almost twenty-five years before his death in 1994. While serving on the District Court for the Eastern District he declared the government of the City of New York to be unconstitutional.

Bob Fiske, the Davis Polk partner who gently pointed me toward a career in government and away from the inhospitable doors of the Wall Street establishment, later took his own advice and became the U.S. attorney for the Southern District of New York, the second most important prosecutor's office in the nation. In that position, he became the scourge of labor racketeers and drug traffickers and later became the first Whitewater special prosecutor. Today, he is one of the most liked and admired lawyers in New York.

Mario Cuomo, who got me my first job in private practice, went on to become governor of New York for three terms and flirted with running for president of the United States before ending up as a highly paid private practitioner, right where his wife Matilda advised him to go in the first place.

Rudy Giuliani, my ally, adversary, and friend, who as a prosecutor made his reputation chasing crooked politicians, became a politician himself—needless to say, a scrupulously honest one. Today, as the first Republican mayor of New York in twenty years, he has surprised no one with his fierce independence and surprised everyone with his political effectiveness. Ironically, his only misstep was to support Democrat Mario Cuomo (whom I had introduced him to back in his prosecutor days) against the nominee of his own party for governor, risking his career over principle. At the time of this writing, he is well on his way to bringing New York back to reality and fiscal integrity. Someday he may be president.

George Moresco, who risked his career as an FBI agent to expose corruption in the FBI and resisted all attempts made to oust him, ultimately retired from the Bureau with his self-respect and honor intact. Today he is inspector general of the State of New York, a long way from the days of the "Sicilian feud." When I hear his voice over the telephone during periodic calls to see how I am doing, I am reminded of his courage and good humor during adversity. I am also reminded of how infectious his enthusiasm was, and I marvel at how courageous he made me.

Frank King, the former detective who was the central figure in the theft of drugs from the Property Clerk's Office of the New York Police Department, served his time in prison for tax evasion and died in relative obscurity. The secrets behind this infamous crime—how it was done and who was involved—died with him.

The Abscam defendants, former Congressmen Murphy, Thompson, Lederer, Myers, Kelley, Jenrette, and former Senator Williams all disappeared from view. John Murtha, who was given immunity and testified against his colleagues, remained in Congress and is still there today where he serves as one of its most powerful members.

Bob DelTufo, who started the bureaucratic war within the Justice Department which almost derailed the Abscam investigation, predictably, ran for the governorship of New Jersey and, also predictably, lost.

Vitas Gerulaitis, the first person of prominence whom I defended after I left the government, tragically died when a faulty heater leaked gas into a Southampton pool house where he was resting after a celebrity tennis match. Vitas had gone from being a great tennis player to a great sportscaster and was ironically at the height of his new career when this bizarre accident occurred. We had kept in touch over the years, but my hectic schedule somehow never allowed me the time to take the "free tennis lessons for life" he had always promised me.

Claus Von Bulow never returned to Rhode Island after his acquittal. Instead he eventually took up residence in London with his daughter Cosima nearby. His trips to New York are infrequent, but when he is in town, I rarely miss the opportunity to have lunch or dinner with him at the Century or one of his other favorite watering holes. Unflappable as ever, he regales me with stories of his life on the continent, comments on the latest doings of his treacherous stepchildren, and expresses sadness about the awful fate of his wife Sunny who still remains in a coma at Columbia Presbyterian Hospital. He always appears happy, especially when he speaks about Cosima. But I know that he must be resigned to the fact that the speculation about him will never end. Victory in the court of public opinion is not as attainable as vindication in a court of law.

Stanley Friedman served his time in jail, and, as well as I could determine, being the ultimate realist, he made the best of a bad thing. Even though the evidence against him ultimately proved overwhelming, I always felt that I had let him down. The last time I saw him was at the Metropolitan Correction Center in New York. Dressed in an orange jumpsuit and smoking his trademark cigar, he appeared subdued but almost unruffled by life in jail. It was hard not to admire his toughness. However, what I most remember about the visit was my rather comic exit. Through an unfortunate screwup, I almost spent the night in jail myself. I paid little attention to an almost invisible stamp which had been placed on the back of my hand as I passed through security going in to visit Stanley. On the way out, when I was asked to place my hand under a light, I noticed the demeanor of the guards quickly change and my way was blocked. I soon found out that instead of being stamped "visitor" I had been stamped "inmate." As much as I looked like Tom Puccio, no one was prepared to let me leave for fear that I was a prisoner planning to escape. It was about forty-five minutes later, after numerous telephone calls to Washington amid my threats of a lawsuit, that I was released.

John Mulheren and I will always be friends. To me he will always be larger than life. In the Wall Street scandals of the 1980s, he is the only one who at the end was able to stand tall. Today, perhaps more successful than ever, he plies his trade in front of a trader's screen, his illness in check. Whenever I am in the Wall Street area and have the time, I know I am always welcome in John's office. More often than not, when I speak to him, however, it is because he has called me to ask for advice or help, not for himself but for a friend. John will never change in his attitude toward people, no matter how much the Boesky experience cost him.

As for me, I can always be found looking for new battles to win and fields to conquer in the name of the law.

INDEX